CU00822081

Famine

In *Famine* (1981), a collection of essays by experts from the developing world and advanced agricultural societies, the authors share their ecological perspectives and provide an insight into the multiple causes of famine. They examine the fact that the main cause of famine is more likely to be as a result of human actions, rather than the vagaries of climate, and look at whether planned intervention by governments and relief agencies may compound the problems already existing.

Famine

Its Causes, Effects and Management

Edited by
John R.K. Robson

First published in 1981
by Gordon and Breach Science Publishers

This edition first published in 2023 by Routledge
4 Park Square, Milton Park, Abingdon, Oxon, OX14 4RN

and by Routledge
605 Third Avenue, New York, NY 10017

Routledge is an imprint of the Taylor & Francis Group, an informa business

Publisher's Note
The publisher has gone to great lengths to ensure the quality of this reprint but points out that some imperfections in the original copies may be apparent.

Disclaimer
The publisher has made every effort to trace copyright holders and welcomes correspondence from those they have been unable to contact.

A Library of Congress record exists under ISBN: 79048035

ISBN: 978-1-032-53498-5 (hbk)
ISBN: 978-1-003-41236-6 (ebk)
ISBN: 978-1-032-53499-2 (pbk)

Book DOI 10.4324/ 9781003412366

FAMINE:

ITS CAUSES, EFFECTS AND MANAGEMENT

Edited by
JOHN R.K. ROBSON
Medical University of South Carolina

GORDON AND BREACH SCIENCE PUBLISHERS
New York   London   Paris

Copyright © *1981 by* Gordon and Breach Science Publishers, Inc.

Gordon and Breach, Science Publishers, Inc.
One Park Avenue
New York, NY 10016

Gordon and Breach Science Publishers Ltd.
42 William IV Street
London WC2N 4DE

Gordon & Breach
7-9 rue Emile Dubois
Paris 75014

With the exception of those by M. Alamgir and A.P. den Hartog, all the articles in this book were first published in the journal of *Ecology of Food and Nutrition* in various issues of Volumes 4, 6, 7 and 8.

Library of Congress Cataloging in Publication Data

Main entry under title:

Famine, its causes, effects, and management.

(Food and nutrition in history and anthropology;
v.2)
 Most of the articles were first published in the
journal Ecology of food and nutrition in various
issues of vols. 4, 6-8.
 Includes index.
 1. Food relief — Addresses, essays, lectures.
2. Famines — Addresses, essays, lectures.
3. Malnutrition — Addresses, essays, lectures.
1. Robson, John R.K. II. Ecology of food and
nutrition. III. Series.
HV696.F6F35   363.8   79-48035
ISBN 0-677-16180-8

Printed and Bound in the U.K. by Mansell (Bookbinders) Ltd., Witham, Essex

CONTENTS

PREFACE

Famine is an absolutely unique phenomenon in society. It is the ultimate breakdown of nutrition, very often of public health, and quite often of society itself. And there is a general opinion, probably reinforced by the way in which we receive news through dramatic television scenes or newspaper headlines, which sees famines as the result of one immediate triggering event — a natural catastrophe, like a drought or flood, an invasion of locusts, an earthquake, diseases of plants, or not infrequently, wars and civil disorders. I am going to try to show as an introduction, taking two particularly striking examples, that this relation of famine to a single event is very largely a delusion except in the case of famines caused by war. What one is usually coping with is indeed a major natural catastrophe, but one that would not normally cause a famine if one were dealing with a well-organized, prosperous society with strong administrative and medical structures and good transportation. Indeed, the truth of the situation is that the natural catastrophe is the last straw, which plunges a society that was not working well into a disastrous situation.

That such a distinction is important is, I think, obvious to all of us who have had to cope with famines. I have had the sad privilege in my life of seeing famines in three continents: in Europe, during World War II and at the liberation of concentration camps, one in India, and several in Africa, particularly during the Biafran war. The reason this is important is that when we speak of relief and, even more, of rehabilitation, if what we are speaking about is simply bringing the situation back to the extremely unsatisfactory state it was in before, probably the next natural catastrophe will, again, cause a famine. And it is only if one understands well the nature of the problem that one can hope that the process of rehabilitation will also be a process of development which makes less likely the reoccurrence of a famine due to a natural catastrophe.

Let me take two examples, which are very clear in terms of the relationship of social disorganization and ecological factors. First, Soviet Russia in 1920-1922. This was brought about, some would say, by a severe drought affecting roughly 1.2 million square miles, a very large area in the middle and lower Volga. A population of about 30 million people was very directly affected. At no time during the worst part of the famine were there less than 24 million people in difficulty. International relief organizations and the Hoover American Relief Commission fed about 10 million people during the height of the famine — an enormous job of organization, particularly for that period. To understand how striking such a famine in Russia was at the time, let me cite some statistics which are astounding in the light of what we know of the present difficulty of the Soviet Union as regards food production. Between 1909 and 1913, the Russians had about three times as much area under cultivation as the United States: 93 million as compared to 38 million. The production of grain was almost twice that of the United States, 724 million quintales to 400 million. Russian grain exports were almost five times as great as the exports of the United States — 87 million to 18 million. Agriculture was somewhat less efficient per acre: the yield was about 7 quintales per hectare to the United States' 10.5, but the enormous area under cultivation explains the gigantic crops that Russia produced and of course Russia was one of the granaries of the world at that time.

The difficulties, however, were mounting. The population doubled between 1860 and 1913. The system of serfs was abolished and in 1906 some land reforms (fairly timid land reforms) were begun. Until then, most of the farming was done either on large estates or on communal lands, and in the curious effort to organize a certain amount of equality in the midst of an extremely unjust system, communal land was divided among the farmers in narrow longitudinal rows, so that many Russian families would have a hundred strips situated in various parts of the landscape, each one only about three or four feet wide — a most extraordinarily inefficient system of agriculture. By 1913, however, as a result of the Stolypia reforms, 28 million hectares had been bought by peasants. At the beginning of World War I, the Russians had three classes of land holdings. Some large ones, some middle-size ones, and small ones which were not enough to feed families, so that the men hired themselves out as labor. Then there were the many landless peasants who worked on the large estates. The war started in 1914. Seventeen million men and 2 million draft animals were conscripted, with the result that there was inadequate labor on the large estates. The railroad system, which had been barely adequate, became completely occupied by transportation to the front, so that the farmers began running out of supplies, even though most of them were operating with very primitive equipment — one-third of Russia still plowed with wooden plows. From 1914 on, things became very difficult for farmers, although production was maintained. The lack of transportation, however, meant that even though there was plenty of grain in the countryside, bread was scarce in the cities. Bread riots began, and eventually the revolution itself. Very rapidly the country completely disintegrated. Production of coal went down by 75 percent between 1916 and 1921, production of iron by 98 percent. The number of working locomotives dropped from 17,000 in 1917 to less than 4,000 in 1920.

At the same time the Soviet government was experimenting with a whole series of contradictory measures as far as land tenure was concerned. In 1917 the Bolsheviks urged the peasants to seize the land, and they did with great relish, believing that they were invited to appropriate it as their private property. The government was aghast, having intended the seizure to be in the name of the state, and the conflict was on between the government and the peasants: proclamation of revolution, seizure of land, private property, private ownership, seizure of grain and orders forbidding the peasants to keep more grain for themselves than was strictly necessary for their families. Production started falling, and it was at that point that a severe drought occurred which brought the rainfall from the usual 14 inches to 2¼ inches in the lower Volga area. The rest of the country, not affected by the drought, produced enough grain to feed the stricken areas, but the combination of total disorganization and lack of transportation meant that very quickly a catastrophic situation arose. The number of dead was estimated variously at 2 million by the League of Nations Commission and at 3 million by Dr. Nansen and some of the members of the Hoover Commission.

Let's look now at the situation in Bengal in 1943. Again, we are dealing with an area which in times past had been a granary of India. Bengal was a grain exporting area until 1933. During the period of 1900 to 1940, however, the available grain per person had fallen from 598 lbs. per person per year to 399 — a very serious fall, not entirely due to the increase in population. In 1933, Bengal became a net importer. There was also a series of localized crop failures starting in 1933, and a poor harvest in 1941, none of which, however, was serious enough to cause starvation and death.

Then in 1941 the war started at Pearl Harbor. Let me point out that once again I am speaking about an area which was not invaded and not affected directly by war. Singapore fell in January 1942 and throughout the first part of 1942 exports were increased to the Middle Eastern theater of operation and to a certain extent to troops in Europe. The Japanese advanced through Southeast Asia with a total loss of Burma, which had been again a granary and a chief source of rice for Bengal, in May 1942. At the same time, the government of India, very much afraid that the

viii

Japanese would go on through Assam and take over Bengal, started what they called the Boat Denial Policy of seizure of all boats large enough to hold ten people, and a re-registration of small boats. All in all, 46,000 coastal boats were seized by the Indian government, eliminating both fishing and coastal transportation.

Then followed the same sort of contradictory policy we saw applied in Russia, in this case not because of a revolution but because the Governor of Bengal, Sir John Herbert, a very clear-sighted man, was dying of cancer and the Viceroy of India, Lord Linlithgow, was never interested, in the two years of the famine, in attempting to control the situation in Bengal. On July 1 prices shot up in Bengal. Price control was set at a completely unrealistic level, roughly half of the actual price at the time. The government did not release stocks, so price control was totally ineffective. By January of 1943, the price tripled, by that April it had doubled again over that tripling, and by June the price was about ten times as high as it had been a year before. There was some slowing down at this point, when some of the stocks of grain which had been seized at the same time as the boats were seized (again to make sure that they would not be taken over by the Japanese) were released. I would spare you then the series of measures and countermeasures taken by the Government of Bengal and the Government of India. At some times, trade was encouraged between various parts of India, at other times it was discouraged. I must point out that at that time, there was a serious cyclone which destroyed 25 percent of the crop. But while the cyclone was severe, the disaster could have been contained if the administrative situation had been different. Again, the combination of administrative ineptitude and a natural disaster caused catastrophe. From then on the famine was rampant. Somewhere between 1½ and 2 million people died, and the famine continued until 1944 when a new Viceroy, Wavell, took some very energetic measures and in a few months re-established a near-normal situation, even though he was laboring under extremely difficult conditions.

The Sahel area again provides a very good illustration of the effects of a combination of an extraordinarily fragile economy and an almost complete lack of an administrative and medical structure, which was hit at the same time by a very serious and prolonged drought and by world conditions created by the massive grain buying by the Soviet Union. This directly pushed up the price of wheat and indirectly the price of rice to the point where the normal trade of millet and other grains growing north from the coastal area, which meanwhile consumed rice, was changed, with the rice from West Africa going for such very high prices to the Far East and the millet which normally went up to feed the people in the north being consumed in the southern area. The people in the north were at the same time being deprived of their normal form of currency, which was livestock — principally goats — because of the serious drought in the north. But, again, I think this combination of a massive natural disaster, lack of governmental organization, and extraneous economic factors is one more illustration of what I am talking about.

The one type of situation which does not lend itself to this analysis and which is far less relevant than that described thus far is famine due to war. Wars, of course, may cause famines in a variety of ways. They destroy the means of production, communication, and transportation, they kill and draft farmers. There is one type of famine, however, that deserves special mention. That is the famines used by man against man: the set patterns of starvation, organized for military purposes. It is a particularly terrible type of famine and it is also an extraordinarily cruel and ineffective weapon. Indeed, it is my thesis that famine should be outlawed as an instrument of war because it is not only indiscriminate, like bacteriological warfare, but beyond this because it specifically attacks those very people who are least likely to be combatants; namely, children, pregnant and nursing women and the elderly, who are the people who die first and in largest numbers in any famine. As an example of what I am talking about, we can begin in our own country with the destruction of crops in Georgia and Sherman's march to the sea. As you look back, it had absolutely no military significance. Certainly Lee capitulated at Appomattox for good and sufficient military reasons which had very little to do with the destruction of grain and other crops. The siege of Paris in 1870-1871 is another example. The siege lasted 129 days. The death rate started up as soon as it began and went up continuously throughout the period — deaths very characteristically were predominantly children, women and the elderly. The death rate of men did not increase. Indeed, in the words of a contemporary historian, the National Guards "had enough to eat and too much to drink". Paris eventually surrendered because of the capitulation of the French armies in Switzerland. The starvation in Paris had no military effect. Conversely, the Allies blockaded the Central Powers in World War I. Famine appeared at Hamburg at the end of 1916, in Berlin at the beginning of 1917, in Vienna and the Rhineland in the middle of 1917, and war went on until the end of 1918 with great victories by the German army in March and June of 1918 and perfectly normal rations as far as the army was concerned. With set starvations, the armed men never starved. The people who starved were the non-combatants. The siege of Leningrad is another example. About 3 million inhabitants were closed into Leningrad on September 8, 1941. For many months, only 45,000 tons of food came by water, air and by ice on Lake Ladoga. Late in 1942, a corridor was opened so that some of the population managed to get out, but the siege was not lifted until 1944, by which time well over a million people had died. The rations were so meager that practically all of them died of starvation or starvation-related diseases. The Russian troops defending Leningrad did have their rations reduced somewhat but still had adequate food, adequate enough so that they broke out of the siege in 1944.

Obviously, one of the priorities any dispassionate observer can deduce from all this is a missing convention — a pact we still do not have — which would outlaw starvation as an instrument of war. I have had the painful privilege of being in Biafra while the war went on, talking to both sides and trying to get some food through and observing the situation. There, again, starvation was used as a weapon of terror by the Nigerians, as a weapon of propaganda by the Biafrans. At no time did I see any shortage of food in the Biafran army, which eventually defeated militarily. The best estimate we could make of the number of civilians dying, through whatever primitive means we could use, was perhaps as many as 1 ½ million people. Today, the very special case of military famines and particularly of set famines is not our topic. But I think we should remember as we look at the natural, ecological factors involved in famine, that at least until and unless we have a natural catastrophe of an order far greater than any we have seen in recent times, it is fair to say that it is only the combination of environmental factors and the disorganization of society which can lead to famine. I hope that one of the results of further discussion of famine will be an ability to think more clearly of what could be the components of an early warning system which would enable us to detect famine before it starts and hopefully to prevent it. In time it should become more and more evident that such an early warning system will have to have a number of components: climatological, economic, organizational and medical. The state of health, mortality and morbidity of the children of the poor or of vulnerable groups in selected poor districts is, sadly, perhaps the most sensitive indicator that the food situation is deteriorating and that an alarm should be sounded.

JEAN MAYER
Tufts University, Massachusetts

SECTION I

**THE ECOLOGICAL SYSTEMATICS
OF FAMINE**

SECTION I

INTRODUCTION

John R.K. ROBSON

The distressing details of the famines in Bangladesh and Ethiopia, the Sahel disaster and the sufferings of the civilian populations during the Nigerian-Biafran War were brought to the homes of the industrialized nations through the miracles of electronics, satellites and the mass media. To the uninitiated, famine appears to be the result of climatological problems, or the consequence of war. Prior to these unfortunate events famine was usually associated with India and its continual struggle to provide adequate food supplies for its rapidly growing population. Looking further back in history, there is ample evidence that industrialized countries were, at one time, also prone to serious food shortages and one of the more surprising aspects of famine is their high frequency of occurence. For example, in Russia 121 years of famine and one hundred years of hunger were recorded in the millenium A.D. 971-1970. On average, this represents one year of hunger or famine in every five, with the number of famine years increasing rapidly with the passage of time, reaching a peak in the 19th century. Increases in global famine are now being predicted because of recognition that there is a finite limit to food production potential in the world and that man appears to be unable to control population growth at a rate that can be supported by the available food resources.

In order to prevent famines in the future there is a need to understand the mechanisms of the cause and effects of food shortages. In response to this need the organizers of prestigious scientific meetings have allocated time for the discussion of this subject. These meetings have shown clearly that not only is the causation of famine complex but also that a high level of expertise is needed to understand and define all of the factors involved. For many years in the more conventional areas of nutrition it was believed that nutrient deficiencies in populations could be corrected by giving the nutrient to persons affected. It is now recognized that this is too simplistic and that in order to

prevent or control a nutrient deficiency, one must understand the events that led to that state. For years vitamin, mineral or protein deficiences were considered from the short-term point of view and the cause was inevitably attributed to the diet. For example, kwashiorkor, the disease resulting from inadequate caloric or protein intake, was believed to be due to a failure to provide the weaning child with adequate protein. While kwashiorkor can usually be cured by protein, experience has shown that all too often after a few weeks in the home environment the child is likely to return to the hospital with the same disease. Kwashiorkor can be attributed in reality to agricultural and economic systems that do not allow parents to provide sufficient amounts of protein foods or variety of such foods during the weaning period. The problems may be compounded by the customs of the society, its land tenure system or the structure of its tribal government or the effectiveness of environmental hygiene. The alleviation of kwashiorkor as a global problem, therefore, depends, not on the provision of food, although this might be essential as a life saving measure, but in the control of the events that resulted in the harmful diet patterns of the child.

A similar situation has arisen with respect to famine. Although drought is usually considered the cause of famine, in Russia this was not found to be true, and drought and famine were not synonymous. Famine occurred in some of Russia's most productive agricultural regions and was the result of the combination of natural phenomena such as climate, disease, rodents, insects, and floods, and an even larger number of man-made factors. These include wars, poor political decisions, transportation problems, serfdom, communication difficulties, incompetence, poverty, disease, panic, and food speculation.

In the Bengal famines, administrative and governmental ineptitude coupled with a cyclone were primarily responsible. Although the loss of

3

25 percent of the crop in Bangladesh was serious enough in itself, it was also coupled with lack of price controls and lack of transport to move grain to needed areas, hence the magnitude of the disaster was greatly increased. The Bengal famine was caused in part by fragile local economics, but it is clear now that any country with marginal food resources is also at the mercy of international economics and marketing. The Sahel situation was precipitated not by drought alone but by the world shortage of grain as well. The latter resulted in grain buying by the Soviet Union, which in turn drove up prices to such an extent that normal trade in grains was severely disrupted. Consequently, locally produced grains were exported, depriving the indigenous population of their main life support.

This monograph recognizes that if famine is to be understood and controlled, there must be an understanding of its ecology. The first section will discuss the systematics of famine, and it will include not only a descriptive analysis of famine, but also mathematical models and a discussion of concepts such as agro-ecosystems.

While the mechanics of famine are important, it is also necessary to recognize the stress imposed by food shortages on individuals. The adaptation of the human body to stress is discussed in detail, but it is also necessary to recognize that, eventually, adaptive mechanisms may be inadequate to meet the demands of continued stress, and a pathological state ensues. The effects of famine on health is important and must be taken into consideration when intervention is planned.

The management of food supplies is not solely a question of mobilizing resources, however. Each component of management is part of a system, and the total efficiency of the food supply system is limited by the individual efficiency of its component parts. These components include not only the production, distribution and consumption of food, but each component may be operating in either a market-dependent food supply system or a subsistence food supply system, which greatly complicates the situation.

Finally, there is a need to look into practical experiences in famine and famine relief and this is achieved by case studies of famines in Bangladesh and an examination of the more historical aspects of famines in Russia.

REFERENCES AND ADDITIONAL READINGS

Mayer, Jean (1969). "Famine in Biafra", *Postgraduate Medicine*, **45**, 236.
Davis, L.E. (1971). Epidemiology of famine in the Nigerian crisis: rapid evaluation of malnutrition by height and arm circumference in large populations. *Am. J. of Clin. Nutr.*, **24**, 358.
Gebre-Medhin, M., Vahlquist, B. (1976). Famine in Ethiopia — a brief review, *Am. J. of Clin. Nutr.*, **29**, 1016.
Robson, J.R.K. (1974). Ecology of malnutrition in a rural African community in Tanzania, *Ecol. Food and Nutr.*, **3**, 61.
Almquist and Wiksell (1971). *"Famine: A Symposium Dealing with Nutrition and Relief Operations in Times of Disaster"*, (Eds. Blix, Hofvander and Vahlquist), Sweden.

THE ECOLOGY OF FAMINE: AN OVERVIEW†

GEORGE W. COX

Department of Biology, San Diego State University, California, U.S.A.

Once upon a time there was a great flood, and involved in this flood were two creatures, a monkey and a fish. The monkey being agile and experienced, succeeded in scrambling up a tree and escaping the raging waters. As he looked down from his safe perch, he saw a poor fish struggling against the swift current. With the best of intentions, he reached down and lifted the fish from the water. Unfortunately, in spite of this aid, the fish died.

Oriental Proverb (Foster, 1962)

Famine may be defined as the regional failure of food production or distribution systems, leading to sharply increased mortality due to starvation and associated disease. Famine is one of the component problems of the global food crisis, but it differs in a significant fashion from other problems, including chronic malnutrition. Chronic insufficiency of foods meeting minimal nutritional requirements leads to suffering and to high mortality rates, but its most significant effect is the long-term physical and mental crippling of members of the affected population. In famine, the short-term impacts of food unavailability dominate: people suddenly die in large numbers. Famine may be characterized as epidemic malnutrition, chronic scarcity as endemic malnutrition.

The world may very well be emerging from a half-century moratorium on famines triggered primarily by climatic factors. Following the famine of 1928–1929 in China, in which an estimated three million people died, the major famines that have occurred were largely induced by war and revolution—until recent years. Setting these aside, the four decades ending with the emergence of the Sahelian crisis represent one of the longest intervals of freedom from a notable famine during the Christian Era (See Keys, *et al.*, 1950). Climatically, the beginning of this period is correlated with an increase in the mean temperature of higher latitudes of the northern hemisphere, and with an increase in the reliability of monsoon conditions in India (Bryson, 1974a). The greatest economic and

technological growth in human history has occurred during this same 40 years, providing man with new tools of production and improved means of transport, both of which have contributed to mitigating problems of food insufficiency.

This period of favorable conditions and relative adequacy may now be at an end. The climates which we have come to think of as normal, and under which national boundaries have grown rigid, may in fact be the most abnormally favorable period of the past thousand or more years (Bryson, 1974b). Return to less favorable climatic conditions may now be under way. Population growth may have eroded the margin of extra productive capability that new technology provided, and may, in fact, be mining the ecological capital of the world's arable lands. Our ability to combat diseases of crops, domestic animals, and indeed, man himself, is increasingly challenged by the counter-evolutionary responses of pathogens (Reeves, 1972).

The specter of famine appears again to be with us. In the past, famine has been dealt with as an unexpected crisis, unplanned for and with little carry-over of experience from previous crises (Mayer, 1974). It is apparent, however, that famine has major ecological roots and impacts. We must therefore examine these, and seek ecologically-sound short-term responses, to alleviate occurring famines, and long-term programs, to prevent future famines.

Our treatment of the famine problem in recent history has been much like that employed by the monkey in assistance of the fish (see Foster, 1962, for a general discussion of this problem in international aid). Famine relief and assistance have

† Based on a paper presented at the American Association for the Advancement of Science Meeting held on February 20, 1976.

5

been predicated on certain unquestioned assumptions about the objectives of these efforts, and concern has centered principally on how best to achieve those objectives. Among these assumptions are the following: first, food and medical relief should be employed to keep alive as many persons as possible, and second, subsequent efforts should be made to modernize food production activity by the introduction of agricultural techniques from the developed countries.

In approaching the problem of famine from an ecological point of view, however, we must examine these basic objectives, as well as considering means of implementation. For each instance of potential or incipient famine, our goal must be to answer the following questions:

What are the dominant relationships influencing food production and availability relative to population?

How are these relationships likely to influence the probability or course of famine?

Is outside aid justified, or are intrinsic mechanisms of human ecology best able to deal with famine crises?

If outside aid is justified, what forms of assistance will enable a stable relation between population and food production to be achieved?

How can such aid be most effectively supplied by groups in a position to assist?

With these questions in mind, let us turn to an examination of the causes of famine.

FAMINE: THE ENVIRONMENTAL CONTEXT

Two ecological characteristics dominate the environmental context of famine: seasonality of climate and major reliance by human populations upon subsistence and local market food production systems. Virtually all naturally-triggered famines have occurred in regions which combine strongly seasonal patterns of temperature or moisture with a high degree of variability of these factors from year to year. Combined with subsistence food production, pastoralism or subsistence cultivation, these conditions mean that production during a favorable season must be stored locally to meet the food needs of a less favorable season. For pastoral or semipastoral peoples, this storage

must largely be in natural form: the biomass of their animals, the standing crop of forage on rangelands, the quantities of supplementary plant and animal foods that may be collected, and the fat and tissue reserves of their own bodies. In subsistence crop production systems, more of this storage must be artificial. In either case, failure of production during the favorable season may lead to starvation conditions during the less favorable season.

ECOLOGICALLY STABILIZED SOCIETIES

The major systems of subsistence agriculture are the products of several thousand years of biological and cultural evolution. These systems, together with even more ancient patterns of hunting and gathering, have enabled man to occupy even the most difficult of the world's natural environments. Few persons outside the field of cultural ecology and its interfacing sciences appreciate the complexity and sophistication of the interrelations between these systems, their practitioners, and the natural environments in which they are found.

Food production is an activity enmeshed in the total pattern of human culture—in a set of beliefs and practices that forms a logically-integrated, functional whole (Foster, 1962). No culture is perfectly tuned to its natural environment, perfectly balanced in the relations between its components, or completely static. Cultural institutions often contain compromises forced by the realities of different conditions of the environment. The natural environment is a changing one, as well, and the responses of cultural institutions to these changes are not always parallel and in perfect harmony.

Nevertheless, many undisturbed human cultures possess strong ecological rationale, and give rise to what may be termed ecologically stabilized societies. In such societies, interactions among cultural components favor the maintenance of long-term balance between the human population and its environment. Often, the mechanisms creating such balance are not obviously directed to this end. Among the various Amerindian tribes of the Amazon Basin, for example, sets of cultural traits dealing with reproduction, relations with strangers, and interpersonal violence apparently act to limit population density and maintain a high degree of dispersion of village groups (Meggers, 1971). The specific traits involved differ, however, from tribe to tribe. Wilkinson (1973, 1974) has summarized evidence that many intact societies possess cultural restraints on reproduction which function to maintain the population in balance with environmental carrying capacity.

Subsistence food production systems of peoples inhabiting seasonal environments show many adjustments to the sharp spatial and temporal variations that may occur in biological productivity. The diversified and mobile systems of pastoralism practiced from Africa through central Asia clearly show such adaptation (Phillips, 1961). In the Cunene and Cuanhama regions of Angola, for example, pastoralist peoples actually carry on a combination of cattle herding, farming, gathering, and fishing activities (Cruz de Carvalho, 1974). Herds are moved seasonally in response to conditions of range favorability. Essentially the same pattern is shown by the Karimojong of northeastern Uganda (R. and N. Dyson-Hudson, 1970). Here, the cultivation of sorghum, maize, and millet by women near permanent village sites is combined with herding of cattle, sheep, and goats by the men and boys. The advantages of these systems are those of diversification: complete dependence is not placed on crop production, which may fail in a given year due to inadequate rainfall, nor is dependence complete on animal herds, which may be decimated by disease or poor range conditions.

Similar arguments may be made for many subsistence systems of crop production. The practice of mixed cropping—the interplanting of several crop species—is widespread in subsistence farming in areas with strongly seasonal distribution of rainfall (Norman, 1974). Analysis of these systems in Nigeria supports the view that such practices act to maximize production and minimize the risk of complete crop failure due to poor weather or pest damage.

In addition to these general adjustments of overall food production systems, many of the native peoples of famine environments have well-developed food procurement technologies serving specifically in times of famine. Bhandari (1974) gives a comprehensive account of the use of wild plant and animal foods in the Rajasthan Desert; some 25 plant species ranging from trees and shrubs to grasses and annual herbs are included. Similar food procurement systems exist in Africa, and undoubtedly occur in most regions in which failures of normal food production means occasionally occur.

The further possibility exists that human populations may be adjusted in their reproductive performance to the instability of their environments (Yellen, 1974). Cultural restraints on reproduction, mentioned earlier, may be best developed in human populations of stable environments, or in cultures in which diversified food production activities and high mobility provide effective responses to environmental instabilities. In other societies, such as those occupying seasonal environments but dependent entirely upon crop production, a more nearly "r-selected" reproductive pattern may exist. In other words, the population may be adjusted to the periodic occurrence of famine mortality by a higher, culturally-conditioned reproductive rate.

Whether or not this last suggestion is actually the case, it is apparent that strong cultural adjustments and responses to famine conditions exist in many undisturbed societies. Cross-cultural comparison of these adjustments may give considerable insight into factors minimizing vulnerability to famine.

HISTORY AND IMMEDIATE CAUSES OF FAMINE

The famines recorded through history number in the hundreds Bhatia, 1963; Cepede and Lengelle, 1953; Keys, et al., 1 950. In some regions, such as China and India, it would be safe to say that prior to the development of modern transportation systems, famine somewhere within the region was a nearly annual occurrence. Unfortunately, the information available on most recorded famines is too incomplete and vague to be of much value in understanding causal relationships.

The major immediate causes of famine are well known: unfavorable weather, disease and pest attacks, war and civil disruption, and other catastrophic factors such as floods and earthquakes. Singly, or more often in combination, these forces have triggered famine at irregular intervals throughout recorded history.

Unfavorable weather is the most frequently cited cause of famine. Drought, generally continued over several years, is the major natural cause of crop failure in arid and semi-arid portions of western China, central Asia, the Indian region, the Middle East, much of Africa, the Mediterranean Littoral, and portions of South and Central America. In some areas, such as Egypt, that depend upon river flow for canal or natural flood irrigation, drought in river headwaters may be the cause, rather than drought in the affected region. Too much rain, through destructive flooding, may also severely damage crop systems and trigger famine. In higher latitudes, especially across Eurasia, cold, wet, and short growing seasons have produced famine-inducing crop failures.

Disease has also served as the major cause of famine by its effects upon crops, domestic animals, or man himself. The most famous example of a famine triggered by crop failure is the Irish Potato Famine of 1845 and 1846, in which over one million people died (Adams, Ellingboe and Rossman, 1971). This failure was caused by an epiphytotic of a blight fungus, *Phytopthora infestans*, which was unknown in Europe much before this time. An associate of potato species in the New World, it apparently reached Europe by natural dispersal or accidental introduction by man. Cool damp summer conditions also favored its development to epiphytotic status.

Diseases of domestic animals have also been responsible for famines among pastoralist peoples. Introduction of European cattle to East Africa in the late 1800's brought previously unknown diseases to the region. In the 1890's, rinderpest epizootics decimated both game herds and the cattle herds of pastoralist peoples such as the Masai, leading to famine conditions (Talbot, 1972). Human disease, as in the case of the great plague of 1345–1348 in Europe, may so disrupt societal function that food production is impaired and secondary starvation compounds the problem of epidemic disease.

War and civil disturbance may act as just as effective agents of destruction of the crops and animals upon which human populations depend. The famines of this century, spread widely from Soviet Russia and India through Europe and even portions of South America have largely been of this sort; they need little further explanation. In similar fashion, wherever weaknesses exist in the food production systems serving major human populations, catastrophes such as earthquakes or cyclones may trigger famine.

Two patterns impress the student of historical famines: the distribution of famines in the Old World, and the differences in recorded frequency of famine in Old and New Worlds. In the Old World, it is possible to recognize two "famine belts." One, extending from the British Isles across Europe and Soviet Russia to northern China, corresponds to a region in which food production failures may occur because of dampness, cold, and shortened growing seasons. The second, extending from Africa and the Mediterranean Littoral eastward through the dry and monsoon lands to China, is a belt of drought-induced famine. Modernization of Europe, Soviet Russia, and more recently, China, has nearly eliminated the threat of natural famine in the northern belt by providing an infra-structure of transportation and governmental assistance that buffers year-to-year variability in food production and prevents local failure from inducing local famine.

Further south, in the drought belt, development of infra-structure and governmental capability have been much less complete. Transportation and communication in some areas are so poor that famine conditions may pass unrecognized. Even when recognized, as in recent experience in Ethiopia, the mechanics of distributing aid over large areas with primitive transportation networks may prove nearly insurmountable.

Recent years have seen food production capacity drastically affected in both the northern and southern famine belts of the Old World. The northern belt, however, has demonstrated its ability to solve the problem by external purchase of food and effective internal distribution. While this, in itself, is laudable, it adds an additional highly variable term to the equation of food availability in other food-short regions. Not only is production at the mercy of the vagaries of rainfall, the capacity to compensate by importation is at the mercy of importation patterns by the more affluent northern countries.

A second pattern is the high frequency of recorded famines in the Old World, the scarcity in the New World. Certainly, a portion of this reflects the fact that recorded history is older in the former area. Likewise, for some portion of the historical period following early colonization of the New World, catastrophes that befall the native peoples of the Americas were probably not described nor graced with the importance attached to similar events in parts of Europe. Yet, over several hundred years following colonization frequent famines were recorded in the Old World, but few in the New World.

Part of this difference may reflect geographical and climatic differences between Old and New Worlds. The New World has nothing comparable in extent to the drought belt spanning Eurasia and northern Africa in the Old World. Nevertheless, arid environments, and environments with equally variable year-to-year conditions of rainfall exist in the New World. At least some of these should furnish conditions of equal potential in triggering famine.

In part, the apparent rarity of famine may be the result of our overlooking it. Da Silva Mello (1964) records some of the most poignant descriptions of famine conditions in northeastern Brazil, together with the statistic that since 1700 an average of one year out of five has been a drought year in this region. May and McLellan (1974) state that between 1948 and 1964, rural strife in Colombia gave rise to pockets of famine. Other students of New World prehistory have suggested that abandonment of cliff dwelling in the American Southwest was the result of drought-induced food crises. The declines of other civilizations, including those of the Mayans and Toltecs, may also have reflected food system failures prior to western colonization.

Nevertheless, real ecological differences relating to the occurrence of famine may exist. Many of the peoples of the New World were hunters and gatherers; others practiced agriculture but retained highly diversified food procurement systems, including activities of hunting and gathering. Greater diversification may have kept native peoples of the New World less tied to specific locations and more flexible and mobile in their response to locally severe conditions.

UNDERLYING CAUSES OF FAMINE

When human food production and emergency procurement systems are closely attuned to the conditions of the environment, their complete breakdown, even in the most severe situations, should be uncommon. The immediate causes of famine described above more easily trigger such failures when the normal relationships between human population and food production have been thrown into imbalance. The factors producing such imbalances are underlying, but equally important, causes of famine. Underlying causes may be climatic, cultural, economic, or political. All lead to imbalances evident in ecological terms.

Most climatologists agree that there have been significant shifts in average conditions of temperature and precipitation within recent historical time, and that some of these changes have persisted for periods of years, decades, or centuries. Although usually small in actual value, many of these changes have influenced human activities and the occupation of regions of marginal climate (Bryson, 1974a). In recent historical time, there is general agreement that mean temperatures, at least for the northern hemisphere, have gradually increased from the late 1800's or early 1900's through the early 1940's and then declined in a progressive and somewhat more rapid fashion (Bryson, 1974b; Lamb, 1974). There is, however, major difference of opinion over the extent to which these changes reflect the impact of human activities on atmospheric CO_2 and particulate levels, as opposed to reflecting other relationships independent of human influence (see Bryson, 1973, for the former viewpoint, Landsberg, 1970, for the latter). The answer to this question is of some importance, since if man is a significant cause of global climatic change, the observed trends are likely to continue or intensify in response to his activities.

Cooling of the northern hemisphere, evident in satellite-recorded changes in ice and snow cover during the winter period (Kukla and Kukla, 1974), has been implicated as a possible causal mechanism of drought in the Sahelian Zone of Africa (Bryson, 1973). This idea is based on the argument that the location of the North Atlantic subtropical high, during the northern hemisphere summer, is determined by latitudinal and altitudinal temperature gradients, and that, in turn, its location influences the northern point reached by the Intertropical Convergence in the Sub-saharan region. Interestingly, the prolonged drought conditions in the Sahelian Zone are positively correlated with drought in the dry northern portion of the Chilean Mediterranean Zone, where winter rains normally occur during the same months (Hajek, Pacheco and Passalacqua 1972).

Whatever may be the involvement of man in these climatic trends, it is evident that they are capable of contributing to crop failures in a number of world regions. Such failures, even when they do not lead to famine in the areas involved, may seriously influence the capacity of the world to deal with food crises elsewhere. In 1975, for example, grain production fell 76.6 million tons below expectations—a shortfall of over 35 percent—in the Soviet Union (Anon., 1975), leading to purchases in international grain markets that effectively exhausted supplies that might have been needed to meet emergency needs in famine areas.

Disruption of the cultural integrity of a society may also initiate trends toward ecological imbalance. The fact that culture is an integrated whole has two important corollaries: first, successful modification of one cultural component requires accommodating change in other components, and second, change in one cultural component may lead to second and third order changes in other components, some of which may not easily be anticipated (Foster, 1962). The introduction of medical services to isolated populations may quickly lead to major reductions in death rates; without accommodating changes in birth rates the result may be rapid growth leading to imbalance with environmental productivity. The construction of wells in arid regions may alleviate critical water shortages; without accommodating regulation of nearby land use, the areas surrounding the wells may be overgrazed and degraded. Introduction of new crop varieties with high-yielding potentials may alleviate overall food calorie deficits; without accommodating changes in the production of protein-rich foods the result may be severe nutritional imbalances.

Unbalanced cultural changes of these sorts may act as underlying causes of famine by eroding the productive capacity of the land, fostering malnutrition in the human population, and increasing vulnerability of the region to severe impacts from bad weather and disease. In the Sahel, there is strong reason to believe that overgrazing has been a major cause of environmental deterioration (Sterling, 1974). During the 1950's and early 1960's, favorable range conditions, construction of water wells, and control of livestock diseases permitted rapid buildup of animal herds (Ormerod, 1976). Together with expanded provision of medical services to peoples of the region, these factors have fostered the development of human and livestock populations out of balance with the drier conditions of the early 1970's. Overgrazing, and accompanying changes in the albedo of the land surface, may also be acting as a positive feedback system, promoting the desertification of the region (Charney, Stone and Quirk, 1975; Otterman, Waisel and Rosenberg, 1975). There is little doubt that similar patterns have occurred in the past; once-occupied landscapes of the Mediterranean Region and the Middle East show the evidence of erosion and salination by past civilizations. In other areas, also as a result of cultural and demographic imbalance, vegetational destruction due to the gathering of woody plants for fuel is reaching crisis proportions (Eckholm, 1975). Extensive deforestation and destructive land use must be considered contributing causes of destructive flooding along major rivers in India and Bangladesh, where such events may trigger famine (Akbar, 1975).

Second and third order changes in cultural institutions may be less obvious but even more important. Here, several generalizations relating to rural societies—those most vulnerable to famine—may be identified (Foster, 1962). First, changes in the basic means of economic livelihood almost invariably lead to changes in family organization. Where activities become more closely tied to the earning of wages or the production of goods for market, for example, the functional unit tends to shift from the extended family to the immediate biological family. Similarly, where cash crop systems are introduced, traditional patterns of cooperative work by members of rural societies tend to deteriorate. Rapid change in basic social institutions also tends to intensify divisive tendencies and factionalism within such societies. Such changes, typical of the shift from purely subsistence farming to active participation in a monetary economy, are commonly reflected in dietary deterioration. As activities become more involved in the earning of wages and the purchase of required foods and other goods, traditional knowledge no longer serves to give balanced nutrition. Education for good nutrition in developing market economy conditions is not often available.

Economic relationships at regional or national levels constitute a third area of underlying causes of famine. Nowhere is this more clearly shown than in Africa south of the Sahara (Lofchie, 1975). Food production inadequacies have existed in many African countries since the 1950's or earlier. Yet the economics of many of these same countries are active in the agricultural sector—producing export crops such as coffee, tea, cacao, cotton, sisal, groundnuts, and cashews. In Mali, for example, production of maize for local consumption declined by more than a third between 1969 and 1971; production of cottonseed, groundnuts, and rice (for export) all reached record levels during the same period. What has evolved in many of these countries is a dualistic agricultural economy; one portion fits into patterns of international trade; the other operates at subsistence or local market levels to provide food for consumption.

Similar imbalances were fostered in the Indian area by policies of the British East India Company and British colonial governments (Gangrade and Dhadda, 1973). Under colonial rule, exports promoted earlier by the East India Company were cut back and imports increased, leading to decline in the numbers of non-agricultural rural craftsmen. The land revenue system established under British rule also forced many small farmers to give up their land. The result of both of these actions was rapid growth in the numbers of landless laborers. It is significant that this period of economic and social upheaval was also the period in which famines in India were most frequent and severe.

Dualistic agricultural economies almost invariably tend to guide technological innovation and investment into the cash crop sector (Lofchie, 1975). In Africa, for example, road and rail systems, irrigation projects, and other developments are planned largely to facilitate food and fiber production for export. Production of food for consumption remains virtually unmodified, the ox-drawn plow even being a rarity in many areas.

Finally, we should note that political inaction and ineffectiveness may permit the occurrence of famine when it might easily be averted. Political difficulties appear to have been major factors in the 1974 famine in Bangladesh (Akbar, 1975). At face value, this famine was triggered by severe flooding which destroyed crops and displaced persons in low-lying areas. The famine, however, occurred during a year of bumper harvest—the second highest in 10 years. Hoarding and illegal smuggling of grain out of the country apparently played a role in reducing availability, but the failure of the government to respond to the aftermath of the flooding until too late seems to have been the single most important underlying cause of famine. As a result, at least 27,000 persons died—and in Rangpur District alone some 711 gruel kitchens were eventually set up to feed 20 percent of the population, or about 1.2 million people.

FAMINE AND THE INDIVIDUAL

The response of individuals, and of the human population as a whole, to failure of food production is a complicated and variable phenomenon. As Jelliffe and Jelliffe (1971) have suggested, we may envision the initial cause of famine conditions as being interpreted by cultural patterns, nutritional history, aggravating factors, and ameliorating factors, to give rise to the response, which may range from actual famine to averted famine. Thus, it can be seen that environmental, and more specifically, ecological, factors are intimately involved in determining the outcome of a potential famine situation.

Let us consider first the impact of food deprivation upon the individual. This topic has received much scientific attention by human physiologists

(Keys, et al., 1950; Young and Scrimshaw, 1971). The physiological response of the human body, in its broadest nature, is one which reflects adaptation to the patterns of food availability and shortage that characterized man's evolutionary history. The dominant features of this history are general omnivorousness and frequent shortage; man is consequently a species with a strong capacity for tolerating food shortages.

The dominating physiological consideration under starvation conditions is the maintenance of an adequate energy supply to the brain and central nervous system. Under basal metabolic conditions, the brain is responsible for about 45 percent of the oxygen consumption of the body, and requires roughly 1.6–2.5 MJ (400–600 Cals) of energy daily (Young and Scrimshaw, 1971). Normally, this is met by the daily consumption of 100 to 145 grams of glucose in cellular respiration. When starvation is imposed, this pattern undergoes profound modification.

Initial shortage of circulating glucose may be compensated for by conversion of liver glycogen to glucose and its release into the blood stream. However, less than 100 grams of liver glycogen normally exist in storage—less than a single day's brain requirement. During the early days and weeks of starvation, most of the glucose requirement is met by gluconeogenesis, the withdrawal of proteins from body tissues and the metabolic reworking of the amino acids of these materials into glucose. Most of this metabolic production of glucose occurs in the liver and the renal cortex. To create adequate glucose to meet brain requirements by this method alone, however, would lead to a rate of protein loss that would lead to fatal depletion of the protein framework of the body in three weeks or less.

As this protein source of glucose becomes stressed, still another mechanism rises to prominance. The respiratory metabolism of brain tissues shifts to heavy dependence upon various fatty acid derivitives mainly the ketones acetoacetic acid, beta-hydroxybutyric acid, and acetone. This dependence may start as early as 7–10 days after the start of fasting (Owen, et al., 1967; Whitehead, 1971; Young and Scrimshaw, 1971). Thereafter, until fat reserves become essentially exhausted, the bulk of the energy needs of brain metabolism are met by this mechanism.

This metabolic sequence functions well as a mechanism of adjustment to short-term conditions of general undernourishment like those presumably experienced by early man. Individuals suffering from general food deprivation in essence meet their internal physiological needs by drawing materials from body tissues. This means, specifically, that in meeting caloric requirements, withdrawals of body proteins, mainly from muscle tissues, occur. The conversion of these materials also serves to maintain levels of amino acids in the blood, and to permit maintenance of near-normal biochemical status of the body fluids (Whitehead, 1971). However, in many present-day food production systems, especially those of subsistence cultivation, complicating nutritional relationships may develop. This is especially true where food scarcity forces increased dependence on manioc, maize, and other carbohydrate-rich, protein-poor items.

Where such foods are available total calorie needs by brain and other tissues may essentially be met, thus inhibiting withdrawal of proteins from body tissue pools. This, combined with inadequacy of protein intake in the food, may lead to severe physiological imbalance, and to the protein deficiency malnutrition or kwashiorkor syndrome. Young children, whose normal protein demands are high to begin with, are highly susceptible to this pattern of disturbance. Protein deficiency in infancy may lead to irreversible stunting of brain development through reduction in the number of brain cells produced. Later, after cell division has produced the normal number of brain cells, protein deficiency may be somewhat more reversible in its effects (Winick and Rosso, 1975). In later life, the physiological disturbances caused by dietary imbalances of this sort are apparently deeply involved with the development of some of the major symptoms and signs (such as oedema), that appear in famished individuals.

Under either of the above patterns of food inadequacy, the long-term response is one of change and adjustment of enzyme systems in various body tissues and organs. Not surprisingly, this influences the response of the individual to food materials that may be presented as a part of a rehabilitation program. The sudden return of individuals having experienced severe protein deficiencies to a normal diet may cause severe physiological repercussions (Viteri and Pineda, 1971). Thus, to intelligently deal with famine situations, much more extensive knowledge of regional nutrition patterns, better methods of diagnosing the physiological state of individuals, and carefully designed rehabilitation strategies are badly needed.

Many other physiological adjustments to starvation conditions have also been documented. Correlated with the patterns of change in mobilization of food materials in the body, described above, there is a rapid decline in both basal metabolic rate and voluntary energy expenditures in activities beyond the basal level. The change in basal metabolic rate is greater and more rapid than can be accounted for by gradual wastage of metabolically active tissues (Viteri and Pineda, 1971), and thus represents an adaptive physiological response to food shortage.

Psychological changes occur as well. As with physiologcal change, many of the patterns of behavior noted under famine conditions can be interpreted as adaptive under some conditions. In densely populated, urbanized, or confined situations, however, they may constitute "social pathologies" that compound the relief problem. In general, starvation conditions direct thought and activity toward food, and most other activities are inhibited (Keys, et al., 1950). Frequently, food-seeking activities may be directed toward what one worker has termed the "cultural super-food," or the major regional staple on which the population normally depends, at the expense of other potential sources (Jelliffe and Jelliffe, 1971). However, in most situations, the range of foods sought and eaten is broadened greatly to include many materials not normally considered edible. Ties with homes, farms, and ultimately even family members also become weaker. Eventually, wandering bands of individuals seeking any available food appear. Under such conditions, it can well be said that famine breeds famine, since organized activities of society may become disrupted to the point that purposeful action to improve conditions becomes impossible. Breeding livestock and seed grain may be consumed, thus compounding future food supply problems. In addition, conditions of sanitation of food and water may deteriorate, setting the stage for disease epidemics.

Starvation, social disruption, and disease form a triad of problems that exist in almost every famine situation (Foege, 1971). Increased threat of infectious disease follows from two main mechanisms: the increased chance of disease transmission, and the increased severity of disease attacks upon malnourished individuals. Factors favoring disease transmission include deterioration of food and water sanitation and the crowding of individuals that have abandoned attention to matters of personal hygiene in food distribution and refugee camps. In general, the diseases that become epidemic during famines are those already endemic in the population. Typhus, in Europe, and cholera and smallpox, in Asia, have been major famine-associated diseases of the past, but virtually any infectious disease may be favored by the transmission conditions created by famine (Foege, 1971).

More recently, the significance of decreased resistance to disease among malnourished persons has been appreciated. Several basic mechanisms of disease resistance are compromised by starvation (Scrimshaw, Taylor and Gordon, 1968): reduced capacity for antibody production, reduced phagocyte activity, reduced epithelial tissue integrity, reduced capacity for wound healing and collagen formation, endocrine imbalance, and modified intestinal flora. Tuberculosis is a disease long known to increase in times of famine (Keys, et al., 1950). In West Africa, recent experience has shown that measles may act as a major agent of mortality among famished children, causing, by one report, mortality as high as 50 percent in the patients in a malnutrition therapy hospital (Foege, 1971). Many other infectious diseases, including many diarrheal and gastrointestinal infections, are similarly made more frequent and serious in nature. These may also become major causes of actual mortality during famines.

The demographic consequences of these physiological, psychological, and disease problems are clearly expressed. Mortality rates are highest for the weakest and most energy-requiring segments of the population: children, the aged and infirm, and pregnant and nursing women. Many of these individuals are not seen by visitors to famine areas, since they remain in seclusion to a greater degree. Among children, perhaps the most vulnerable are those recently weaned due to the arrival of a later child which must be nursed. In many parts of Africa, children at this age receive very little protein-rich food, even when it is available. Reasons for this are varied, and include various superstitions and misconceptions about the need for certain protein foods or about their digestibility (Bailey, 1975).

FAMINE PREDICTION

Famine prediction is perhaps the least developed aspect of the famine problem, as well as being an area in which little relevance of ecological relationships is generally admitted. Famine, however, represents a culminating crisis in a sequence of events having certain predictable developmental aspects. In essence, it is a catastrophic event triggered by immediate factors under circumstances of high vulnerability created by underlying causes. Vulnerability is a situation of strained balance between human populations and their productive resources in environments in which major variations in productivity tend to occur.

The topic of famine prediction thus has two aspects: assessment of vulnerability, and prediction or early recognition of triggering events. The indicators of vulnerability are factors such as density and age structure of human populations, levels of nutrition and disease resistance of individuals, condition and trend of cultivated and range lands, strength and diversity of genetic resistance of crops to pathogens and pests, and various other factors. Information on some of these indicators is already available through various international agencies such as the World Health Organization and the Food and Agriculture Organization of the United Nations. Improvements in the quality, coverage, and currency of these data can obviously be made. Such indicators might possibly be put to better use by combining them in some fashion into an index of vulnerability to internal food inadeauacy episodes—an activity that might logically be attempted through the U. N. Environmental Program.

Prediction of the triggering events that turn vulnerability into food production failure is more difficult. Here, perhaps, the strategy may be akin to the location of upstream observation stations in river basins subject to flooding. For famine, upstream becomes principally a temporal concept. Most severe famines do not result from the failure of crops in a single year, but rather from the culmination of a sequence of partial and major failures. Thus, advance warnings often exist. To turn the general system of indicators suggested above into prediction or early diagnosis of famine outbreak, only organizational changes are needed. Statements of indicators may be combined with statements of the deviation from existing values at which serious food insufficiency problems may arise. When conditions approach these critical points, a "close-watch" system may be instituted and advance preparations made for relief. Remote sensing capabilities and long-range weather forecasting represent technologies which are likely to undergo major improvement, and which may contribute toward increased accuracy in dealing with famine indicators and their projection into the future.

FAMINE RELIEF

The literature dealing with famine relief is extensive. Two recent general summaries have been done by Masefield (1963, 1967), but much additional information has been published following the experiences in Biafra in 1967 through 1969, and more recently in the Sahelian Region in Africa. Here, we can only comment on some of the more general aspects of relief efforts. The objectives of relief efforts must be to improve nutrition while disrupting cultural patterns as little as possible. To accomplish this, a relief organization must have strength, scientific competence, and cultural compatability.

Relief efforts must be adjusted to the nature of the local crisis. In some circumstances, such as the recent earthquake crisis in Guatemala, immediate aid of predictably short duration is appropriate. In other situations, as in the Sahel, relief and aid over a longer period may be necessary to deal meaningfully with the basic condition.

Many of the difficulties in relief operations arise due to the lack of coordination among individual efforts undertaken by various national and international groups, and by failure of these groups to work effectively with local governments. Both Mayer (1971, 1975) and Omololu (1971) emphasize the need for efforts to be coordinated through a single relief unit, and Mayer has further argued that this unit should be headed by an individual of calibre and authority, a "famine dictator" with the ability to force operations to move quickly.

An effective relief organization requires more than food and nutrition personnel, although such individuals clearly form the area of focus of relief activities. Several other groups are indispensible: intelligence personnel, to gather information on all aspects of the famine situation; medical and public health personnel, to treat and prevent famine-associated disease; logistics and communication personnel, to handle the logistics of acquisition, transport, and distribution of materials; business and economics personnel, to handle financial matters and advise on integration of relief activities with the local economy; and liaison personnel, to mesh relief work with local civil authority (Mayer, 1971). The need for a continuing organization with the above mix of capabilities may be appreciated when it is remembered that an effective operation requires that relief workers with little knowledge of the local scene must generally be brought in and trained quickly, a large variety of foods and other

materials must be mobilized from distant supply areas, and a fleet of vehicles of some size and diversity must be employed, maintained, and repaired during the period of relief operations.

Scientific competence is required in determining the food and other needs of the population in distress. In almost all famine areas, some foods are available, and relief activities must be planned to effectively complement these in nutritional terms. In some cases, food proteins may be extremely critical in supply and special efforts must be made to meet protein needs. In other instances specific deficiencies, such as Vitamin A, may be important considerations. Balancing the materials that are available to the relief operation also requires skill; expensive protein supplements employed in an overall diet short in total calories may result in the protein being metabolized to yield calories, rather than meeting body protein requirements (Masefield, 1971). Other considerations relating to foods concern price, bulk and transport cost, storage ability, processing and cooking requirements, potential black market value, and familiarity to local people.

Cultural compatability is likewise essential to the relief operation. Familiarity of food materials, of course, promotes their effective use by recipients. Workers must also understand how family relationships may influence food distribution and how to achieve nutritional objectives for various target individuals—children, nursing mothers, etc.—in the context of interpersonal relationships characteristic of the society. Giving bulk food to children or women, for example, is no guarantee that these individuals will be the ones to consume this food in many societies. If such is the case, direct feeding of target individuals may be the only technique possible. When such is done, however, recognition must be taken of the fact that some portion of the target group may be too weak or ill to leave home and go to the location at which food is provided.

Another strategy important in maintaining normal societal structure is the employment of many small food and medical relief centers rather than a few large ones. The existence of large centers acts as a stimulus for migration, as well as creating an increased potential for disease transmission (Mayer, 1971). The more normal the distribution of the population that can be maintained, the easier it will be for individuals to re-initiate normal life when famine conditions have abated.

In addition to relief in the form of food and medical treatment during the height of a famine, certain longer-range forms of assistance may be desirable. Specialized medical rehabilitation may be needed for some individuals for some time after food production returns to pre-famine levels. Assistance in the reuniting of broken families and in return to homes and lands abandoned during famine conditions may be necessary. During and following famine, the import of items such as tents, clothing, tools, fertilizers, and seeds must all be considered. Proper clothing and shelter can reduce food needs by reducing metabolic heat losses. Tools and supplies useful in food production are essential to reestablishing food production. The cost of importing these materials, at the proper time, may be less, relative to the relief effects obtained, than that of importing actual food (Masefield, 1971).

FAMINE PROTECTION

We have seen that famine is not a catastrophe without a history; it is the culmination of a developmental sequence leading a regional human population toward a more and more precarious balance with food production. While humanitarian relief cannot be withheld, such relief alone—reaction as if famine were nothing more than an unforeseen emergency—is likely only to magnify the problem in the long run (Dow, 1975). Much of the approach taken by the United States, the United Nations, and, in fact, many of the nations experiencing famine problems, is predicated on this assumption. Famine prevention, however, requires elimination of the conditions of vulnerability by establishing a new, more stable relationship between the population and its food supply system.

Throughout much of the underdeveloped areas of the world today, vulnerability to famine is largely the product of forces external to the regions involved. The growth of Western industrial civilization, in particular, has fostered uneven impacts on indigenous cultures and economies in most of the rest of the world. Rich deposits of minerals are systematically located and exploited, but agriculture in the same areas is given scant attention. Cash crop production has been promoted on the best available land by national and international interests, but the diets of cash crop laborers are given only passing interest. Medical and public health activities have reduced death rates, while birth rates remain high. Business and industry in urban areas have been subsidized and aided, with rural development left to its own initiative. Not

surprisingly, the disparity of change in such contrasting portions of the national system creates ecological imbalance: the vulnerability of food production systems, upon which human populations are absolutely dependent, to massive failures.

These disparities have been accentuated in the period following World War II. Economic planners, in effect, encouraged under-developed countries to short-cut the development process by rapid industrialization without previous or concomitant formation of a strong agricultural sector (Schaefer, May, and McLellan, 1970). This approach was adopted by influential groups such as the U.S. Agency for International Development. Unfortunately, many Third World nations, in their call for a "new economic order," seem to be continuing this emphasis. Unbalanced development arising from such efforts may only increase famine vulnerability.

The basic causes of the problem of famine require much more than massive "single approach" programs for their elimination. Food banks may serve to assist with relief operations in times of crisis, but their existence has little to do with preventing the development of famine situations and may weaken or deter programs of more basic importance. Resettlement may alleviate local trouble spots, but the long range effect may be to turn occasional famine into perennial chronic malnutrition—unoccupied areas with favorable conditions for human settlement are few in number in the modern world.

Solution to famine vulnerability requires cultural and economic readjustment to reduce the imbalances that created vulnerability. To obtain an idea of some of the factors involved in such an effort, let us examine a specific case, the Bihar Famine Threat of 1966–1967, a situation now regarded as a model for dealing with famine (Berg, 1971). Bihar, in eastern India, possessed a population of 53 million, about 90 percent of whom were engaged in agriculture. The system of land tenure still retained strong holdovers from the landlord system instituted by the British East India Company in the 1700's—a system that left over a quarter of the agricultural workers as landless laborers. Systems of labor bondage were still common. Of the total acreage of cultivated land, about 20 percent was irrigated, with only 7 percent being from assured sources of water that reduced their vulnerability to failure of the monsoon. Two successive years of drought caused grain production in India to fall from 88 million tons in 1965 to 72 million in 1966 and 74 million in 1967.

Famine was nevertheless averted. More than 20 million tons of grain were moved into drought affected areas and distributed through thousands of fair price stores and free food distribution centers. One of the key factors to famine prevention was the existence of an adequate transportation infrastructure. Perhaps more importantly, a number of rural development programs were set in motion. Water wells were dug and improved. During the two famine years, for example, as many wells were dug in Bihar as had been constructed during the preceding 15 years. Water storage, irrigation, and drainage facilities were also improved. Furthermore, the government provided major loans to facilitate reactivation of agricultural production following the disruptions caused by drought conditions. In 1968 and 1969 production levels consequently rose well above the levels achieved in the pre-crisis years. Of course, the gains achieved in this case were only modest, and not nearly great enough to eliminate the threat of famine from the monsoon areas of eastern India. Nevertheless, the situation does demonstrate the fact that development effort, concentrated for many years by the Indian government in urban and industrial development, permitted the development of a rural condition—demonstrably improvable by concerted effort—that threatened to trigger a major famine.

Probably no nation has done more to eliminate the threat of famine in recent years than has the People's Republic of China. Located where the northern and southern famine belts converge, it has been suggested that for two thousand or more years, famine was a nearly annual event somewhere in China. With a present population of somewhere in the vicinity of 850 to 900 million people, China has apparently achieved self-sufficiency in food production (Wortman, 1975). This has been the result of a strong, centrally-controlled program of agricultural development that has maintained between 80 and 85 percent of the population engaged in some kind of agricultural activity. One of the major emphases in Chinese agriculture has been the improvement of irrigation; about one-third of the arable land of China is irrigated. By contrast, in the United States, where reclamation and water resource development have been pursued for decades, slightly more than 10 percent of all arable land is irrigated. In a number of other ways, such as the development of fertilizer technology, labor-intensive systems for the efficient use of productive resources in agriculture have been promoted. These activities, combined with improvements in transportation and communication within the country, have apparently greatly reduced the threat of famine in China. We should also note that significant reductions in the growth rate of the human population have also occurred in China. In the relatively near future, of course, stabilization of this population must be achieved, otherwise no amount of labor or energy-intensive technology applied to food production will be able to maintain a stable relationship with food production.

Reestablishing a balance of developmental emphasis within both the developed and the developing nations of the world requires, in almost all cases, increasing attention to rural development (Power, 1975). Existing patterns of emphasis have spawned urban systems that, worldwide, are acting as magnets, drawing the rural segment away from the land, and producing massive problems of poverty and unemployment in the cities. Resource limitations preclude the infinite expansion of consumer product economies everywhere; any solution must be one which adjusts human populations to the productive level of renewable resources, including agricultural ecosystems. To prevent famine, therefore, requires the establishment of programs of rural development that attract and hold major population components in culturally rewarded food production activities. Fortunately, a number of programs of this intent are now under way, sponsored by international agencies such as the World Bank (Lele, 1975) and by private groups such as the Intermediate Technology Development Group (Schumacher, 1973). Simultaneously, however, human populations as a whole must be brought into balance with regional productive capacity through reduction in growth rates to replacement levels.

Rural development implies land reform and the application of an appropriate level of technology in many of the areas where rural-urban imbalance is most critical (Schumacher, 1973). Contrary to the opinion of some economists, the members of peasant societies are not totally resistant to innovative change. They are rational in their economic actions (Firth, 1969), efficient in the use of available resources, and interested in improving their economic status. They must be able to justify each modification in terms of the incremental effect upon their own productive position, and the risks associated with such change must be small. In areas where chronic poverty, unemployment, and inadequate food production are combined, however, the introduction of mechanized, energy-intensive methods is likely to worsen rather than alleviate the overall problem. Farmlands are likely to become increasingly concentrated, and rural dwellers displaced to cities where not only are jobs unavailable, but food costs are rising proportionate to the increased costs of inputs to the "factory farming" activity that displaced them.

Thus, a new pattern of international assistance is needed: one that combines balanced economic development, using technologies of appropriate scale, with programs to modify human population increase. The objective must be the achievement of an ecologically stabilized society; an objective that can only be realized by accommodating patterns of change in many of the cultural institutions distorted by population growth and unbalanced economic development. Care must be taken to avoid programs of high political visibility and impact, but which tend to create long-term problems and trends toward further imbalance. Central to any such goal of ecological stabilization are programs of reducing population growth rates. Without such programs the specter of famine will rise and spread over an increasing portion of the human population.

CONCLUSION

Both the potential of famine and the capability of human society to avoid famine are greater today than ever before. The population explosion shows only scattered signs of abatement; throughout most of the world existing populations are now approaching what many feel to be the limits of sustainable food production (Brown, 1974). Many terrestrial, freshwater, and marine environments are being damaged or overexploited, and immediate needs force many nations to pursue resource use strategies predicated only on short-run considerations.

Communication and transportation, however, give man a greater capability of response to local crises. Scientific and technological capacities are greater than ever—the trick is to make them a part of the solution and not of the problem. Solution to the problem of famine is thus coincident with solution of the overall world food problem. Resolution of this problem can only occur by the bringing of human populations into balance with the sustainable productive capacities of world agricultural and food productive systems.

ACKNOWLEDGEMENTS

I wish to thank the following persons for constructive comments on an earlier version of this paper: Michael D. Atkins, Frederick B. Bang, Shyam S. Bhatia, Charles F. Cooper, Warren A. Johnson, Dwain W. Parrack, and William C. Sloan.

REFERENCES

Adams, M. W., A. H. Ellingboe, and E. C. Rossman (1971). Biological uniformity and disease epidemics. *Bio-Science*, **21**, 1067–1070.
Akbar, A. (1975). 1974 famine in Bangladesh. Unpublished report, Rajshahi University, Dacca, Bangladesh. 62 pp.
Anonymous (1975). Reaping a bad harvest. *Time*, **106**(24), 35 (Dec. 15).
Bailey, K. V. (1975). Malnutrition in the African region. *WHO Chronicle*, **29**, 354–364.
Berg, A. (1971). Famine contained: Notes and lessons from the Bihar experience. *In* Blix, G., Y. Hofvander, and B. Vahlquist (Eds.), *Famine. A symposium dealing with nutrition and relief operations in time of disaster*. Swedish Nutrition Foundation, Symposium No. IX, Almquist and Wiksells, Uppsala. pp. 113–129.
Bhandari, M. M. (1974). Famine foods in the Rajasthan Desert. *Econ. Bot.*, **28**, 73–81.
Bhatia, B. M. (1963). *Famines in India*. Asia Publishing House, Bombay.
Brown, L. R. (1974). *In the human interest*. W. W. Norton and Co., N.Y. 190 pp.
Bryson, R. A. (1973). Drought in Sahelia: Who or what is to blame? *Ecologist*, **3**, 366–371.
Bryson, R. A. (1974a). World climate and world food systems III: The lessons of climatic history. University of Wisconsin Institute of Environmental Studies, Report No. 27. 17 pp.
Bryson, R. A. (1974b). A perspective on climatic change. *Science*, **184**, 753–760.
Cepede, M. and M. Lengelle (1953). *Economic Alimentaire du Globe*. Librairie de Medicis, Paris.
Charney, J., P. H. Stone,.and W. J. Quirk (1975). Drought in the Sahara: A biogeophysical feedback mechanism. *Science*, **187**, 434–435.
Cruz de Carvalho, E. (1974). "Traditional" and "modern" patterns of cattle raising in southwestern Angola: A critical evaluation of change from pastoralism to ranching. *J. of Developing Areas*, **8**, 199–226.
Da Silva Mello, A. (1964). *Nordeste Brasileiro*. Livraria Jose Olympio Editora, Rio de Janeiro. xxiv + 382 pp.
Dow, T. E., Jr. (1975). Famine in the Sahel: A dilemma for United States aid. *Current History*, **68**, 197–201.
Dyson-Hudson, R. and N. Dyson-Hudson (1970). The food production system of a semi-nomadic society: the Karimojong, Uganda. *In* P. F. M. McLoughlin (Ed.), *African food production systems*. Johns Hopkins Press, Baltimore. pp. 91–123.
Eckholm, E. P. (1975). The deterioration of mountain environments. *Science*, **189**, 764–770.
Firth, R. (1969). Social structure and peasant economy: The influence of social structure upon peasant economics. In C. R. Wharton, Jr. (Ed.), *Subsistence agriculture and economic development*. Aldine Publishing Co., Chicago. pp. 23–37.

Foege, W. H. (1971). Famine, infections, and epidemics. In Blix, G., Y. Hofvander, and B. Vahlquist (Eds.). *Op. cit.*, pp. 65–72.

Foster, G. M. (1962). *Traditional cultures: And the impact of technological change.* Harper and Row, N.Y. xi + 292 pp.

Gangrade, K. D. and S. Dhadda (1973). *Challenge and response. A study of famines in India.* Rachana Publications, Delhi. viii + 124 pp.

Hajek, E. R., M. Pacheco, and A. Passalacqua (1972). Analisis bioclimático de la sequia en la zona de tendencia mediterranea de Chile. Pub. No. 45, Laboratorio de Ecología, Universidad Católica de Chile, Santiago.

Jelliffe, D. B. and E. F. P. Jelliffe (1971). The effects of starvation on the function of the family and of society. In Blix, G., Y. Hofvander and B. Vahlquist., *Op. cit.*, pp. 54–61.

Keys, A., J. Brozek, A. Henschel, O. Mickelsen, and H. L. Taylor (1950). *The biology of human starvation.* Univ. of Minn. Press, Minneapolis. Vol. I and II. 1385 pp.

Kukla, G. J. and H. J. Kukla (1974). Increased surface albedo in the northern hemisphere. *Science*, 183, 709–714.

Lamb, H. H. (1974). Is the earth's climate changing? *Ecologist*, 4, 10–15.

Landsberg, H. E. (1970). Man-made climatic changes. *Science*, 170, 1265–1274.

Lele, U. (1975). *The design of rural development.* Johns Hopkins Univ. Press, Baltimore. xiii + 246 pp.

Lofchie, M. F. (1975). Political and economic origins of African hunger. *J. Mod. Afr. Stud.*, 13, 551–567.

Masefield, G. G. (1963). *Famine: Its prevention and relief.* Oxford Univ. Press, London.

Masefield G. G. (1967). *Food and nutrition procedures in times of disaster.* FAO Nutrition Studies No. 21.

Masefield G. G. (1971). Calculations of the amounts of different foods to be imported in the famine area—emergency subsistence level; temporary maintenance level. In Blix, G., Y. Hofvander and B. Vahlquist., *Op. cit.*, pp. 170–175.

May, J. M. and D. L. McLellan (1974). *The ecology of malnutrition in western South America.* Hafner Press, N.Y. xiii + 365 pp.

Mayer, J. (1971). Famine relief. In Blix, G., Y. Hofvander, and B. Vahlquist., *Op. cit.*, pp. 178–185.

Mayer, J. (1974). Coping with famine. *Foreign Affairs*, 53, 98–120.

Mayer, J. (1975). Management of famine relief. *Science*, 188, 571–577.

Meggers, B. J. (1971). *Amazonia: Man and culture in a counterfeit paradise.* Aldine-Atherton, Chicago. viii + 182 pp.

Norman, D. W. (1974). Rationalizing mixed cropping under indigenous conditions: The example of northern Nigeria. *J. of Development Studies*, 11, 3–21.

Omololu, A. (1971). Nutrition and relief operations—the Nigerian experience. In Blix, G., Y. Hofvander and B. Vahlquist., *Op. cit.*, pp. 130–135.

Ormerod, W. E. (1976). Ecological effect of control of African trypanosomiasis. *Science*, 191, 815–821.

Otterman, J., Y. Waisel, and E. Rosenberg (1975). Western Negev and Sinai ecosystems: comparative study of vegetation, albedo, and temperatures. *Agro-ecosystems*, 2, 47–60.

Owen, O. E., A. P. Morgan, H. G. Kemp, J. M. Sullivan, M. G. Herrera, and G. F. Cahill, Jr. (1967). Brain metabolism during fasting. *J. Clinical Investigation*, 46, 1589–1595.

Phillips, J. (1961). *The development of agriculture and forestry in the tropics: Patterns, problems, and promises.* Faber and Faber, London.

Power, J. (1975). The alternative to starvation. *Encounter*, 45, 11–35.

Reeves, W. C. (1972). Can the war to contain infectious disease be lost? *Am. J. Trop. Med. Hyg.*, 21, 251–259.

Schaefer, A. E., J. M. May, and D. L. McLellan (1970). Nutrition and technical assistance. In P. Gyorgy and O. L. Kline (Eds.), *Malnutrition is a problem of ecology.* Bibliotheca Nutritio et Dieta, No. 14. S. Karger, Basel. pp. 101–109.

Schumacher, E. F. (1973). *Small is beautiful.* Blond and Briggs, London. 290 pp.

Scrimshaw, N. S., C. E. Taylor, and J. E. Gordon (1968). *Interactions of nutrition and infection.* WHO Monograph Series, No. 57. 329 pp.

Sterling, C. (1974). The making of the sub-Saharan wasteland. *Atlantic Monthly*, 233, 98–105.

Talbot, L. M. (1972). Ecological consequences of rangeland development in Masailand, East Africa. In M. T. Farvar and J. P. Milton (Eds.), *The careless technology.* Natural History Press, Garden City, N.Y. pp. 694–711.

Viteri, F. E. and O. Pineda (1971). Effects on body composition and body function. Physiological effects. In Blix, G., Y. Hofvander and B. Vahlquist., *Op. cit.*, pp. 25–40.

Whitehead, R. G. (1971). The causes, effects and reversibility of protein-calorie malnutrition. In Blix, G., Y. Hofvander and B. Vahlquist., *Op. cit.*, pp. 41–51.

Wilkinson, R. G. (1973). *Poverty and progress.* Praeger, N.Y. xxi + 225 pp.

Wilkinson, R. G. (1974). Reproductive constraints in ecologically stabilized societies. In H. B. Parry (Ed.), *Population and its problems: A plain man's guide.* Clarendon Press, Oxford. pp. 294–299.

Winick, M. and P. Rosso (1975). Brain DNA synthesis in protein-calorie malnutrition. In R. E. Olson (Ed.), *Protein-calorie malnutrition.* Academic Press, N.Y. pp. 94–102.

Wortman, S. (1975). Agriculture in China. *Scientific American*, 232, 13–21.

Yellen, J. (1974). Quoted in G. B. Kolata, Human biogeography: Similarities between man and beast. *Science*, 185, 134–135.

Young, V. R. and N. S. Scrimshaw (1971). The physiology of starvation. *Scientific American*, 224, 14–21.

AN APPROACH TOWARDS A THEORY OF FAMINE

MOHIUDDIN ALAMGIR

Harvard Institute for International Development,
Harvard University

Famine is best defined in terms of a community syndrome, represented by a general state of prolonged foodgrain intake decline *per capita* giving rise to a number of sub-states which lead, directly or indirectly, to excess deaths in the country or region. It has been argued in this paper that no attempt should be made to build into the definition any theory of famine. The causal analysis should be carried out separately, although it must explain the sequence of events before and after the famine so as to establish an organic link with it. The situation prevailing in many Third World countries can be characterized as a quasi-famine "below poverty level equilibrium trap." Famine is a disequilibrium situation which occurs only when a number of exogenous forces combine to produce a shock of considerable magnitude under the pressure of which the existing institutions give in, at least temporarily. Three different types of famine have been identified here, general famine, regional famine and class famine. In the modern world class famine is the most important type of famine. Famine is a complex socio-economic phenomenon. A large number of possible scenarios can be worked out to describe the sequence of events leading to famine. Each specific instance of famine needs to be examined separately to establish the causal sequence that triggered off the famine syndrome.

KEY WORDS: Famine, Disequilibrium, Community syndrome, Theory, Third World, Socio-economic phenomenon, Excess death, Class famine.

INTRODUCTION: DEFINING THE "FAMINE" PHENOMENON?

Today there are many academics and political leaders alike who are concerned with the prevalence of widespread hunger and starvation in the world. Starvation persists over time and seems to be engulfing an increasing proportion of the population of the world. This is happening in spite of the advances made by science and technlogy in various spheres of life. Controversies have arisen as to whether the world has reached the limits to growth so that mankind is unable to feed itself any longer. A contrary view holds that even with the present level of technology and resources the world can feed a multiple of the present population, provided production and distribution (consumption) are more rationally organized. Obviously, the alternative views represent different underlying theories of hunger and starvation.

Hunger and starvation, as the terms are generally used, do not give rise to much of a problem of definition and interpretation. But when attention is drawn to famine, the term seems to carry with it many overtones and undertones. Governments and politicians, given their interest base, do not like to use this term to describe a situation unless they are forced to, while others concerned with hunger and starvation quarrel as to when a situation can be precisely described as having turned to famine. The problem is one of definition coupled with the need for providing a causal interpretation (explanation) of the phenomenon.

If one looks at the relevant literature, one comes across a large number of definitions of famine which attempt to combine a description of the phenomenon with a partial and truncated causal sequence. The United Nations Research Institute for Social Development (1975) states in a document that a famine occurs when many people in the same place and at the same time lack resources that will provide them with command over food stuff, for example, adequate income, inter-personal solidarity, etc., and the institutional aid can no longer cope with the situation. The document continues:

Famine is an economic and social phenomenon characterized by the widespread lack of food resources which, in the absence of outside aid, leads to the death of those affected.

In a later revised version of the document (United Nations Research Institute for Social

19

Development, 1976), a more formal and wider definition of famine is provided:

"... the word 'famine' is used to refer to a societal crisis induced by the breakdown of the accustomed availability of and access to basic foods, on a scale sufficient to threaten the lives of a significant number of people."

G.B. Masefield (1963) quotes two definitions from the *Shorter Oxford English Dictionary* and the *Chamber's Encyclopaedia*. The former defines famine as "extreme and general scarcity of food" and the latter as "a lack of food over a large geographical area sufficiently long and severe to cause widespread disease and death from starvation." According to Masefield, the first definition is rather general, while the second is more specific. He himself holds the view that,

On balance it seems clear that any satisfactory definition of famine must provide that the food shortage is either widespread or extreme if not both, that the degree of extremity is best measured by human mortality from starvation. A time element should probably also be included. The minimum acceptable definition would then imply a wide and prolonged shortage of food resulting in an increased human death rate.

The Food and Agriculture Organization of the United Nations would characterize famine as a food situation in which there are prolonged shortages of food resulting in an increased human death rate. However, in a report it comes out with the following:

definition of famine as appropriate for the purpose of assessing the need for international action: It is a food situation in which there are clear indications, based on careful and impartial study, that serious catastrophe and extensive suffering will occur if international assistance is not rendered."

(as quoted in Masefield, 1963).

The basic problem with these and other definitions is that they only present a partial picture, whether in terms of describing the phenomenon under consideration or in terms of suggesting a causal theory. The definition is expected to fulfill a number of objectives. First, one should be able to clearly distinguish between a famine situation and a non-famine situation. Therefore, emphasis on excess deaths is important. Second, the definition should include the symptoms associated with famine so that governments and the potential victims could be forewarned and relief instruments activated. Finally, it should point towards the most obvious immediate reason after the

ultimate manifestation of famine. This will thus provide a point of departure for developing a causal theory of famine. It is then meaningful to keep the focus on death, which seems to be the ultimate distinction for the potential famine victims. Therefore, hunger and starvation, prolonged or not, should not be confused with famine unless, of course, it is accompanied or followed by excess deaths. "Excess" refers to death rates above the 'normal' observed level. Similarly, death should not be linked merely to foodgrain shortage. It must be understood that foodgrain shortage only when translated into prolonged foodgrain intake decline causes death. So, foodgrain intake decline should be considered as the most proximate cause of famine which operates through the sequence of one or more intermediate steps to bring about the ultimate and essential manifestation of famine, that is, excess deaths. In this study, famine is considered to represent a general state of prolonged foodgrain intake decline per capita giving rise to a number of sub-states (symptoms) involving individuals and the community as a whole which ultimately lead, directly or indirectly, to excess deaths in the country or region. The sub-states referred to, include increase in inter-regional migration, increase in crime, increased incidence of fatal diseases, loss of body weight, eating of alternative "famine foods," changes in nutritional status, mental disorientation, uprooting of families, separation of families, transfer of assets, "wandering" and breakdown of traditional social bondage. Among these, crime, disease, loss of body weight, changes in nutritional status and eating of alternative "famine foods" can combine to produce significant excess deaths. According to this definition, the following syndrome can be constructed to describe the famine phenomenon (Figure 1).

It should be observed that famine must be characterized by the presence of the initial and the ultimate state while one or more of the intermediate states may be missing. Clearly, this view is presented to distinguish famine from poverty, hunger and starvation. This is not to say that the others are not important, but it indicates that famine includes poverty, hunger, starvation, and something more, death. No attempt has been made here to build into the definition any theory of famine. The causal analysis should be carried out separately, although it must explain the sequence of events before and after the famine so as to establish an organic link with it.

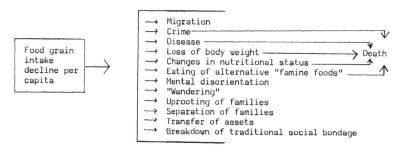

FIGURE 1   Effects of decline per capita in food grain intake.

FROM THE DEFINITION TO A THEORY OF FAMINE

In the literature on famine, no systematic attempt has been made to develop a comprehensive theory of famine under any given situation. Most of the writings have been descriptive and emphasis has varied with the interest and professional training of the scholar. Attempts have been made to look into the causes of each famine under consideration, but such investigations have not been carried out with a broad analytic framework. However, such studies have done a lot in terms of improving our understanding of the causal sequence of events underlying famine, although none has presented a complete sequence. There has been a general tendency to present an oversimplified analysis of famine. By and large, three general approaches have emerged in the analysis of famine which derive clearly from the definitions considered above. The first indicates that famine is caused by foodgrain availability decline; the second attributes it to lack of purchasing power, and the third combines the two. Professor A.K. Sen (1977), in a recent contribution, has formalized the lack of purchasing power approach in terms of what he calls deterioration of exchange entitlements. This is a new dimension in that it is more analytic, although he admits that, "the exchange entitlements approach provides a *structure* for analysing famines rather than presenting a particular theory of 'ultimate' explanation."

A theory of famine should provide the complete chain of causation that may lead to famine under different situations and it should also indicate the possible scenarios following famine which reflect the process of adjustment of the individuals and the society to a post-famine situation. In essence, one needs a combined theory of the economy and the society to understand how these operate under normal circumstances, what kinds of shocks induce a chain of reactions leading to famine, what happens during a famine, and finally whether the economy and the society adjust back to the original position or to a new position. While hypothetically such a theory should be applicable to all countries of the world at all times, the emphasis here will be primarily on the famine-prone regions of the Third World in modern times. More specifically, since the theory will be applied to study the 1974 famine in Bangladesh, the scenarios considered will be those of Bangladesh, although it will be clear from the following presentation that the basic approach is general enough to be applicable elsewhere in the world.

It is likely that under the prevailing circumstances quasi-famine situations (understood as widespread hunger and starvation) will affect an increasingly larger proportion of the population of the Third World, famine occurring only occasionally as a result of breakdown of the existing equilibrating forces. This is closely related to the phenomenon of "below poverty level equilibrium trap," which many Third World countries have experienced in recent decades. Famine is a disequilibrium situation which occurs only when a number of exogenous forces combine to produce a shock of considerable magnitude under the pressure of which the existing institutions give in, at least temporarily.

Before proceeding any further with the construction of a general theory of famine, it may be worthwhile to point out that there are three

TABLE I
Major famines of the world

Date	Area	Notes and Comments
c. 3500 B.C.	Egypt	Earliest written famine reference.
436 B.C.	Rome	Thousands of starving people threw themselves into the Tiber.
A.D. 310	England	40,000 deaths.
917-18	India, Kashmir	Great mortality. "One could scarcely see the water of the Vitasta (Jhelum) entirely covered as the river was with corpses, soaked and swollen by the water in which they had all been lying. The land became densely covered with bones."
1051 (circa)	Mexico	Caused migration of Toltecs. Said to have originated human sacrifice.
1064-72	Egypt	Failure of Nile to flood for seven years. Cannibalism.
1069	England	Norman invasion. Cannibalism.
1235	England	20,000 deaths in London. People ate bark of trees, grass.
1315-17	Central and Western Europe	Caused by excessive rain in the spring and summer of 1315. Deaths from starvation and disease may have been 10% over wide area.
1334-35	India	Severe famine which lasted for seven years. Many thousands of deaths.
1333-37	China	Great famine, reported 4,000,000 dead in one region only.
1344-45	India	Many thousands of deaths.
1347-48	Italy	Famine followed by plague (the 'Black Death') caused great mortality.
1396	India, South	A severe famine in which it was reported that everywhere "innumerable skulls were rolling about."
1540	India	"A large number of people died in the Vijainegar Kingdom due to a famine caused by war. It was so severe that cannibalism was reported."
1555-56	India, North	Scarcity was so severe that men "ate their own kind and the appearance of the famished sufferers was so hideous that one could scarcely look upon them."
1557	Russia	Widespread, but especially upper Volga. "Very severe: a great many starved in cities, villages and along the roads." Caused by rains and severe cold.
1594-95	India	Great mortality, cannibalism, and bodies not disposed of. Plague.
1600	Russia	500,000 deaths from famine and plague.
1630	India, Deccan	Famine due to drought and war. Parents sold children. 30,000 people died in one city, Surat. "Life was offered for a loaf, dogs' flesh was sold for goats' flesh, and pounded bones of the dead were mixed with flour and sold. Men began to devour each other and the flesh of a son was preferred to his love."
1650-52	Russia	Excessive rain and floods. "People ate sawdust." Many died despite tsar's permitting free grain imports. High grain prices prevented purchase of seed.
1660-61	India	"Unfavourable seasons, and want of rain, combined with war and movement of armies."
1677	India, Hydrabad	Great mortality. Caused by excessive rain. "All persons were destroyed by famine excepting two or three in each village."

TABLE 1 *(continued)*

Date	Area	Notes and Comments
1687	India, Golconda	Siege during war. Scarcity of grain so great "that even rich men were reduced to beggary, while the condition of the poor baffled description."
1693	France	Awful famine — described by Voltaire.
1702-04	India, Deccan	Famine and plague taking a toll of about 2 million lives.
1747	Western India	Failure of rain. "The country was desolated, and men and cattle perished in large numbers."
1769	France	Five percent of population said to have died.
1769-70	India, Bengal	Caused by drought. 10 million deaths.
1770	Eastern Europe	Famine and disease caused 168,000 deaths in Bohemia, 20,000 in Russia and Poland.
1775	Cape Verde Island	Great famine — 16,000 people died.
1783	India, North	"Failure of rain, excessive revenue assessments, wars and locusts, all combined to make 1783 a year of intense suffering."
1790-93	India, Hydrabad, Bombay, Orissa, Madras, Gujrat	The "Dogi Bara" or skull famine. Countryside littered with skulls. Dead were too numerous to be buried. Cannibalism.
1803-04	Western India	Caused by drought, locusts, war and migration of starving people. Thousands died.
1837-38	Northwest India	Drought. 2.8 million people affected. 800,000 dead. It is reported, "The misery was intense, the poorer classes resorted to jungles, children were sold for a few seers of grain, villages were desolated, and even orthodox Brahmins 'were now seen . . . stealing scraps from . . . dogs'."
1846-47	Ireland	Due to potato blight. 2-3 million deaths.
1860	India, Northwestern Provinces	Drought. Mortality in the famine was "a minimum of 2 lakh (200,000) deaths." Alternative estimate says "two to three percent of the people died due to famine in the affected areas."
1868-70	India, Rajputna, Northwest and Central Provinces, Punjab and Bombay	Drought. Famine followed by fever. Deaths estimated at a fourth to a third of the total population of Rajputna. 1.5 million deaths. In one district 90% of the cattle died.
1874-75	Asia Minor	150,000 deaths.
1876-79	India	Drought. 3.6 million people affected. Deaths estimated at 5 million.
1876-79	North China	No rain for 3 years. Deaths estimated at 9-13 million.
1891-92	Russia	Widespread distress, mortality relatively small.
1892-94	China	Drought. Deaths estimated at 1,000,000.
1896-97	India	Drought. Widespread disease. Estimates of death range up to 5,000,000.
1899-1900	India	Drought. 1 million deaths.
1918-19	Uganda	4,400 deaths.
1920-21	N. China	Drought. Estimated 20 million affected, 500,000 deaths.
1921-22	Russia, Ukraine and Volga region	Drought. 20-24 million people affected. Estimates of death vary between 1.3 million and 5 million.
1928-29	China, Shensi, Honan and Kansu	In Shensi alone an estimated 3 million died.
1932-33	Russia	Due to collectivization. Excess mortality estimated at 3-10 million.

TABLE 1 *(continued)*

Date	Area	Notes and Comments
1941-43	Greece	War. Losses because of increased mortality and reduced births estimated at 450,000.
1941-42	Poland, Warsaw	War. Starvation, directly or indirectly estimated to have taken 43,000 lives.
1943	Ruanda-Urundi	35,000 to 50,000 deaths.
1943-49	India, Bengal	Drought. Burmese rice cut-off by war. 3 million deaths.
1947	Russia	Drought and political decisions. Reported by Khruschev in 1963.
1960-61	Congo, Kasai	Due to civil disturbance.
1967	India, Bihar	Drought. A great disaster but excess mortality avoided through major relief operation.
1971-73	Ethiopia	Drought. Deaths estimated at 1.5 million.

Sources: Johnson (1973); Bhatia (1967; Aykroyd (1974); Masefield (1963); Srivastava (1968); Walford (1878).

different types of famines. Different causal sequences give rise to different types of famine. Analyzing the history of famines, it is found that different parts of the famine-prone regions of the world have suffered from different types of famine at different points of time. The three types of famine are; (i) famine as a general phenomenon, (ii) famine as a local/regional phenomenon, and (iii) famine as a class phenomenon. Taking the national boundary as a point of reference, famine as a general phenomenon implies a situation in which all classes of people in all regions of a country are affected, although not to the same degree. The time sequence may differ somewhat between regions and between classes of people. Secondly, famine may affect only a part/region of a country, but all groups of people within the region are more or less affected. Finally, the most interesting of all is the type of famine in which only specific groups/classes of people are affected with or without any reference to the geographic area of concentration. This is the most important type of famine. The above typology of famine also suggests that different countries can be affected by different types of famine at about the same time depending on the initial conditions and the particular causal sequences leading to the famine situation. Once we have presented the complete causal sequence of events leading to famine, it will be clear which combination leads to what type of famine.

We emphasize the need for clearly identifying the different sequences of events that may lead to famine, because this is the most essential dimension for building a theory of famine. Without such a sequence, it will not be possible to locate the vulnerable points in the rather long chain of events. Neither will it be possible to decide upon the possible course of intervention on the part of the government and other relevant national and international agencies.

Let us now turn to the theory of famine. We will consider a typical famine-prone country like Bangladesh. The economy is primarily rural, single crop rice is the most important rural production activity. There is non-rice rural production activity, mainly agricultural. In addition, there is some non-agricultural production activity. Land is given, other capital stock is growing very slowly but for any given period of production it is given. The labor force is growing at a rate higher than the population growth, which itself is quite high. Distribution of landholding and other assets is highly skewed. Land is cultivated mainly under owner-management and on a crop-sharing basis. Agricultural laborers work as family labor as well as hired labor. Crops are mostly consumed by the producing units, roughly one third entering the market. Land use pattern between different activities is determined by relative prices and subsistence requirement. Production technology adopted in the three sectors reflects relatively high labor intensity in rice and non-rice rural production activities, but somewhat high capital intensity in relation to internal factor endowments for non-agricultural production activity. But in all sectors the scope for factor substitution is limited, which along with a low rate of capital accumulation produces a low rate of growth of employment. Land being limited and population and labor force increasing, pressure on land increases. Thus, in the land market a large number of potential tenants are bidding for limited land and on the other hand, in the labor market, a reserve army of unemployed and underemployed is competing for the few job opportunities. The whole situation is compounded by the underlying social structure characterized by a low level of productive forces and exploitative production relations, which have unleashed a set of laws of motion that sustain a zone of very low level living in which the majority of the population is seemingly trapped. We may venture a step further to examine what happens at any point of time in a society like this.

Land and labor being the two most important factors, a large part of the income of households originates from these. The land market is shown in Figure 2. The two bargaining parties are landowners and potential tenants. For the landowners, two options are available. They may rent out a portion of the land under sharecropping arrangement*, or they may cultivate it themselves. On the other hand, the tenants can either rent land or can offer themselves as wage laborers. The landowners also have the option of working as hired labor. The horizontal axis represents percentage of land (*l*) and the vertical axis percentage of share of the crop (*c*), the maximum in each case being one hundred. The offer curves of the landowners and tenants are marked as *O* and *T* respectively. These curves simply show that at zero crop-share the landowners would like to rent out all land while the potential tenants would take none. At the other extreme, when the crop-share is one hundred percent (that is tenants get it all), the situation will be exactly opposite. Both of these offer curves can actually be considered as the outcome of optimizing exercises carried out by the two parties. Each maximizes total income from land and labor subject to the various constraints operating on the system. Under normal market operations, the distribution of land between owner cultivation and sharecropping would be determined by the marked clearing cropshare arrangement *C*. But in reality conditions of sharecropping are determined, among others, by social and institutional norms. The usual practice is 50 percent of the crop, with the tenant bearing the entire cost of cultivation. At this level usually excess demand for land is the outcome. Given the productivity of land, with this arrangement the tenant apparently obtains only a subsistence level

---

* For simplicity only sharecropping arrangements are considered here.

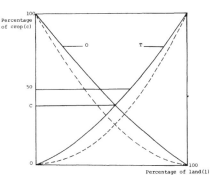

FIGURE 2   Inter-relationships between crop production, land availability ownership and tenancy of land.

of income. The institutional crop-share seems to come under two types of pressures. With population growth and growing pauperization and polarization in the society, *T* curve moves to the right, and also with the diffusion of new technology, *O* curve moves to the left as it becomes more profitable for the owners to cultivate land themselves, both having the effect of lowering the market clearing share arrangement, which in turn tends to lower the institutional share. This has been observed in many countries.

The labor market is differentiated between a market for rural activities and one for non-agricultural activity. The respective labor supply and demand curves are shown in Figures 3 and 4. In Figure 3, w_F represents famine wage level below which the laborer cannot maintain the desired level of work effort. Some labor power will be available at that wage level, but the wage rate must increase to draw labour supply beyond L_F. $\bar{L}$ represents the maximum supply of labor at any point of time. The labor supply curve, $S(L_R)$, represents roughly the situation prevailing in a typical developing country like Bangladesh. Underlying this supply schedule is the utility maximization process of individuals with respect to income and leisure and also the total contribution of individual labor supply to the community labor supply schedule. Income, as mentioned before, originates from sale of labor power as well as from family labor and crop-share, if any. The demand curve for labor, $D(L_R)$, reflects underlying production technology characterized by non-substitutability between labor and capital beyond a certain point. Marginal condition

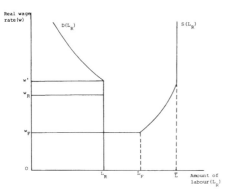

FIGURE 3   Inter-relationships between wages, labor availability and labor supply and demand in a rural market.

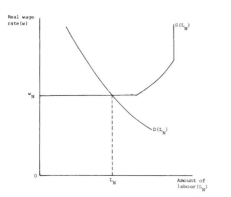

FIGURE 4   Inter-relationships between wages, labor availability, and labor supply and demand in a non-rural labor market.

for profit maximization, although not strictly applicable because of discontinuity involved, dictates a wage level w with excess labor supply, while market clearing wage is obviously w_F. However, actual wage rate, w_R, is established from time to time through a process of social arbitration, thus producing excess supply of labor. w_R is usually observed to be at around the subsistence level in these societies. w_R itself fluctuates depending on the variation of L_F and $\bar{L}$ over time, which is organically linked at any point of time with, among others, shift of labor from rural activity to non-agricultural activity, thus affecting $S(L_N)$ and employment opportunity in this sector

given by $D(L_N)$ (Figure 4). $S(L_N)$ is comparable to $S(L_R)$ except that w_N is a shade above w_R, the difference representing transfer cost between the two sectors. This sector too carries excess labor supply at wage level w_N.

In the three product markets, prices are determined by simple demand and supply considerations. For a given level of income and money supply, demand for non-rice product and non-agricultural product can be taken to be a function of prices. Supply is given by cost considerations which are derived, in turn, from production condition. Other things remaining the same, supply is a function of price. For rice, the situation needs to be specially investigated because of its importance in the matter of survival in these countries. Producers of rice consume a part and sell a part. Consumption by the producer has both a pure survival component and an income and price induced component. Higher production will imply a higher real income and will increase the producer's own consumption. On the other hand, market price will determine how much of the output in excess of pure subsistence requirement will be marketed. Thus, given the production level and prices of other commodities, marketed supply of rice will be a function of its own price. On the other hand, given the production level and wages, demand for rice will be a function of price. The participants in this market are surplus farmers on the supply side and deficit farmers and other wage earners on the demand side. The situation is often compounded by government invervention in terms of internal and external procurement of rice and its sale in the domestic market at a subsidized price through a system of rationing, thus having the effect of raising the real income of those who can avail themselves of this facility. To the extent that the system of rationing is effective in the sense that people buy as much as they can at rationed price and no rice from the rationing system leaks into the free market, the market price itself will be determined by supply and demand, although the extent of transaction is reduced by the amount of rationed supply. The rice market is shown in Figure 5.

The above system of production activities and market relations in the countries under consideration produce a quasi-equilibrium solution with a low level of real income per capita, which in turn implies a low level of foodgrain intake per capita. While, over time, values of other variables change, there is little or no change in income and basic

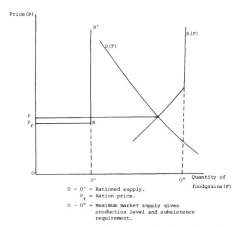

FIGURE 5 Inter-relationships between the price and quantity of food grains and demand for the grain.

consumption. This equilibrium is associated with unemployment and underemployment of factors, especially labor, and with quasi-survival of some individuals. Essential economic characteristics of the solution are price differentials in different markets and non-market clearing prices. Social arbitration, patron-client relationship, kinship bondage and occasional intervention from the government and international agencies keep the system from sliding below a crisis point in terms of decline in real income and consequent fall in foodgrain intake. The relationship between per capita real income and foodgrain intake is shown in Figure 6. An upper limit to per capita intake is indicated at $\bar{f}$. For simplicity, the relationship is assumed to be linear. In reality, the per capita income of the majority is observed to be fluctuating between the poverty income (y_P) and famine income (y_F), which give foodgrain intake between f_P and f_F. The former refers to nutritional minimum norm and the latter to survival norm. As foodgrain intake persists between these two levels or move towards f_P, death rate rises above normal D_N, but the difference with the norm does not become very pronounced until f falls below f_F (Figure 6). This is where the society enters the famine zone. As explained above, the normal experience of the societies under consideration is that the majority are trapped between f_P and f_F or y_P and y_F. This presentation is admittedly a simplified version of the real world complexities

that characterize the societies of the developing countries, Bangladesh included. However, it is important that one gets a feel of how these societies and economies operate under normal circumstances, so as to be able to investigate what kind of exogenous shocks can produce the large change in the initial condition of foodgrain intake to produce the famine syndrome shown in Figure 1, which, as mentioned before, is a disequilibrium phenomenon.

As shown in Figure 6, foodgrain intake decline can occur due to a fall in real income. But there are other factors which may directly affect the existing level of foodgrain intake. From Figure 7 one can easily see that the other immediate factors causing a drastic fall in foodgrain intake include a sharp fall in foodgrain availability per capita, a sharp increase in foodgrain prices, absence of social security and inadequate institutional arrangements to cope with the effect of food

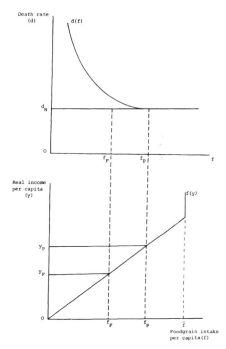

FIGURE 6 Relationships between real income and food grain intake and death rebel.

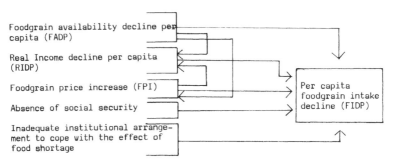

FIGURE 7   Inter-relationships of income and other factors on per capita foodgrain intake.

shortage. A certain amount of interaction between these factors is also indicated in Figure 7. Although the relative importance of each of these factors may differ depending on the situation under consideration, yet any analysis of famine must include a careful investigation of all of them. Famine as a general phenomenon may occur through a combination of foodgrain availability decline per capita and inadequate institutional arrangements to cope with the effect of food shortage. This type of famine, therefore, is unlikely to occur in modern times except under some exceptional circumstances such as war. In the past also, there have not been many instances in which general famine occurred. The great famine of 1344-45 in India was of this type. In the recent decades the Dutch famine during 1944 approached this dimension due to war-created blockade of supplies. Similarly, famine as a local/regional phenomenon can occur through foodgrain availability decline per capita, inadequate institutional arrangements to cope with the effect of food shortage and real income decline per capita. The 1630 Indian famine of Deccan is an example. Finally, famine as a class phenomenon can occur through any one or a combination of situations depicted in Figure 7. This type of famine, as suggested earlier, is characterized by the fact that the burden of foodgrain intake decline per capita and excess mortality falls primarily on the weaker sections of the population with little staying power. The world has perhaps witnessed more of this type of famine than the other two. The great Bengal famine of 1943 falls into this category, and the famine of 1974 in Bangladesh was no different (Sen, 1977; Mahalanobis, Mukherjee, Ghosh, 1946). There is,

however, no unanimity of experience regarding the relationship between declines in food intake and death, more appropriately say, between loss of body weight and death (Aykroyd, 1974). But it seems inevitable that for death to occur on a large scale within a relatively short period as experienced during famine, the average observed figure for foodgrain intake must fall much below the notional level of f_F. Such a drastic decline in foodgrain intake is likely to be concentrated among the poorer sections of the population for whom no institutional support exists to replace the support provided by the traditional society in times of emergency. In order to establish the typology of famine, the geographical and class characteristics of the famine victims must be investigated. Next, in order to determine which of the different possible combinations of causal sequences may have precipitated a particular famine situation, each one of the items on the left hand side of Figure 7 must be investigated carefully. In particular, quantitative analysis of the first three factors will be essential.

FOODGRAIN AVAILABILITY DECLINE PER CAPITA

Other things remaining the same, a decline in foodgrain availability for a consuming unit will reduce its intake. In a purely subsistence economy, where each accounting unit consumes what it produces (except saving for input requirement), a famine may occur from availability decline precipitated by production shortfall and each unit will be affected to the extent of availability shortfall. In an exchange economy, availability shortfall will imply shortfall in own production and/or shortfall in the amount that could be obtained through exchange. However, for the purpose of analysis, the conventional definition of availability needs to be further developed. Availability per capita admittedly hides a lot of information, in the sense that unless carefully specified, it says little about geogrpahical distribution, inter-class distribution and seasonal distribution. From the point of view of analysis of famine all are important. It is also necessary to distinguish between the stock and flow concepts of availability. On the one hand, one should know what was the stock of foodgrains at different points of time before and during the famine and on the other hand, it is also important to capture the flow variables. The famine intervention policies should be directed towards both. For the country as a whole, stock of foodgrains at time period t is given by:

$$S(t) = Q(t-1) + M(t-1) + A^P(t-1) + A^G(t-1)$$
$$+ A^T(t-1) - C(t-1) - X(t-1) - L_{t-1}$$

(1)

where,

$S(t)$ = stock at the beginning of period t;
$Q(t-1)$ = net production during period $t-1$;
$M(t-1)$ = imports during period $t-1$;
$A^P(t-1)$ = private stock carry-over from period $t-2$;
$A^G(t-1)$ = government stock carry-over from period $t-2$;
$A^T(t-1)$ = trading stock carry-over from period $t-2$;
$C(t-1)$ = consumption during period $t-1$;
$X(t-1)$ = exports during period $t-1$;
$L(t-1)$ = leakage from the system during period $t-1$.

Production is considered as net, after account has been taken of seed, feed and wastages. Leakage here refers to smuggling or some unforeseen loss, if any. For a particular region, the above relationship must be modified slightly. We use superscript R to refer to a region.

$$S^R(t) = Q^R(t-1) + O^R(t-1) - I^R(t-1) +$$
$$+ A^{PR}(t-1) + A^{TR}(t-1) + M^R(t-1) -$$
$$- C^R(t-1) - X^R(t-1) - L^R(t-1)$$

(2)

where,

$O^R(t-1)$ = government offtake in region R during period $t-1$;

$I^R(t-1)$ = internal procurement in region R during period $t-1$.

Here offtake from government stocks is relevant, since neither imports nor government stock carry-over can be related directly to any specific region, although probably one could refer to a policy parameter α_R which will represent the fraction of imports preassigned to region R and also to $A^{GR}(t-1)$ which will stand for government stock carry-over from period $T-2$ located in region R. If a region does not have government storage facility, this term will be zero. M and X now refer to interregional trade flows.

For any household, stock at the beginning of the period t will be given by:

$$S^H(t) = Q^H(t-1) + R_m^H(t-1) - R_x^H(t-1) +$$
$$+ A^H(t-1) + E_m^H(t-1) - E_x^H(t-1) -$$
$$- C^H(t-1) - I^H(t-1) + O^H(t-1) +$$
$$+ G^H(t-1) + w_m^H(t-1) - w_x^H(t-1) -$$
$$- L^H(t-1)$$

(3)

where,

$R_m^H(t-1)$ = produce share rental receipt by household H in period $t-1$;
$R_x^H(t-1)$ = produce share rental payment by household H in period $t-1$;
$E_m^H(t-1)$ = receipt from other units (household or trading) through market exchange by household H during period $t-1$;
$E_x^H(t-1)$ = transfer to other units through market exchange by household H during period $t-1$;
$G^H(t-1)$ = gifts and credit received (net) in kind by household H during period $t-1$;
$w_m^H(t-1)$ = wages received in kind by household H during period $t-1$;
$w_x^H(t-1)$ = wages paid in kind by household H during period $t-1$;
$O^H(t-1)$ = purchase from government offtake by household H during period $t-1$.

Availability during a period of time considered as a flow will be given by the following:

At national level:

$$F(t) = Q(t) + M(t) - \triangle S(t) - X(t) - L(t) \quad (4)$$
$$\text{or} = Q(t) + S^P(t) - \triangle S^P(t) - \triangle S^T(t)$$
$$+ O(t) - I(t) - X(t) - L(t) \quad (5)$$
$$f(t) = F(t)/P(t) \text{ or } F(t)/\overline{P}(t) \quad (6)$$

where,

$\triangle S(t)$ = net changes in total stock during period t;

$\triangle S^p(t)$ = net changes in private stock during period t;

$\triangle S^T(t)$ = net changes in trading stock during period t;

$S^p(t)$ = private stock at the beginning of period t;

$P(t)$ = mid-period population during period t;

$\bar{P}(t)$ = mid-period adjusted (for adult equivalence) population during period t;

$f(t)$ = foodgrain availability per capita during period t.

Emphasis here is placed on determining the amount that is available for consumption, whether actually consumed or not. Therefore, current production, private stocks and government offtake adds to current availability; increases in trading stock, internal procurement, exports and leakages reduce it. One should, however, be careful about double counting. For example, if a part or the entire amount of $I(t)$ is exported, then this should be deducted from $X(t)$. During periods of crisis, knowledge about adjusted population may turn out to be crucial from the point of view of organizing famine relief. Besides, for the same P, a bottom-heavy population will require less foodgrain. It is also important to realize that if there appears an acute shortage the children are likely to be the first victims, if not for any reason other than the inequitable distribution of foodgrains within the family. This has been observed both during normal times as well as during famines (Aykroyd, 1974; Chen, 1975).

At the regional level, foodgrain availability can be defined as:

$$F^R(t) = Q^R(t) + O^R(t) - \triangle S^R(t) + M^R(t) - X^R(t-1) - I^R(t) - L^R(t) \qquad (7)$$

or $= Q^R(t) + O^R(t) + S^{PR}(t) - \triangle S^{PR}(t) - \triangle S^{TR}(t) + M^R(t) - X^R(t) - I^R(t) - L^R(t) \qquad (8)$

$$f^R(t) = \frac{F^R(t)}{P^R(t)} \text{ or } \frac{F^R(t)}{\bar{P}(t)} \qquad (9)$$

For a typical household, foodgrain availability can be defined in terms of potential flow within the command of the household. Therefore,

$$F^H(t) = Q^H(t) + S^H(t) + R^H_m(t) - R^H_x(t) - I^H(t)$$
$$+ G^H(t) + w^H_m(t) - w^H_x(t) - L^H(t) +$$
$$\bar{O}^H(t) - E^H_x(t-1) + \Big[P^H_{F_s}(t) \cdot E^H_x(t) +$$
$$Y^H_{NF}(t) + W_R(t)L^H_R(t) + \sum_{i=1}^{n} P_{Ki}K_i(t)$$
$$+ W_N(t)L^H_N(t) - P_r(t)\bar{O}^H(t)\Big]/P_F(t) \qquad (10)$$

$$f^H(t) = \frac{F^H(t)}{P^H(t)} \text{ or } F^H(t)/\bar{P}^H(t) \qquad (11)$$

where,

$\bar{O}^H(t)$ = amount of government-distributed foodgrain assigned to household H during period t;

$P^H_{F_s}(t)$ = sale price of foodgrain during period t;

$Y^H_{NF}(t)$ = non-foodgrain income of household H during period t;

W_R = wage rate (money) in rural activity during period t;

W_N = wage rate (money) in non-rural activity during period t;

$L^H_R(t)$ = wage employment in rural activity for household H during period t;

$L^H_N(t)$ = wage employment in non-rural activity for household H during t;

$K_i(t)$ = amount of asset i available for sale during period t;

P_{Ki} = sale price of capital asset i during period t;

$P_r(t)$ = price of government-distributed foodgrain during period t;

$P_F(t)$ = purchase price of foodgrain during period t.

In the above, time reference t can be so adjusted as to enable one to analyze the seasonal dimension of the problem. Foodgrain availability, real income and foodgrain prices have often been found to observe certain seasonal patterns and if there are exogenous shocks occurring during the lean season, it is possible that the situation will assume catastrophic proportions and many people will be victims of famine. Relationships (5), (8) and (10) provide a basic framework to analyze famine. They combine all of the elements in Figure 7 that may precipitate a famine situation. A shortfall in $F(t)$, $F^R(t)$ and $F^H(t)$ is an indication of a general famine. Regional famine can occur with no change in $F(t)$, but with a sharp decline in $F^R(t)$ and $F^H(t)$, while a class famine can occur with or without a decline in $F(t)$ and/or $F^R_H(t)$, the important characteristics in this case being that decline in $F^H(t)$ is limited to specific groups. Shortfall or decline should be measured in relation to a non-famine normal period. Therefore, a slightly modified definition of foodgrain availability in terms of command over flow of foodgrains has provided us with a relatively simple theoretical framework to study famine. A sharp decline in foodgrain availability per capita will necessarily lead to a decline in foodgrain intake per capita and to a sequence of events culminating in excess deaths. Clearly, this can happen with foodgrain availability decline as conventionally measured (reference to relation (5) and (8)), real income decline and sharp increase in food prices. Also, the other two factors are entered into the above relations through mechanisms of transfer embodied in government foodgrain distribution and gifts and credit. If past famine was to be analyzed the above three relationships could be used to determine the extent to which each factor was responsible for initiating the famine syndrome and which regions or classes of people suffered most. This framework can also be used to predict what can happen in the future and where possibly government and relevant agencies can intervene to prevent a recurrence of famine.

However, a complete analysis will require further penetration in terms of causative analysis, so that each one of the components on the right hand side of (5), (8) and (10) can be predicted with

a certain degree of confidence. Some of the components could, of course, be treated as policy instruments under the control of the government which could be manipulated so as to avoid or achieve a certain outcome. Figure 8 shows that a decline in $F(t)$, or $F^R(t)$ can be caused by any combination of a given number of factors.

Let us start with production. At the national level, production is determined by land, crop yield, natural environment and socio-political and administrative environment. At the household level, social structures reflected in, say, tenurial status, size of landholding and asset are also factors affecting production. From time series and/or cross sectional data one can estimate relationships explaining level of foodgrain production. One can now say that foodgrain availability decline may occur due to a shortfall in production which can be caused by natural factors, low crop yield, war, civil commotion, inefficient government management and changes in agrarian structure (Figure 9). Natural factors causing shortfall in foodgrain production include flood, drought, excessive rainfall, earthquake, volcanic eruption, cyclone, wind storm, river erosion, changes in the course of rivers, waterlogging, salinity, tidal bore, frost and snow, crop disease, crop pest and locusts, livestock disease and epidemics.

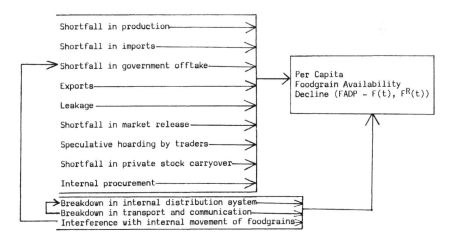

FIGURE 8   Inter-relationships of various factors affecting decline in per capita foodgrain availability.

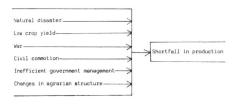

FIGURE 9   Factors affecting shortfall in food production.

Flood may be caused by silting of rivers and/or excessive rainfall, while the flood itself sometimes causes changes in the course of rivers. Shortfall in waterflow in rivers will lead to the problem of salinity intrusions in the lower reaches of rivers. Excessive withdrawal of ground and surface water is likely to aggravate the situation (Figure 10). Similarly, drought may be caused by deforestation. Apparently, natural disaster is a purely exogenous shock to the system and it can occur quite unexpectedly with such an intensity that the existing institutions completely fail to cope with the situation. At the present state of the art, it is almost impossible to predict a natural calamity too far ahead, although in certain cases, for example with respect to flood, longitudinal cycles can be found with given degree of intensity. However, some forewarning mechanism exists in almost all cases mentioned in Figure 10 with a

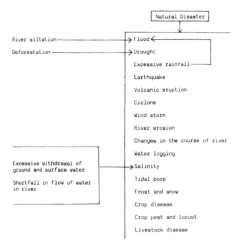

FIGURE 10   Factors affecting food production.

variable time lag. This may sometimes be useful in avoiding major catastrophy in terms of direct loss of human lives and property damage, but so far as reducing impact on standing or stored crops nothing much can be done within a very short period. Prevention in such cases requires long-term measures. Most famine-prone areas of the world today, unfortunately, are also areas frequented by natural disasters.

Crop yield is a function of rainfall, irrigation water, fertilizer, other inputs, labor, supervision and draft power. Therefore, a decline in crop yield must originate from a shortfall or inadequacy of any one of these factors. Shortfall in rainfall can affect crop yield directly; it can also do so indirectly thereby reducing the supply of water for irrigation. In addition to shortage or rainfall, irrigation may be adversely affected due to interruption of flow of water in the main channel as a result of withdrawal in the upper reaches (which sometimes causes interregional or international disputes), depletion of groundwater reserve, breakdown of irrigation equipment and non-availability of fuel. Inefficient management at various levels often leads to breakdown of irrigation equipment and a sudden scarcity of fuel. Similarly, inefficient management and shortage of credit may affect adversely the supply of irrigation water, fertilizer, other inputs and draft animals. The situation is further compounded by the prevailing agrarian structure which perpetuates a management problem, including a skewed distribution of power and resources, which leads to low crop yield and production among certain groups in the society. This lays the foundation for or aggravates a class famine situation. Availability of credit reflects the internal resource position of the rural society, intersectoral flow of funds through government and private channels and, above all, the influence of government policy with respect to allocation of resources between the floodgrain sector and other sectors. Needless to say, the overall resource position of the country will depend on the effectiveness of instruments for mobilization of domestic and foreign resources. On the other hand, overall supply of fertilizer and other inputs to the ultimate users may decline due to production shortfall, import shortfall and distribution bottlenecks. Imports may be related to production through the supply of inputs. Natural disaster, war, etc., not only affect production of inputs and create a distribution bottleneck but they also lead to a shortage of

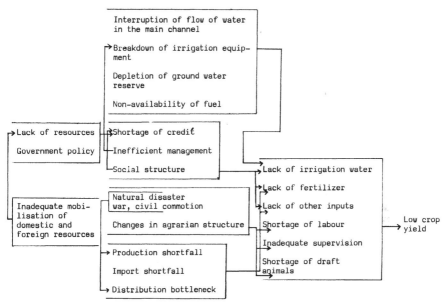

FIGURE 11   Factors affecting crop yield.

labor, inadequate supervision and shortage of draft animals. A sudden change in agrarian structure could upset the balance in a manner such that all factors will be adversely affected. The causal sequence with respect to low crop yield is shown in Figure 11.

Import is a function of domestic production, population, total foreign exchange resource, import price and government policy. However, import planning and the international supply situation also figure prominently in the determination of imports. Therefore, a shortfall in imports may occur on the one hand due to inadequate foreign exchange resources, sharp increases in import price, supply shortages at the international market, poor import planning and government policy with respect to allocation of foreign exchange between purchase of foodgrains and inputs for foodgrain production, and import of other items on the other hand. Lack of foreign exchange resource may arise from poor export performance, inadequate foreign capital inflow, and unusual international price movements. Import price rises and supply shortages at the international market are caused by any one or a combination of such factors as production shortfall in exporting countries, depletion of world stock, increased world absorption, domestic policies of exporting countries, increased cost of production and international inflation. Factors involved in a shortfall in imports is shown in Figure 12.

Reasons for shortfalls in production, as indicated in Figure 9, can also be responsible for breakdown of internal distribution systems, breakdown of transport and communication, speculative hoarding by traders, shortfall in market release and shortfall in private stock carry-over. Trading stock and market release are also influenced by the rate of inflation, rate of increase of foodgrain prices, previous period's production level, status of standing crop and prolonged retention of marketable foodgrain by farmers. A shortfall in government offtake can be caused by inadequate stock and storage carry-over and unforeseen storage loss or destruction. Poor planning and government policy may affect foodgrain stock, while natural disaster, war, etc., will lead to storage loss. Furthermore, the government offtake may be directly affected by breakdown of

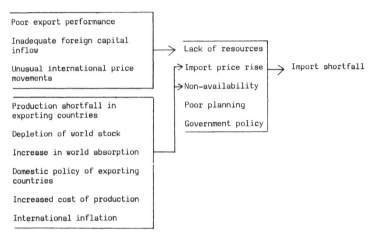

FIGURE 12   Factors affecting a shortfall in food imports.

transport and communication systems. Leakage through smuggling is caused by price differentials between neighboring countries, maintenance of artificial exchange rates at home, inadequate border policing and general lack of confidence in the economy, giving rise to a strong tendency for capital flight. War and inefficient government management feed into this process. Government policy and price differentials are responsible for exports across boundaries of nations and regions. This can clearly aggravate a simple shortage situation into a famine situation. Government policy of internal procurement and interference in the internal movement of foodgrains may worsen the situation during shortages, thus leading to famine. The above causal sequences leading ultimately to per capital decline in foodgrain availability are shown in Figure 13.

Relationships (5), (8) and (10) show that food-grain availability, understood broadly, is also linked with the real income of households and foodgrain prices. In other words, a decline in $FH(t)$ may be contributed to by real income decline and foodgrain price increase. Besides, a fall in the value of saleable assets may also adversely affect the situation. Real income is affected by output, level of economic activity, employment, rate of inflation, real wages, demand, terms of trade and social (agrarian) structure. In addition to the factors already considered. Output, particularly of non-foodgrain type, may be affected by government policy and inefficient management. Similarly, disruption in normal economic activity and fall in employment may be caused by natural disaster, war, etc., and also by a shortfall in demand, which in turn is caused by a shortfall in output. It is well known that a shortfall in output also contributes to inflation. Monetary expansion and international inflation may add to domestic inflation and all of these are affected by government policy. Inflation leads to a fall in real wages, and such a fall is aggravated by a shortfall in demand. Government policy has a direct bearing on intersectoral terms of trade. The other factor, foodgrain price increases, is influenced by foodgrain availability decline [$F(t)$, $F^R(t)$], incidence of panic purchase by consumers, increase in cost of imports, increase in money supply and government policy. It will be necessary to carefully analyze the foodgrain market. For prediction of foodgrain prices one can estimate a price equation, while the problem is more complex in the case of real income. One may either extrapolate the values of certain determinants of income or construct a simple model to determine employment and wage level which, along with prices, will give real income. The relevant causal sequences for real income and foodgrain price are shown in Figure 14.

Famine is caused by a decline in foodgrain availability as given in (5), (8) and (10) above. One can also refer to the corresponding per capita

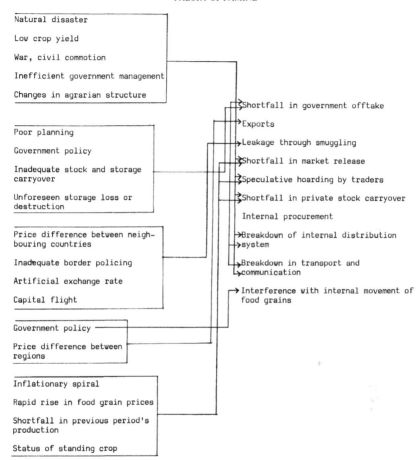

FIGURE 13   Factors and sequence of events leading to a decline in per capita food grain availability.

relationships. From the above it is apparent that a large number of causal sequences may lead to the famine syndrome. However, it is contended here that possibly more than one sequence operates simultaneously, and that they reinforce one another so as to finally cause excess deaths. This has been characterized as a disequilibrium phenomenon in the context of a country like Bangladesh in modern times. As the famine syndrome reaches its climax, a set of forces gets underway to establish a new equilibrium for the society and economy. However, while certain things (parameters) change as a consequence of famine (for example a reduction in population), the society basically reverts back to the low income-low food-grain intake equilibrium as shown in Figure 6.

The process of adjustment to the original equilibrium through a sequence of events is shown in Figure 15. As excess deaths continue to occur, society within and outsided reacts to soften the pace of human mortality. Thus one comes across government-sponsored gruel kitchens, emergency

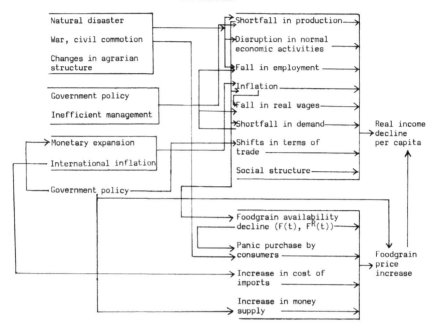

FIGURE 14   Factors and sequence of events leading to a decline in per capita income.

international aid and relief efforts, voluntary social service temporarily establishing an interpersonal resource transfer mechanism, personal acts of charity, medical relief work, work programs, acceleration of import, augmented public distribution at subsidized prices and emergency supply of agricultural inputs and credit. The time lag in which each one of these relief instruments comes into operation depends on the situation under consideration, particularly on the sensitivity of the government to the catastrophies and human suffering. By and large, such relief efforts continue until the worst in terms of excess deaths is over. In Bangladesh, during 1974, gruel kitchens were operating on a regular basis between August and November, while starvation deaths are known to have occurred before and after this period.

The famine syndrome initiates a number of processes in the society, which facilitate restoration of the low income-low foodgrain intake equilibrium. Excess deaths reduce the labor force, thus improving the bargaining power of labor in certain localities. But this gain is very shortlived,

since new additions to the rank through the process of pauperization and marginalization (because of distress sale of assets) in rural areas and permanent migration into urban squatters, wipe it out. The power of the local elites is clearly enhanced, since they gain command over a greater amount of productive resources. A general famine, however, can bring about a leveling of the society. It should be noted that all types of famine do this to the lower strata of the society which becomes even more homogenous. Following famine, the agrarian structure tends to undergo changes. In the context of Bangladesh, it can be said that the process of pauperization and polarization strengthens the semi-feudal mode of production in agriculture, although there is an opposing view that in modern times famine opens up a new vista for capitalist penetration in agriculture. The process of breakdown of the traditional social bondage continues, thus eliminating an informal support mechanism without replacing it with anything new. Sometimes a slow change in dietary pattern sets in,

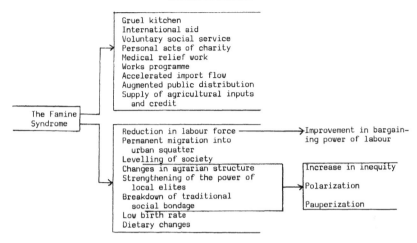

FIGURE 15 Characteristics of the famine syndrome and establishment of a new post-famine equilibrium.

which may simplify the famine relief work or improve the normal foodgrain availability situation. Introduction of wheat in rice-eating regions is a case in point. Finally, famine reduces birth rate and increases death rate, thus having a long-term decelerating effect on high population growth regions with consequent positive impact on foodgrain availability. With normal production activities restored, the society is confronted with the outcome of a few processes, some of which have a positive and others a negative impact on foodgrain availability per capita. Admittedly, the outcome on balance is quite uncertain, but recent history of the societies under consideration indicates that any gain is unlikely to be sustained over a long period of time. Given the fact that following the famine the society is basically back to the operational framework represented in Figures 1 through 6, one can only predict the restoration of the original equilibrium.

SOME HYPOTHESES AND POSSIBLE SCENARIOS

The analytic framework to study famine presented above can be applied to any situation, although a specific case may require some modification of the basic structure. In the present context, it will be necessary to carry out a fairly elaborate analysis to identify the causal sequence in a typical famine-prone region of the third world and also to indicate the nature, timing and point of intervention by the government and other concerned institutions. Out of a large number of hypotheses that emerge from the causal sequences described, a few are singled out because they emerge naturally and can be put to empirical tests.

Hypothesis 1

The most obvious hypothesis is that a famine is caused by a serious shortage in the total availability of foodgrains and substitutes. This, of course, will apply to all types of famine. One can then proceed to examine whether all of the famines of the past occurred due to food shortage or whether there are instances of famine without food shortage. Rejection of this hypothesis in one case could not be taken as its being invalid universally.

Hypothesis 2

A second hypothesis would call for the examination of the proposition that famine can occur from lack of purchasing power or, "from a sharp deterioration of exchange entitlement". (Sen, 1977) A shift in exchange entitlement reflects a shift in the balance of class power in the society, which may lead to class famine. One can examine the trend of real income of various classes in the society to determine whether there was a significant decline during the period under consideration. In addition, one can look at the market for assets to analyze the price trend so as to establish how far people were able to sustain themselves through liquidation of assets. The most likely outcome is that both of these hypotheses will be accepted in a typical situation, since they are interrelated.

Hypothesis 3

Substitution of market and exchange for subsistence economy increases the possibility of famine. The argument here runs as follows. In a purely subsistence economy, a consuming unit faces the prospect of famine only when there is a natural or man-made calamity having adverse effects on its physical means of direct subsistence. As the economy moves to market and exchange, new factors emerge which may cause famine. In other words, the probability of a famine occurring increases, since there are more ways now than before in which it can happen. It must be understood that these hypotheses have two dimensions; one is the theoretical possibility of a cause and effect sequence occurring, the other is the actual experience. However, if the hypothesis is rejected, one should not reject the logic of the argument, because the real cause of empirical test failing may be that insufficient account was taken in the beginning of the possible countervailing forces operating on the system. Admittedly, it is not easy to test this hypothesis. History of famines in purely subsistence economies of the past is not well recorded. It is possible to look at the famine-prone regions of the modern world to test if there is a significant positive correlation between famine incidence and/or intensity on the one hand and a measure of market and exchange penetration in the economy, on the other.

Hypothesis 4

A hypothesis related to 2 and 3 has been proposed by A.K. Sen (1977). Famine possibility increases with "the emergence of labor-power as a commodity, with neither the protection of the family system of peasant agriculture, nor the insurance of unemployment compensation — nor, of course, the guarantee of the right to work at a living wage." One can put forward a

corresponding hypothesis that in modern times, a simple food shortage situation is aggravated into a famine situation due to the breakdown of traditional dependency relationships. While it is not very difficult to see the logic of the arguments underlying these hypotheses, their validity is difficult to establish because sufficient data may not be available for a particular region covering a relatively long horizon. Cross-country or cross-regional data may be used instead, but it is unlikely that sufficient information can be gathered without serious differences as to the underlying quality. The reason we emphasize the need for carefully looking into these hypotheses is that they have important welfare implications for societies in transition. The issue is, "is it so bad to be traditional?" as some would like us to believe.

Hypothesis 5

There are three contending hypotheses regarding the relationship between agrarian structure and famine in the third world. These are; first, famine in the modern times strengthens semi-feudalism in agriculture, second, famine facilitates penetration of capitalism in agriculture, and third, penetration of capitalism in agriculture increases the possibility of famine. An examination of these hypotheses will require analysis of the mode of production dominating the agriculture sector and the laws of motion operating in the society. However, empirical tests may be devised to compare the situation before and after famine to determine the extent to which any one of the above assertions can be validated. But purely mechanistic tests may be misleading, if they fail to reveal the internal dialectics of antagonistic classes in the society.

Hypothesis 6

A famine situation can be created or aggravated through the arbitration of the state in the distribution of foodgrains between regions or classes of people. While government intervention is unavoidable in a crisis situation, it can often be counterproductive, either because the underlying strategy was misconceived and could not be applied effectively, or because a deliberate bias was introduced in such an action program as to affect the well-being of a region or a group of people in a certain predetermined manner. A test of this hypothesis will naturally call for a thorough analysis of the government intervention policies before, during and after a famine.

Hypothesis 7

The more unequal the distribution of income-generating assets, the greater the probability or intensity of famine. A class famine situation is triggered off or accentuated by an exogenous shock more easily if the command over productive assets is unevenly distributed. Empirically this can be tested with both longitudinal and cross-sectional data.

Hypothesis 8

A region characterized by low level of productive forces and a high rate of population growth is relatively more susceptible to famine. This is rather obvious and many instances can be found in history. While in the short run nothing can be done on either front, long run measures will have to be initiated to remove them as causes of famine.

Hypothesis 9

Exploitative production relations aggravate the effect of a famine situation. Other things remaining the same, sharecroppers, tenants and wage laborers are squeezed even more during or prior to famine than at normal times by landowners, moneylenders and other exploitative elements in the society. This is reflected in the post-famine societal adjustment sequence described above. It can be empirically established how the weaker sections of the population suffer specifically from a famine situation because of their low bargaining position. Data on land sale, indebtedness, real wage level, etc., can be analyzed to test this hypothesis.

Hypothesis 10

Destabilizing price speculation in foodgrains can lead to or worsen a famine situation. This can be demonstrated very easily. A foodgrain price spiral will very soon reach a crisis point and in no time will victimize a large section of the population which depends on the market for foodgrains.

Hypothesis 11

Lack of seasonal or spatial arbitrage mechanism can create and/or accentuate a famine situation.

This is again easily verified. Seasonality in availability has in many cases created severe distress, although temporarily. On the other hand, regional price differential due to absence of smooth inter-regional flow of foodgrains can cause a regional famine.

Hypothesis 12

Uncoordinated world production, consumption and storage policies will make the famine-prone regions of the world even more vulnerable to the hazards of famine. This has been observed in the international foodgrain crisis of recent years reflected in unusual stock and price movements.

CONCLUSIONS

Famine has both long-term and short-term causes and consequences. Careful analysis must be done before one can say how a particular famine occurred, who were the victims and how did the society adjust to the post-famine situation. While hypothetically famine can occur anywhere at any time, in reality it is apparent that certain regions of the world are today more vulnerable to famine than others. Similarly, within each region, the consequence of famine is not equitably shared by all. A large number of possible scenarios can be worked out to describe the sequence of events leading to famine. In this sense, there probably does not exist a single theory of famine. As a matter of fact, it was somewhat of an over-simplification when we claimed that famine occurs due to a sharp decline in foodgrain availability per capita. It is important to realize that we can only make an approach towards a theory of famine, without really establishing *the theory*. This is because situations vary widely over time and space and it would be unrealistic to capture all of them in one sweep and bind them or hide them within a narrowly conceived theory of famine. Instead a rather elaborate analytic framework has been presented here, so that one can test a set of alternative hypotheses and carefully work out a causal sequence that may have precipitated a particular famine syndrome. The famine syndrome itself needs to be carefully outlined, so that one can establish an appropriate typology of famine, which will then facilitate an examination of the post-famine scenario and the process of societal adjustment. What one expects to be able

M. ALAMGIR

to do from such an analysis is to work out a possible policy framework involving famine forewarning, prevention and relief for consideration of relevant national and international agencies. Admittedly, in this paper greater emphasis has been placed on internal factors as opposed to external factors, but this is done because of the present author's belief that in the absence of an effective mechanism to establish a just world order, countries will be well advised to look inside for a solution to the famine phenomenon.

REFERENCES

Aykroyd, W.R. (1974). *The Conquest of Famine.* Chatto and Windus, London. pp. 13-16.

Bhatia, B.M. (1967). *Famines in India 1960-1965,* 2nd edition. Asia Publishing House, New Delhi.

Chen, L.C. (1975). An analysis of per capita foodgrain availability, consumption and requirements in Bangladesh: A systematic approach to food planning. *Bangladesh Development Studies* 3, 93-110.

Johnson, D.G. (1973). Famine. In *Encyclopaedia Britannica* (1973 edition). p. 58.

Mahalanobis, P.C., R. Mukherjee, and A. Ghosh (1946). A sample survey of after-effects of the Bengal famine of 1943. *Sankhya* 7, Part 4.

Masefield, G.B. (1963). *Famine: Its Prevention and Relief.* Oxford University Press, Cambridge. pp. 2-5.

Sen, A.K. (1977). Starvation and exchange entitlements: A general approach and its application to the great Bengal famine. *Cambridge J. Economics* 1, p.35, p.56.

Srivastava, H.S. (1968). *The History of Indian Famines and Development of Famine Policy.* Sri Ram Mehra & Co., Agra.

United Nations Research Institute for Social Development. (1975). *Famine Risk in the Modern World.* Geneva, 18 August.

United Nations Research Institute for Social Development. (1976). *Famine Risk in the Modern World: Studies in Food Systems under Conditions of Recurrent Scarcity.* Geneva, June.

Walford, C. (1878). The famines of the world: Past and present. *J. Statist. Soc.* 41, Part 3.

ECOSYSTEMS AND FAMINE†

DWAIN W. PARRACK

Department of Pathobiology, The Johns Hopkins University, School of Hygiene and Public Health, Baltimore, Maryland 21205.

In discussing famine, its causes and its results, we immediately run into problems of terminology. It seems to me, however, to be useful to think of the ontogeny of famine as involving three major sets of factors: first, background factors; second, pathological factors (precursors); and third, precipitating factors. (See Table I).

For example, the 1974 famine in Rangpur District of Bangladesh, was precipitated by flooding of the Brahmaputra River. The flooding, in turn, had its causes in a set of pathological factors (meteorological, ecological, geographical), which were the precursors of the famine and which were pathological because they were distortions of the basic ecological relationships (background factors). Reading the chain of causation of the famine forward, rather than backward, we have a situation in which a fairly stable ecosystem (background factor) becomes diseased and produces a series of pathological biotic and social conditions (the pathologies, the precursors). The stage is set for the floods which precipitate the famine.

It is the purpose of this paper to examine some of the features of ecosystems and to see how these become pathological and serve as precursors of the tragedy.

ECOSYSTEMS

Natural and agricultural ecosystems have many features that are too numerous to be included in the present discussion. A few are basic, however, and they are common to both the natural and the agricultural ecosystems, to the oak-hickory forest and to the rice field. They also have a direct bearing on famine. Five such features have been selected for discussion.

TABLE I

Ontogeny of famine

Background factors	Pathological factors (precursors)	Precipitating factors
Basic biotic and ecological factors (ecosystems)	Meteorological	Floods
	Biotic	Storms
	Economic	Drought
	Social (including political), etc.	War
		Blight

† Based on a paper presented at the American Association for the Advancement of Science Meeting held on February 20, 1976.

Structure

Natural ecosystems and farmlands are similar in trophic structure. They are composed of diverse species of plants and animals which can be fairly easily assigned to three trophic levels. These have been traditionally called the primary producers (green plants), the primary consumers (herbivores), and the secondary (and sometimes tertiary) consumers (carnivores). Completing the classification is a large group, the decomposers. This concept is based on Eltonian pyramids and each succeeding trophic level, as we go up the pyramid, becomes smaller both in numbers of individuals and in the total biomass of those individuals.

Flow of Energy Through the Trophic Levels

Some of the energy of sunlight which is fixed by plants (the gross production) in the producer trophic level is used for the plants' respiration and some (the net production) is used in growth or reproduction. Energy in the form of the tissue of these plants is harvested by the primary consumers, which likewise use it in respiration or in growth and reproduction. The flesh-eating consumers of the third trophic level, in turn, harvest some of the herbivores of the level below them and, like them, use the energy for general metabolism and in increasing the size of the individual (growth) or of the population (reproduction). Golley's (1960) famous study of an old-field community will illustrate the flow of energy through an ecosystem (Table II).

Carrying Capacity

The conditions operating in an ecosystem limit the system to a certain number of individuals at a given time. This limitation is the carrying capacity of the ecosystem. It varies greatly, for example, the carrying capacity of a well-watered grassland is obviously greater than that of a desert. The capacity also varies from season to season and from year to year, and can be greatly influenced by man's behaviour.

Fluctuation of Populations

The number of individuals within a species in a trophic level adjusts, sometimes very rapidly, to the level imposed upon it by the carrying capacity of the system. In good years, when the requirements of life are plentiful, members of the species may increase so rapidly that the carrying capacity is temporarily surpassed. This overshoot is usually quickly corrected through the emigration or death of individuals or by reduced reproduction. Under certain conditions, these adjustments can appear as very dramatic population crashes.

Reserves of Energy

The organisms in an ecosystem have the ability to survive hard times because of energy reserves. In animals the reserves often are in the form of body fat (and in a few, they are food stored in caches), while in plants reserves are usually stored in underground parts, such as roots or rhizomes. In

either case, some sort of reserve system is necessary to buffer the effects of a changing environment.

Recognizing these five characteristics of these ecosystems, comparisons will now be made between ecosystems and man's agricultural fields, which are truncated ecosystems.

Except for the fringes of grasses, trees, and shrubs, whose growth is sometimes permitted by man at the periphery of his agricultural fields, farm lands represent, almost of necessity, depauperized biological communities, often dominated by a single species of plant (wheat, corn or rice) and by man. In much of the world, where farmers are essentially vegetarians by necessity, if not by choice, the structure of the ecosystem essentially consists of only two levels, the primary producer (say, rice) and the primary consumers (the farmer and his draft animals, which are essential for farming the rice). In more sophisticated agricultural systems, producing domestic animals primarily for their consumption by man, humans occupy both the herbivorous and carnivorous levels of the consumers. For the vast majority of people, however, the trophic role of man is much closer to that of the grazing cow than to that of the hunting tiger. For the purposes of this discussion in both the sophisticated and the less sophisticated situation, the agricultural ecosystem is simplified, by combining the primary and secondary consumers to form a system of two trophic levels namely: crops and man-domestic animal, or plants and animals.

The development of modern agriculture has led to changes in the flow of energy within some agroecosystems, especially in those which emphasize beef production. The omnivorous farmer of Iowa competes, to some extent, with his own cows, for they both eat some of the same parts of the same crop plants (corn). The essentially herbivorous farmer of Bengal, on the other hand, avoids this

TABLE II

Energy relationships in an old-field community (based on Golley, 1960)

Food Item	Consumption	Energy used in respiration (% of assimilated energy)	Net production (% of assimilated energy)
Grass		15	85
Meadow mice	2% of the grass	68	32
Weasels	31% of the mice	93	7

competition by dividing his chief crop, rice, into grain for himself and straw for his cattle (Fig. 1). The situation in Bengal makes ecological sense and would be good, were it not for relatively recent growth in human population which has, at times, surpassed the carrying capacity of the land.

The plant/animal (producer/consumer) ratio of the biomass is of fundamental importance to the ecosystems. Data on this ratio in several natural tropical ecosystems have been summarized (Farnworth and Golley, 1973) and vary from high ratios in forests (4383 g of plants to 1 g of animals and 2264 to 1 in Panamanian and Puerto Rican forests, respectively) to a low ratio in East Africa savanna land (15 to 1). The forest ratios are high because of the immense amount of dead material in the trees which is indigestable to most animals. The ratio for the savanna land is much closer to that of man's agricultural fields. Data on plant/animal relationships in farming communities are

not common and are often in crude forms. Odend'hal (1972) actually counted the humans and domestic animals in an area of almost 6 square miles in West Bengal. Cattle were the most common livestock and averaged 653 per square mile, while the average density for humans was 2850 per square mile.

Makhijani and Poole (1975) have described the village Mangaon in Bihar, just west of West Bengal, a village where all available land was cultivated and where the forests have long since been cut and where even the wealthiest 10 percent of the people were usually poor. The 1000 residents of the village owned some 1213 animals (cattle, goats) and, annually, produced some 585 tons of crops (rice, wheat, maize, sugar cane). It is the ratio of animals, particularly humans and cattle, to plants that concerns us here. The crudest form of this relationship can be expressed as numbers of individuals, animals, and weight of the crops, as

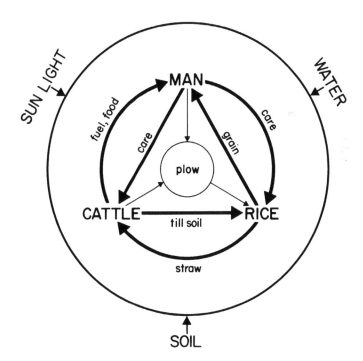

FIGURE 1 The relationship of man, cattle and rice in the Gangetic delta.

above. This can be made more meaningful by expressing it in terms of biomass of the elements of the system. At some point in the growth of the populations of consumers, a ratio between plant and animal biomass is reached and this represents the carrying capacity. According to Makhijani's and Poole's description, Mangaon is, at best, at that point or perhaps beyond it.

When the carrying capacity has been reached, an area may slowly slip into a famine as the result of several years of drought, or famine conditions may suddenly develop as in the case of severe storms, floods or war. The point is that an area at carrying capacity is extremely vulnerable, for it has little or no reserves to buffer the temporary loss of food. There is little chance of building up reserves, even in good years, when the demands of the human population are so great, and it is especially difficult when the surplus food (Fig. 2) is siphoned off by rodents, insects, microorganisms and smugglers and legitimate sales.

Although records are imperfect they indicate that the consumer/producer ratio reached the pathological condition thousands of times in the past. In Europe, from the first century A.D. until near the end of the 19th century, there was a famine or serious food shortage in one place or another every two or three years (Nichol, 1971). Yao (1943) reported 3106 floods and 1873 droughts in China from 206 B.C. to 1911 A.D. During approximately the same period, there were 1828 famines in China (Nichol, 1971) or one famine somewhere in China every 0.9 year.

As pointed out by Bourne (1975), our modern ecosystem is artificial and fragile. The present situation indicates that a new balance will come about by reduction of food production and a reduction of human biomass. In other words, the consumer/

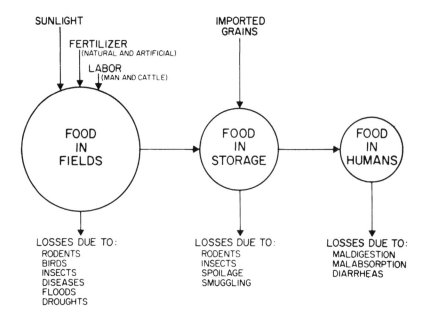

FOOD-ENERGY RELATIONSHIPS

FIGURE 2   Food and energy relationships in the rural Gangetic delta. Man's food in all three stages (in fields, storage, or stomachs) is subject to various losses to other members of the ecosystem.

producer problem will likely be solved by widespread starvation.

In summary, it seems fruitful to consider agroecosystems as being similar to natural ecosystems in having several common basic biological characteristics which serve as the background factors for famine. These factors become pathological when distorted by the development of harmful conditions of weather, economy or society. Under such conditions, famine is precipitated by a specific event (such as flood or drought or wars).

REFERENCES

Bourne, A. (1975). The man/food equation. *In: The Man/Food Equation*. Steele and Bourne (eds.). (Proceedings of a symposium held at The Royal Institution, London, September 1973). Academic Press, New York.

Farnworth, E. G. and F. B. Golley (eds.). (1973). *Fragile Ecosystems, Evaluation of Research and Applications in the Neotropics*. Springer Verlag, New York. 258 pp.

Golley, F. B. (1960). Energy dynamics of a food chain of an old-field community. *Ecological Monographs 30:* 187–206.

Makhijani, A. and A. Poole. (1975). *Energy and Agriculture in the Third World*. Ballinger, Cambridge, Mass. 168 pp.

Nicol, B. M. (1971). Causes of famine in the past and in the future. *In: Famine: A Symposium Dealing with Nutrition and Relief Operations in Times of Disaster*. Eds.: G. Blix, Y. Hofvander and B. Vahlquist. Almquist and Wiksell, Stockholm, Sweden.

Odend'hal, S. (1972). Energetics of Indian cattle in their environment. *Human Ecology* I, 3–22.

Yao, S.-Y. (1943). The geographical distribution of the floods and droughts in Chinese history, 206 B.C. – A.D. 1911. *Far Eastern Quarterly* II, 357–378.

SECTION II

**THE INDIVIDUAL'S HEALTH
DURING FAMINE**

SECTION II

INTRODUCTION

John R.K. ROBSON

Death and disease are acknowledged as an inevitable outcome of famine, yet little recognition is given to the resilience of the human body to nutritional insult. In the affluent regions of the world, it is recognized that body weight can be maintained on a wide range of caloric intakes. For example, forty years ago Widdowson (1962) showed that for any 20 people of the same age, sex and occupation one could be found eating twice as much as another. Thus there is a wide individual variation in what might be considered a normal intake. Demographic studies (FAO, 1975) demonstrate that the affluent Westerner maintains energy balance at a higher caloric intake, whereas the less fortunate in developing countries maintain weight at a much lower level of intake. In this situation it may be assumed that the affluent could adjust downwards should they be exposed to food shortages. The same question, when directed towards those maintaining weight at lower caloric intakes, reveals that a surprising amount of adaptation to even smaller intakes of energy is possible. When the supply of energy fails to meet demands, one of the first adaptations of the body is to conserve energy, and the individual learns to be extremely economic in movement. As the deprivation continues, the effects become increasingly apparent among groups. For example, in Africa one was alerted to possible energy shortages in an area by the behavior of the children during their morning break or at lunch time. Children usually run out of school, and most play games. When calories are in short supply, however, it was common to observe the children to be moving slowly and showing little evidence of normal physical activity. For the most part, they would rest under the trees, often sleeping. Similarly, the heavy manual laborer in the developing parts of the world learns to conserve energy at every opportunity. This is often manifested as sleeping. This habit, contrary to past beliefs, is not an expression of natural indolence, but a physiological adaptation to stress caused by inadequate food intake.

This is just one aspect of the changes that a human body is prepared to make in order to survive food shortages. Cahill, in the next section, describes the metabolic adaptations that enable reserves of fat and body tissue to be used most economically and to allow the famine victim to survive.

It is not generally realized that the changes that take place in response to deprivation of energy are immediate. Even after short periods of food inadequacy of only a few hours' duration, the body is starting to withdraw protein from the tissues for breakdown and use as a source of energy. While fat is mobilized, in these early days of starvation, the body seems to be reluctant to utilize its adipose tissue stores. In fact, the whole of the physiological mechanisms are geared to facilitate the storage of fat when the calorific intake is in excess of immediate requirements, and to inhibit the mobilization of fat when there is a short term deficit of calories. This facility has important practical implications. First, it allows the body to build up stores of fat during times of plenty for subsequent use in times of energy shortage. Secondly when food shortages reoccur repeatedly for long periods, it could well permit the survival of the individual whose metabolic responses are especially well adapted to store fat. This metabolic phenomenon may be under genetic control and this advantageous property could be passed on to the offspring. It is possible to visualize population groups that may be better able to resist famines because of their metabolic efficiency. Unfortunately, such persons could well be especially prone to obesity if they are provided with a continuous supply of calories and experience no bouts of caloric inadequacy. These considerations have not been the subject of much research, but they need to be taken into consideration if long term efforts are successful in bringing about caloric sufficiency.

Eventually, the effect of the famine begins to

exceed the adaptive capabilities of the body and, as a consequence, bodily dysfunction occurs. The ultimate measure of the deleterious effects of food shortages on human health is mortality; but before this the dysfunction is manifested in disease. These are described by Dr. Bang, who provides evidence that susceptibility to dysentery, tuberculosis and other infections is increased during famine. In the normal, fit person the natural defence mechanisms of the body would usually be expected to counter these diseases. In the malnourished, however, natural immunity and host defenses are impaired so that the mortality from these diseases is far higher than expected. Recently there has been recognition that the small intestine plays a major role in adaptation to food insufficiency. (Bowie, 1967; Williamson, 1978a, 1978b.) Normally, a considerable amount of the protein needed by the body is provided by the cells lining the small intestine. The protein in these cells is absorbed and is available for reconstructing new cells. In starvation, however, new cells can not be produced so that the intestinal tract is virtually

absorbed by its own body. The atrophy of the intestines adversely affects efficiency of digestion and absorption, and diarrhea of non-bacterial origins can add to the stress of the starvation. This phenomenon also has implications for the refeeding of starving patients.

REFERENCES AND ADDITIONAL READINGS

Bowie, M.D., G.O. Barbezat, J.D.L. Hansen (1967). Carbohydrate malabsorption in malnourished children. *Am. J. Clin. Nutr.*, **20**, 89-97.

The State of Food and Agriculture, Food and Agriculture Organization of the United Nations, Rome, 1975.

Widdowson, E.M. Nutritional individuality. *Proc. Nutr. Soc.,* **21**, 121, 1962.

Williamson, R.C.N. (1978a). Intestinal adaptation, Part 1. *New Eng. J. Med.,* **298**, 1393.

Williamson, R.C.N. (1978b). Intestinal adaptation, Part 2. *New Eng. J. Med.,* **298**, 1444.

Beisel, W.R. (1977). Magnitude of the host nutritional responses to infection. *Am. J. Clin. Nutr.,* **30**, 1236.

Scrimshaw, N.S., C.E. Taylor, J.E. Gordon (1968). *Interaction of nutrition and infection.* Monograph No. 57 W.H.O., Geneva.

PHYSIOLOGY OF ACUTE STARVATION IN MAN †

GEORGE F. CAHILL, JR.

Joslin Research Laboratories and the Department of Medicine, Medical School, Harvard University, and Peter Bent Brigham Hospital, Boston, Massachusetts, U.S.A.

The far greater efficiency of storage of excess energy as fat instead of protein or carbohydrate is crucial in animals in whom mobility plays an important role, particularly for those who must struggle against gravity. Thus for man, who once survived as a hunter and gatherer, and in whom mobility certainly played a critical role in his competition with other creatures, storage of energy as triglyceride in adipose tissue was mandatory for survival. As man eats, his first priority is to provide fuel for immediate metabolic requirements, displacing endogenous fuels, the second is to expand his modest glycogen reserves in liver and muscle and also to replace the amount of protein broken down in various tissues since the last meal, particularly in muscle. The third priority is to convert the excess, be the originally-ingested energy as carbohydrate or as protein or as fat, into triglyceride and then to store the energy in his adipose tissue.

In fasting, the priorities are reversed. The body undergoes a series of hormonal and metabolic changes to draw selectively on its extensive supply of energy in adipose tissue, and thereby to spare the breakdown of vitally needed proteins, such as muscle or enzymes in critical structures such as heart or liver, or, even more important, proteins involved in nervous tissues, particularly brain, which appear not to be mobilized at all during starvation.

First, an overall accounting of calories in various forms and tissues is necessary to provide perspective to fuel economy and mobilization in man. A normal adult uses 4–5 kJ (1–1.2 Cals)/minute to maintain basal energy needs, or 6–7.5 MJ (1500–1800 Cals)/day. With standard physical acti-

vity or in a cold environment without insulation, this is doubled, and with strong physical activity, daily expenditures may increase to 20–25 MJ (5,000–6,000 Cals)/day. Thus the 400–600 MJ (100,000–150,000 Cals) in the 12–16 kilograms of triglyceride in fat provides 1–3 months of survival-fuel depending on physical activity, again, providing that the supply of energy is the rate-limiting factor for survival. In a very fat human, survival would be for much longer, and total starvation of a year has been documented in some very obese subjects under carefully observed conditions in which cheating would be most difficult.

PHASES OF STARVATION

In the transition from the fed to the fasted state, a sequence of metabolic alterations occurs, listed as follows with their approximate duration:

1) Gastrointestinal absorption of substrate   1–6 hours
2) Glycogenolysis   1–2 days
3) Gluconeogenesis   first week
4) Ketosis   3–4 days onward
5) Diminishing gluconeogenesis and increasing cerebral ketone consumption   second week onward

Gastrointestinal Phase

Although this is beyond the general scope of this essay, a few words on the disposition of a meal is appropriate, especially concerning the variations in energy content and the distribution in carbohydrate, protein and fat. With a large meal, mainly carbohydrate, the entire body oxidizes glucose. This is a result of two phenomena, both involving insulin. Liver actively removes glucose due to the elevation in insulin levels, as well as a lowering of glucagon.

† Supported in part by USPHS Grants AM 15191 and AM 05077 and RR 05073

Based on a paper presented at the American Association for the advancement of Science Meeting held on February 20, 1976.

51

The glucose is incorporated into glycogen and is also glycolysed to pyruvate and lactate. The pyruvate is subsequently oxidized to acetyl CoA which is used for both liver's energy needs via the tricarboxylic acid cycle and for fatty acid synthesis. Subsequently fatty acid is incorporated into triglyceride and fat is then exported to adipose tissue as very low density lipoprotein (VLDL). Brain continues to use glucose for fuel, as it did before the meal. Again because of elevated insulin levels, muscle preferentially utilizes glucose to replenish its previously depleted glycogen reserves, as well as fuel for energy. This preferential glucose metabolism in muscle is also a function of low levels of free fatty acids, a result of insulin's effect on adipose tissue. In adipose tissue, insulin also stimulates glucose uptake and the conversion of glucose to fatty acid and subsequent incorporation into the triglyceride vacuole in the center of the adipocyte. Triglyceride hydrolysis (lipolysis) of the stored triglyceride is inhibited by insulin resulting in a decreased release of free fatty acid, and in lower circulating levels of free fatty acids. The larger the meal, the more rapid the rate of glucose uptake by these various tissues, this is in response again to the higher levels of circulating insulin. Thus in adipose tissue insulin increases fat synthesis and decreases its mobilization.

The ingested fats from the meal enter into the blood stream as chylomicrons via the lymphatics, and the simple sugars and amino acids from the meal are absorbed into the portal circulation going to the liver. The glucogenic amino acids, for the main part, as well as certain essential amino acids like trytophan, are removed and metabolized by liver. The three branched chain amino acids, leucine, isoleucine, and valine, which will be discussed in further detail later, are mainly removed by muscle and adipose tissues. Because of the availability of insulin and the increase in amino acid levels, peripheral protein, particularly in muscle, is replenished. The chylomicrons serve to transport absorbed fat directly to adipose tissue where the fatty acids are released, and then incorporated as a new triglyceride molecule and stored inside the triglyceride vacuole in the center of the adipocyte along with the newly synthesized fatty acids.

Should the meal be low in carbohydrate, so that the rate of carbohydrate entry into the blood stream be less than that needed by brain and other obligatory glucose users, insulin is still released at a greater rate than basal. This greater rate allows the initiation of peripheral protein synthesis, especially, again, in muscles, and also the stimulation of some lipogenesis in adipose tissue from amino acids (particularly the branched-chain amino acids), and the uptake of circulating triglyceride into adipose tissue. However, glucose levels must be maintained in the presence of this increased insulin, and thus the liver need be poised toward glucose production in spite of the increased insulin levels. This appears to be the primary biological role of glucagon in mammals (Lefebvre and Unger, 1972), whose release is stimulated by both the increase in blood levels of amino acids themselves, particularly arginine, as well as sensitization of the alpha cells to release more glucagon per change in substrate level. This latter sensitization is probably mediated by pancreozymin, which appears to be the "gut" hormone which stimulates not only exocrine pancreatic activity during a meal, but also the endocrine alpha and Beta cells, the former to release glucagon and the latter to release insulin, especially after protein ingestion.

Thus in meals containing little or no carbohydrate, by initiating increased insulin activity as well as that of glucagon, the non-hepatic tissues receive the "fed" signal to take up circulating fuels, but the liver remains in the "fasting" mode in order to maintain blood glucose concentration by continuing to produce glucose, and this it does as a result of the increase in glucagon levels. Thus, whether liver is glucogenic or glycogenic-glycolytic is a function of the ratio of the two hormones, insulin and glucagon, as originally postulated by Unger and subsequently corroborated by a number of investigators. If the meal contains sufficient carbohydrate to be able to displace the need for hepatic glucose production, in other words, enough carbohydrate to enter into blood at a rate of over 100–200 mg/minute, then the slight rise in glucose concentration is sufficient to increase Beta cell insulin release and to suppress completely the alpha cell from releasing glucagon, and as a result, hepatic glucose production is suppressed. In addition, this slight increase in glucose level markedly synergizes the Beta cells to produce even more insulin as a response to the increase in amino acids, so the glucagon/insulin ratio is even more altered.

In summary, the gastrointestinal phase of starvation varies as a function of the fuel ingested, and if deficient in carbohydrate, the liver is signalled to produce glucose as if no meal had been eaten. Should this type of diet be continued for periods of time, experimental animal data have shown that the liver becomes more and more poised toward gluconeogenesis due to the increased activities of the key rate-limiting enzymes involved and the liver is thus metabolically similar to that in total starvation.

Glycogenolysis Phase

Total body free glucose amounts to only 15 grams, or about one hour's worth of fuel for basal energy needs. If one permits a "physiologic excursion" from the fasting level of 80 mg/100 ml in plasma to 60 mg/100 ml, that would be 15 minutes fuel for for the whole body, or if it was limited to brain's needs, about 45–50 minutes. Thus there must be exquisitely sensitive mechanisms to respond to small change in glucose concentrations which can result in increased or decreased rates of glucose production by liver in order to maintain glucose concentrations. Insulin and glucagon play central roles, and there is also evidence that the glucose molecule itself may be important in liver in controlling its own destiny.

First, the liver cell membrane does have a specific glucose transporting mechanism, but its rate (Vmax) is so great that the concentration of glucose inside the liver cell closely approximates that in the circulation. Second, the kinase in liver responsible for forming glucose-6-phosphate is unique in that it has a low affinity for glucose, one within the physiologic range, meaning the higher the blood glucose level, the more is phosphorylated. This is different from the enzyme in muscle and adipose tissue, where the rate-limiting step is glucose entry across the membrane into the cell. But once the glucose molecule has entered, as a result of insulin's effect on the membrane, it is rapidly phosphorylated because of the very high affinity (low Km) that the hexokinase in muscle and adipose tissue has for glucose. Thus, hyperglycemia results in increased glucose phosphorylation, in the liver and thereby in glucose uptake, this being simply a function of the concentration of glucose. In other tissues, permeability, as controlled by insulin, is rate-limiting.

To return to glucagon and insulin, the ratio of these two hormones plays a central role in controlling the level of cyclic AMP (CAMP) inside the liver cell, and thereby the rate of glucose synthesis and release. It has been suggested that CAMP serves as a signal of carbohydrate lack (Tomkins, 1975), and this seems to be particularly applicable to man.

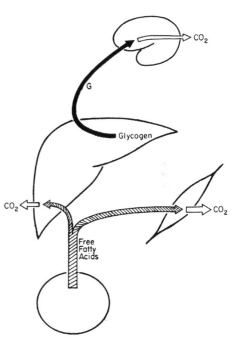

FIGURE 1   Metabolism in the immediate period following digestion of a meal. Brain glucose consumption is provided by liver glycogen. Adipose tissue (bottom) supplies free fatty acids for fuel for both liver and for muscle (the cell on the right).

As glucose absorption from the gut decreases at the end of the gastrointestinal phase, insulin levels fall also, and the liver gradually stops removing glucose; it then is more or less in a "neutral" state and subsequently begins to produce glucose. About 4–5 hours after a meal, and perhaps longer if it was a very large meal, liver begins to return its stored glycogen as free glucose back into the blood to provide fuel needs, mainly for the central nervous system (Figure 1). The signals are twofold, a lower insulin level and a lower level of portal blood glucose. Whether glucagon, no longer suppressed, increases or not in this brief time is not yet clearly documented. It is the author's guess that the "fine-tuning" is primarily a function of insulin and glucose, and not glucagon. For example, in experiments in fasted humans, doubling the glucagon concentration by infusion had little effect on glucose homeostasis (Sherwin, *et al.*, 1976). However, suppression of both glucagon and insulin by somatostatin infusion lowers blood glucose (Gerich, *et al.*, 1975), suggesting the presence of glucagon to be necessary for hepatic glucose production, but not regulatory.

During this phase of decreasing glucose and insulin levels, peripheral tissues such as muscle and adipose progressively diminish glucose utilization, so that after 8–10 hours, over one half of muscle fuel needs are met by free fatty acid oxidation. Simultaneously the levels of free fatty acids increase as the insulin levels fall, primarily due to increased levels of CAMP stimulating triglyceride lipolysis in adipose tissue. Whereas in liver, insulin is pitted against glucagon in controlling CAMP concentration, in adipose tissue it is insulin versus norepinephrine released locally from sympathetic nerve endings. Knowledge of the contribution of muscle glycogen to fuel utilization as a direct result of fasting without exercise is limited. After a meal the glycogen content of human muscle may be as high as one percent. With exercise it is rapidly diminished, and, if fasting persists it is not replenished. At a glycogen content of one percent the 30 kg of muscle in a normal man would provide 300 g of glycogen or 5.0 MJ (1200 Cals). This is a nominal supply, possibly explaining the persistence of a higher respiratory quotient in starving man than can be explained solely by release and oxidation of the glucose stored as glycogen in liver.

Gluconeogenesis

Although there are few data concerning liver glycogen levels after a large meal, extrapolating backward from the 4–5 percent glycogen content in liver in the post-absorptive state, the amount may be as much as 10 percent or more. Thus liver glycogen maintains blood glucose for 12–16 hours, and studies in the post-absorptive state show glycogen providing 75 percent of splanchnic glucose output, gluconeogenesis provides the remainder (Figure 2).

As gluconegenesis is initiated, a number of metabolic changes occur in the liver. These changes result from two processes, the first involves a higher glucagon/insulin ratio due to a significant decrease in insulin, thereby increasing levels of CAMP. In the second process, a higher level of free fatty acids, increases fat oxidation and produces a higher level of fat-derived materials such as acetyl CoA and fatty acyl CoA. As these enzymes

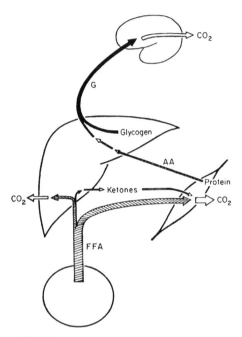

OVERNIGHT FAST
(postabsorptive)

FIGURE 2   In the postabsorptive state, hepatic glycogen begins to run out and gluconeogenesis in liver from amino acids from muscle protein takes over. Ketogenesis is also initiated by liver.

and co-factors all change over 12–24 hours, the rate of liver glucose output begins to be controlled by the level of substrate coming to it, and the rate-control is thus transferred from liver to the release of precursors from peripheral tissues.

Over the ensuing 2–3 days of starvation, muscle and adipose tissue become progressively more efficient in decreasing their glucose utilization, both by blocking glucose uptake, and as a further check, by preventing glycolysis of the glucose to pyruvate. As a final check, pyruvate is completely prevented from being oxidized to acetyl CoA (pyruvic dehydrogenase), so what little pyruvate is formed is either exported as such, or is reduced to lactate and exported, or transaminated to alanine and then sent back to the liver for gluconeogenesis. Thus muscle stops using carbohydrate or its potential precursors.

Returning to the liver, its own energy needs are met by oxidation of free fatty acids, but as starvation progresses, and the oxalacetate is utilized more for gluconeogenesis, less is available for tricarboxylic acid cycle activity. Furthermore, what oxalacetate is available is reduced to malate as the liver is flooded with free fatty acids and with the reducing equivalents resulting from their oxidation. Thus, as the fatty acids are dehydrogenated and split into 2 carbon units of acetyl CoA, the diminished acceptor, oxalacetate, decreases acetyl CoA entry into the cycle and the liver's alternative is to export the acetyl CoA, two at a time, as β-hydroxybutyrate or acetoacetate, the "ketone" bodies. Ketone production thus appears to be the result of two phenomena, the glucagon/insulin ratio being high, increasing the enzymatic machinery for ketone production, and an increase in the delivery of free fatty acids from adipose tissue (Grey, Karl, Kipnis, 1975).

Thus, to summarize the gluconeogenic phase, liver enzymes become poised toward glucose synthesis, fat becomes the hepatic fuel, but the fatty acids eventually are only partly oxidized to acetate units, and then exported to the periphery two at a time as acetoacetate or β-OH butyrate. Adipose tissue hydrolyzes its triglyceride to free fatty acids and glycerol (lipolysis), the former serving as fuel for muscle and liver, and the latter, like amino acids from muscle, or like lactate and pyruvate from muscle and other tissues, is used by liver as gluconeogenic substrate.

Quantitative estimates for 24 hour substrate turnover in a normal man fasted for 3–4 days are given in Table I.

Thus brain begins to utilize ketoacids as their levels increase in blood; glucose utilization begins to diminish; splanchnic ketoacid production is maximal and the bulk of ketoacids are utilized by skeletal muscle and heart. In fact, heart has been shown to satisfy 75 percent of its energy needs by ketoacid metabolism in 3-day fasted man. Ketoacid loss in the urine is minimal calorically, but their acidic properties necessitate ammonia production by kidney to prevent loss of sodium or potassium and thus to preserve body fluid volume (Sapir and Owen, 1975).

Ketosis

By the 3rd day of starvation, ketoacid production by the splanchnic bed is maximal (Garber, et al., 1974) but blood levels continue to increase progressively until the end of the second week when a plateau is achieved (Cahill, et al., 1966). Owen and Reichard (1971), have shown that this progressive increase is mainly a function of decreased ketoacid metabolism by muscle as fasting progresses. Thus by the 3rd or 4th day, ketoacid levels are 1–2 mM but by the second week they may be 6–10 mM. Serum bicarbonate levels are reduced accordingly, and there is a mild but compensated metabolic acidosis. The purpose of this ketoacidosis is to provide a sufficient gradient for the facilitated diffusion of these water soluble fat products across the blood brain barrier to satisfy brain's energy needs (Owen, et al., 1967). Again, this production of ketoacid by liver is a result of a high glucagon/insulin ratio and an increase in the levels of free fatty acids released from adipose tissue, another function of low insulin.

Diminished Gluconegenesis and Increasing Marked Ketoacid Consumption

The final phase in starvation occurs as ketoacid levels reach a plateau and the brain is preferentially using ketoacids as fuel and diminishing glucose utilization accordingly (Figure 3). The net effect is to decrease the need for gluconegenesis and thus spare mobilization of muscle protein. Nitrogen excretion diminishes from 12 g/24 hours to 3–4 g/24 hours, signifying a reduction of protein breakdown from 75 g daily to 12–20 g daily. Thus in starvation the body can continue to utilize the plentiful energy provided by fat while sparing necessary protein. Insulin levels continue to be low, but insulin appears yet to be the controlling signal for integrating the various metabolic processes. Glucagon appears to return to post-absorp-

TABLE I

Quantitative estimates for 24-hour substrate turnover in a normal man fasted for 3–4 days.

Component	Amount g
Brain glucose utilization	100
Brain ketone utilization	50
Splanchnic glucose output (Felig, et al., 1969)	150
Glucose utilization by other tissues	50
Muscle proteolysis (Cahill, et al., 1966)	75
Adipose lipolysis	180
Splanchnic ketogenesis (Reichard, Owen, Haff, 1974)	150

G. F. CAHILL, JR.

PROLONGED STARVATION

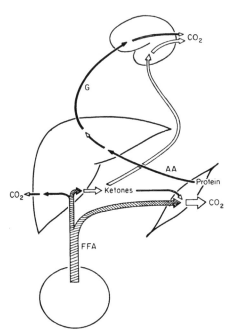

FIGURE 3   In prolonged starvation, brain now also uses ketoacids. Liver energy is derived mainly by the partial oxidation of fatty acids to ketoacids. Muscle diminishes its use of ketoacids and selectively utilizes free fatty acids. The overall effect is to spare nitrogen.

TABLE II

Quantitative estimates of 24-hour substrate turnovers in prolonged starvation

	Amount g
Brain glucose utilization	40
Brain ketone utilization (Owen, *et al.*, 1967)	100
Splanchnic glucose output (Owen, *et al.*, 1969)	80
from amino acid	20
from glycerol	20
from returning lactate and pyruvate	40
Muscle proteolysis	20
Adipose lipolysis	180
Splanchnic ketogenesis (Reichard, Owen, Haff, 1974)	150

tive levels, but the glucagon/insulin ratio is still in favor of glucagon so the liver is poised in the direction of gluconeogenesis. Quantitative estimates of 24-hour substrate turnovers are shown in Table II.

With starvation, as mentioned earlier, the overall rate-control for gluconeogenesis is switched from liver to muscle, or in other words, liver becomes substrate-regulated by muscle proteolysis. As shown over 50 years ago by Van Slyke, circulating amino acid levels respond to insulin, and Wool and Cavicchi (1967) and others have shown a very important role of insulin in promoting and maintaining the protein synthetic machinery inside muscle. Thus a major effect of increased insulin is to initiate uptake of certain amino acids and their incorporation into protein. A more recently described effect of insulin is also to decrease muscle proteolysis, as shown by several workers including Jefferson *et al.*, (1974) and Fulks, Li and Goldberg (1975). Thus insulin appears to control the rate of net muscle proteolysis, the lower the insulin, the more rapid the net proteolysis. However, as discussed above, muscle proteolysis diminishes with more prolonged starvation, and yet insulin levels are, if anything, even lower; thus we have a paradox needing explanation. Factors other than insulin must be playing a role.

Much emphasis has been recently directed to the role of amino acids in intermediary metabolism in man. In the post-absorptive state and in prolonged starvation, alanine and glutamine are released in greater quantities than explicable by their contents in muscle protein (Marliss, *et al.*, 1971). Apparently, there is rearrangement of amino acids resulting from proteolysis with the branched chain amino acids transaminating to pyruvate to form alanine or donating ammonia for glutamine synthesis. Other amino acids contribute carbons to form the pyruvate or α-ketoglutarate for the formation of alanine, or glutamate and glutamine. Some of the glutamate for glutamine formation is taken up from the blood as it courses through muscle. The preferential release of alanine and glutamine is teleologically sound, since alanine is the preferred gluconeogenic substrate for liver and glutamine for kidney. Also, some of the glutamine is made into alanine by the non-hepatic splanchnic bed, so alanine becomes even a greater hepatic gluconeogenic precursor (Felig, 1975).

The explanation for the nitrogen-sparing appears to lie in the unique interrelationships between ketoacids, fatty acids and the metabolism of the branched chain amino acids in muscle mitochondria. As was previously mentioned, early in starvation, ketoacids serve as muscle fuel, but with more prolonged starvation they are less well used. In fact, as acetoacetate is taken up by the muscle, it is returned back to the blood as β-hydroxybutyrate, signifying a more reduced state of the muscle mitochondria, secondary to free fatty acid utilization. Thus fatty acids appear to take preference for oxidation and ketoacid oxidation ceases, sparing the ketoacids for brain, a superb overall survival process. But, the excess oxidation of fatty acids also seems to result in a decrease in oxidation of the deaminated residues of the three branched-chain amino acids, leucine, isoleucine and valine (Aoki, et al., 1975a). Thus fat spares oxidation of these amino acids, which appear to play a central role in maintaining muscle protein, this is particularly true for leucine (Fulks, Li, Goldberg, 1975; Buse and Reid, 1975).

Thus the "nitrogen-sparing" of prolonged starvation results really from fat being selectively used in muscle. One can show in experimental animals that fat prevents the terminal nitrogen catabolic phase in starvation (Cuendet, et al., 1975). As will be discussed later, feeding only a small amount of energy as protein is able to replace the nitrogen depletion of otherwise total starvation, and this concept has been capitalized by Blackburn and co-workers (Blackburn et al., 1973) in their proposal that endogenous fat, if allowed to be mobilized by not giving carbohydrate, may even be more efficient in sparing nitrogen in patients receiving parenteral alimentation.

Under normal circumstances, kidney in man provides less than 10 percent of glucose production, although the data are scant. In prolonged starvation, as overall gluconeogenesis decreases, the component provided by liver decreases dramatically and that of kidney increases in proportion to the increase in ketoacid loss in urine. This loss necessitates ammonia excretion to prevent loss of cation in urine, and this in turn appears to be coupled with increased glucose synthesis. After several weeks of starvation, kidney provides up to one half of total gluconeogenesis, using the same substrates as liver, but the proportions are different so that the order of use is: amino acids, glycerol, lactate and pyruvate in that order (Owen, et al., 1969). The amino acids, primarily glutamine, are used for ammonia synthesis, and in fact, there is more nitrogen in the urine as ammonia than as urea in prolonged starvation. Thus, as far as amino-acid-derived gluconeogenesis is concerned, the kidney is even more imporant than liver.

During the gluconeogenic phase, up to 500 g of lean flesh may be lost daily in addition to the 150–200 g of fat, the total tissue weight loss being approximately 500–750 g. However, total weight loss is far greater, unless the subject has previously been on a restricted carbohydrate intake. This weight loss is due to a saline diuresis, the precise mechanism of which has yet to be adequately explained. Some evidence suggests that it may be related to an increase in the glucagon/insulin ratio (Spark, et al., 1975; DeFronzo, et al., 1975). In grossly overweight individuals, this diuresis may result in 5, 10 or even 15 Kg or more of weight loss. In normal, non-obese subjects, 2–2.5 Kg may be lost, particularly in females. Administration of NaCl, or of adrenal mineralocorticoids has essentially no effect (Spark, et al., 1975). This saline diuresis is exquisitely sensitive to the intake of even small amounts of carbohydrate and on refeeding a previously fasted individual, sodium excretion may fall to less than 1 mEq/day. In some subjects, if placed on a liberal salt intake during refeeding, gross edema may occur. Occasionally circulatory stability may be compromised leading to congestive failure in those with heart disease. This has been called "refeeding edema."

Later in total starvation, after the gluconeogenic phase and the saline diuresis, weight loss falls to what one would calculate, 100–200 g of lean tissue and 150–200 g of fat, for a total of approximately 500 g per day.

A frequently asked question is how well the brain functions when using predominantly ketoacids as fuel. Intellectual function appears to remain intact, but emotional alterations are noted, such as depression or lability. Most individuals decrease spontaneous activity, obviously as a mechanism to spare calories, but physical activity can be marked, as in one marathon runner whose pre-race preparation was total calorie abstention for one week! Of much interest is the elevation of the electro-convulsive threshold of the brain utilizing ketoacids as fuel. In the 1920's this was initiated as a form of therapy in children with seizure disorders and has again been resurrected for those children in whom use of multiple anticonvulsive agents is yet ineffective.

The hypothalamic area appears to be significantly altered in the ketosis of prolonged starvation. Appetite is diminished and this may be part of the success of the ketogenic diets used in the treatment of obesity. More dramatically, the desire for fluid intake is diminished, and fasting subjects usually need to be encouraged to drink water. On this point, the markedly diminished urea excretion diminishes the osmotic excretory load, and urine output of 100 to 200 ml/day may be all that is necessary. Again, the survival value is obvious; fasting man need drink very little water, and the 200–300 ml/day produced by metabolism may permit him to survive water deficits for literally several days to a week or more, providing he is not in a hot, dry, dehydrating climate (Cahill and Owen, 1967).

Of greater interest, libido is markedly decreased in starvation, and there are significant reductions in the release of pituitary gonadotropins, (Newmark, et al., 1976). Thus in the female there is first anovulation and subsequently amenorrhea. In the male there is decreased testicular function. These changes are similar to those noted in subjects with anorexia nervosa by Boyar (1974).

With progressive ketosis and the mild metabolic acidosis, there is a gradual and continual excretion of calcium and phosphorus in amounts beyond that lost from the lean tissue being catabolized. Thus bone mineral is gradually being dissolved, similar to that noted in chronic renal acidosis, but to a much lesser degree. This phenomenon has made some clinicians reluctant to use starvation or ketogenic diets in individuals prone to osteoporosis, such as Caucasian females for prolonged periods of time.

More significant, as ketosis becomes moderate, the kidney retains uric acid to a greater degree, and serum urate levels rise to 8–10 mg/100 ml, and in some individuals to levels as high as 15–18 mg/100 ml. Amazingly, episodes of gout are rare in spite of this super-saturation, and what attacks have been precipitated have usually been in individuals with previous disease.

Rarely, hepatic decompensation may occur, the first sign being liver enlargement which on examination shows the typical changes of fatty infiltration. The mechanism for this is allegedly mobilization of excess free fatty acids to the liver with deficient synthesis of lipoprotein to provide export back to the periphery. Most of the affected subjects probably had either hepatic disease or were on an imbalanced diet prior to starting the fast. Probably contributing to the rare hepatic decompensation in starvation is the decreased splanchnic flow (Drenick, 1968), and thus total starvation is contraindicated in individuals with liver disease. It should be

remembered that small increases in bilirubin can occur even in fasting normals and need not signify hepatic disease (Barrett, 1971).

It is of interest that vitamins are probably unnecessary with total starvation, the need for the B vitamins, particularly B_1 and for vitamin C occurring only when carbohydrates are eaten. The Arctic explorer died with scurvy and beriberi eating his crackers while his Eskimo guide survived on blubber!

A decrease in metabolic rate has been noted in starvation for decades, having been extensively studied by Dubois, Benedict and others. Part of this is explained by the progressively decreasing lean body mass, but the decrease appears to be more than accounted for by decreased metabolizable mass. The selective use of fat as fuel, everything else being equal, would be expected to increase oxygen consumption, since it is slightly less efficient than glucose as an energy source, yet, total oxygen consumption is decreased about 10–15 percent.

Recently investigators have noted that the levels of thyroxine remain normal during starvation, but those of triiodothyronine decrease strikingly into the hypothyroid range (Portnay, et al., 1974; Vagenakis, et al., 1975). In contrast, the level of the inactive triiodo form ("reverse" T_3 in endocrine jargon) increases. When refed with carbohydrate, fasted man reverses the levels of the two triiodo thyronines and the active form returns to euthyroid levels. Whether the decrease in active T_3 is the sole mediator of the decreased oxygen consumption remains to be demonstrated. In any case, administration of triiodothyronine to fasted subjects not only increases oxygen consumption, but also nitrogen excretion (Carter, et al., 1975); however, feeding a high protein intake is able to maintain nitrogen balance (Lamki, et al., 1973).

Carbohydrate supplementation. Administration of small amounts of carbohydrate to prolonged fasted man results in a decrease in the level of ketosis and urinary nitrogen excretion (Aoki, et al., 1975b). Levels of free fatty acids were unaffected, and this might be predicted. Since the administered glucose (120 grams/day) was sufficient just for brain and as ketone levels had fallen dramatically, the remainder of the body would need to continue to use free fatty acids as fuel. Total urinary nitrogen decreased from 3 grams daily with total starvation to 1–2 grams/day with the supplemental carbohydrate. Similar effects were observed by simply infusing insulin; thus the observed metabolic effects are probably secondary to this hormone.

In clinical terms, giving small meals of carbohydrate to totally starved individuals in the amount of 400–500 Calories/day does decrease net N-loss, but the nitrogen sparing already achieved by the fat oxidation is so efficient, that the relative practical economy is small.

Protein or amino acid supplementation. Giving totally fasted humans small amounts of protein, as discussed by Folin over 60 years ago, can maintain nitrogen balance and permit selective utilization of fat calories as fuel. This concept has been used by Blackburn and Flatt (Blackburn, *et al.*, 1973) and others (Hoover, *et al.*, 1975) as a mode of therapy for subjects unable to eat. This technique has been used in postoperative patients in whom total starvation plus added amino acids maintain better nitrogen balance than total starvation, or by administration of equicaloric amounts of glucose without amino acids.

The mechanism whereby this is achieved appears to lie mainly in the branched-chain amino acids which not only are rate-limiting essential precursors to muscle protein synthesis but also, especially leucine, promote the synthesis of protein and decrease its breakdown directly (Fulks, Li, Goldberg, 1975; Buse and Reid, 1975). Proof of their essential role is the ability to use the non-amino carboxylic acid analogues of the branched-chain amino acids in totally fasting man (Sapir, *et al.*, 1974), and these result in a significant reduction in nitrogen excretion. Thus, it is far more logical to feed small amounts of protein to otherwise fasted man in the basal condition to spare his body nitrogen and yet provide the barest minimum of calories from external sources, than a similar amount of calories in the form of carbohydrates.

In summary, starvation entails a progressive selection of fat as body fuel. Soon after a meal glucose utilization by muscle ceases and fatty acids are used instead. Ketoacid levels in blood become elevated over the first week, and brain preferentially uses these instead of glucose. The net effect is to spare protein even further, as glucose utilization by brain is diminished. Nevertheless there is still net negative nitrogen balance, but this can be nullified by amino acid or protein supplementation. Insulin appears to be the principal regulatory hormone. Recent data suggest that decreased levels of active T_3 may play a role by sparing otherwise obligated calories by decreasing metabolic needs.

REFERENCES

Aoki, T. T., C. J. Toews, A. A. Rossini, N. B. Ruderman, G. F. Cahill, Jr. (1975a). Glucogenic substrate levels in fasting man. *Adv. Enzyme Regulation*, 13, 329–336.
Aoki, T. T., W. A. Muller, M. R. Brennan, G. F. Cahill, Jr. (1975b). The metabolic effects of glucose in brief and prolonged fasted man. *Am. J. Clin. Nutr.* 28, 507–511.
Barrett, P. V. D. (1971). Hyperbilirubinemia of fasting. *J. Am. Med. Assoc.*, 217, 1349–1353.
Blackburn, G. L., J. P. Fatt, G. H. A. Clowes, T. E. O'Donnell (1973). Peripheral intravenous feeding with isotonic amino acid solutions. *Am. J. Surg.*, 125, 947–959.
Boyar, R. M., J. Katz, J. W. Finklestein, S. Kapen, H. Weiner, E. D. Weitzman, L. Hellman (1974). Anorexia nervosa: immaturity of the 24-hour luteinizing hormone secretory pattern. *New Eng. J. Med.*, 291, 861–865.
Buse, M. G., S. S. Reid (1975). Leucine. A possible regulator of protein turnover in muscle. *J. Clin. Invest.*, 56, 1250–1261.
Cahill, G. F., Jr., O. E. Owen (1967). Starvation and survival. *Trans. Am. Clin. Climat. Assn.*, 79, 13–18.
Cahill, G. F., Jr., M. G. Herrera, A. P. Morgan, J. S. Soeldner, J. Steinke, P. L. Levy, G. A. Reichard, D. M. Kipnis (1966). Hormone-fuel interrelationships during fasting. *J. Clin. Invest.*, 45, 1751–1769.
Cahill, G. F. Jr. (1971). Physiology of insulin in man. *Diabetes*, 20, 785–799.
Carter, W. V., K. M. Shakir, S. Hodges, F. H. Faas, J. O. Wynn (1975). Effect of thyroid hormone on metabolic adaptation to fasting. *Metabolism*, 24, 1117–1183.
Cuendet, G. S., E. G. Loten, D. P. Cameron, A. E. Renold, E. B. Marliss (1975). Hormone-substrate responses to total fasting in lean and obese mice. *Am. J. Physiol.*, 228, 276–283.
De Fronzo, R. A., C. A. Cooke, R. Andres, G. R. Faloona, P. J. Davis (1975). The effect of insulin on the renal handling of sodium, potassium, calcium and phosphate in man. *J. Clin. Invest.*, 55, 845–855.
Drenick, E. J. (1968). The relation of BSP retention during prolonged fasts to changes in plasma volume. *Metabolism*, 17, 522–527.
Felig, P., O. E. Owen, J. Wahren, G. F. Cahill, Jr. (1969). Amino acid metabolism during prolonged starvation. *J. Clin. Invest.*, 48, 584–594.
Felig, P. (1975). Amino acid metabolism in man. *Ann. Rev. Biochem.*, 44, 933–955.
Fulks, R. M., F. Li, A. Goldberg (1975). Effects of insulin, glucose, and amino acids on protein turnover in rat diaphragm. *J. Biol. Chem.* 250, 290–298.
Garber, A. J., P. H. Menzel, G. Boden, O. E. Owen (1974). Hepatic ketogenesis and gluconeogenesis in humans. *J. Clin. Invest.*, 54, 981–989.
Gerich, J. E., M. Lorenzi, S. Hane, G. Gustafson, R. Guillemin, P. H. Forsham (1975). Evidence for a physiologic role of pancreatic glucagon in human glucose homeostasis: studies with somatostatin. *Metabolism*, 24, 175–182.
Grey, N. J., I. Karl, D. M. Kipnis (1975). Physiologic mechanisms in the development of starvation ketosis in man. *Diabetes*, 24, 10–16.
Hoover, H. C., Jr., J. P. Grant, C. Gorschboth, A. J. Ketcham (1975). Nitrogen-sparing intravenous fluids in

postoperative patients. *New Eng. J. Med.*, **293**, 172–175.

Jefferson, L., D. Rannels, B. Munger, H. Morgan (1974). Insulin in the regulation of protein turnover in heart and skeletal muscle. *Fed. Proceed.*, **33**, 1098–1104.

Lamki, L., C. Ezrin, I. Koven, G. Steiner (1973). L-thyroxine in the treatment of obesity with no increase in loss of lean body mass. *Metabolism*, **22**, 617–622.

Lefebvre, P. J., R. H. Unger (1972). *Glucagon. Molecular Physiology, Clinical and Therapeutic Implications.* Pergamon Press, New York.

Marliss, E. B., T. T. Aoki, T. Pozefsky, A. S. Most, G. F. Cahill, Jr. (1971). Muscle and splanchnic glutamine and glutamate metabolism in post-absorptive and starved man. *J. Clin. Invest.*, **50**, 814–817.

Newmark, R., A. A. Rossini, G. F. Cahill, F. Naftolin (1976). In preparation.

Owen, O. E., A. P. Morgan, H. G. Kemp, J. M. Sullivan, M. G. Herrera, G. F. Cahill, Jr. (1967). Brain metabolism during fasting. *J. Clin. Invest.*, **46**, 1589–1595.

Owen, O. E., P. Felig, A. P. Morgan, J. Wahren, G. F. Cahill, Jr. (1969). Liver and kidney metabolism during prolonged starvation. *J. Clin. Invest.*, **48**, 574–583.

Owen, O. E., G. A. Reichard (1971). Human forearm metabolism during progressive starvation. *J. Clin. Invest.*, **50**, 1538–1545.

Portnay, G. I., J. T. O'Brian, J. Bush, A. G. Vagenaikis, F. Azizi, R. A. Arky, S. H. Ingbar, L. E. Braverman (1974). The effect of starvation on the concentration and binding of thyroxine and triiodothyroxine in serum and the

response to TRH. *J. Clin. End. and Metab.*, **39**, 191–194.

Reichard, G. A., O. E. Owen, A. C. Haff (1974). Ketone body production and oxidation in fasting obese subjects. *J. Clin. Invest.*, **53**, 508–515.

Sapir, D. G., O. E. Owen (1975). Renal conservation of ketone bodies during starvation. *Metabolism*, **24**, 23–33.

Sapir, D. G., O. E. Owen, T. Pozefsky, M. Walser (1974). Nitrogen sparing induced by a mixture of essential amino acids given chiefly as their keto-analogues during prolonged starvation in obese subjects. *J. Clin. Invest.*, **54**, 974–980.

Sherwin, R., M. Fisher, R. Hendler, P. Felig (1976). Hyperglucagonemia and blood glucose regulation in normal, obese and diabetic subjects. *New Eng. J. Med.*, **294**(9), 455–461.

Spark, R. F., R. A. Arky, P. R. Boulter, C. D. Saudek, J. T. O'Brian (1975). Renin, aldosterone and glucagon in the natriuresis of fasting. *New Eng. J. Med.*, **292**, 1335–1340.

Tomkins, G. M. (1975). The metabolic code. *Science*, **189**, 760–763.

Vagenakis, A. G., A. Burger, G. I. Portnay, M. Rudolph, J. T. O'Brian, F. Aziza, R. A. Arky, P. Nirod, S. H. Ingbzr, L. E. Braverman (1975). Diversion of peripheral thyroxine metabolism from activating to inactivating pathways during complete fasting. *J. Clin. End. and Metab.*, **41**, 191–194.

Wool, I. G., P. Cavicchi (1967). Protein synthesis by skeletal muscle ribsomes: effect of diabetes and insulin. *Biochemistry*, **6**, 1231–1242.

THE ROLE OF
DISEASE IN THE ECOLOGY OF FAMINE†

FREDERIK B. BANG

*Johns Hopkins University, Center for Medical Research, Dacca,
and Department of Pathobiology, Johns Hopkins School of Hygiene
and Public Health, Baltimore 21205, U.S.A.*

INTRODUCTION

The frequent appearance of epidemics of infectious disease in times of famine has led to a number of special studies of the relationship of the two (Gontzea, 1974). In discussing this we will refer to the immense literature on the interaction of endemic malnutrition and endemic infections (Scrimshaw, Taylor and Gordon, 1968; Mata, 1975), but will deal only with these issues as they bear directly, on famine.

Using a basic ecological approach to the subject we will first review several individual famines and analyze the prevalent diseases associated with each of them. We will then review the known effects of starvation on certain diseases that were important during these famines, and will attempt to determine retrospectively whether immune mechanisms were disturbed in these situations. Unfortunately, much of the literature deals with chronic undernutrition or unbalanced nutrition rather than starvation, and it may be that each has strikingly different effects.

The effect of disease during famine will be considered as part of the total ecological collapse. Famine usually occurs as a sudden acute shortage of food in an area where malnutrition due to poverty and nutritional ignorance already exists, and where there is already a narrow margin between available food and nutritional demand. Not only is the stabilizing energy reserve of well nourished people very low, but food productivity of man is greatly decreased by disease. Thus, the ability to rebuild a reserve is eliminated. The system then must be restabilized by energy input from outside.

† Based on a paper presented at the American Association for the Advancement of Science Meeting held on February 20, 1976.

Sanitation becomes minimal, patterns of behavior are grossly altered, and populations migrate and mix. These social factors alone often provoke infectious disease. As the destitute victims of a famine are massed together in refugee camps there is a constant accession of both actively infected and non immune people.

The sequence of events is shown in Figure 1. All three conditions must be considered when discussing disease during famine.

DISEASE DURING FAMINE

*Ireland and Epidemic Louse
Borne Diseases*

A disease of potatoes initiated the famine years of 1849–1951 in Ireland (MacArthur, 1956). In an economy almost entirely dependent upon potatoes for food, a localized epidemic fungus disease of the potato showed itself in 1843, causing severe want in some localities while food was abundant in others. The summer of 1846 was damp and of unprecedented heat. The fungus disease swept the country. One day the fields were covered with a luxuriant growth, a few days later the stalks were black and dead. And so, famine started and spread. In such a cold damp climate, louse borne typhus and relapsing fever became rampant. Dysentery spread so that

it was easy to know if any of the inmates in the hospital cabins were suffering from dysentery as the ground in such places was usually found marked with blood.

This famine had many ecological similarities with those of the Indian subcontinent, for it occurred following a catastrophe in a country dependent upon one crop (potatoes compared with rice in India) in a population of families crowded in small houses, and with each family having tiny individual farm plots.

FIGURE 1.   Sequence of events in famines.

The devastation was such that adequate figures are not available. Many of the doctors themselves died of typhus. The tremendous role of disease is inherent in the following figures taken from MacArthur's account of the Medical History of the Famine (MacArthur, 1956) (Table I).

Probably somewhat under a million people died. A disease of the staplé crop initiated the famine, a number of human diseases accelerated it, and these diseases then invaded areas free of famine.

The Madras Famine and Dysentery

The Madras famine of 1876–1878, was part of "The Great Famine of India." During this famine a Brigade-Surgeon of Her Majesty's Indian Army, Alexander Porter (Porter, 1889), studied the diseases which occurred in the relief camps attached to the hospital. He used his leisure time to perform 459 consecutive autopsies on those who died of starvation and its complications between December 1876 and July 1877. Though there is little histological data with the gross autopsies, the study remains extremely useful and thought provocative even a hundred years later.

TABLE I

1851 census of deaths during famine years

	Numbers
Fever (typhus and relapsing fever)	192,937
Dysentery and diarrhea	125,148
Starvation	20,402
Dropsy	22,384
Scurvy	200
Unspecified	99,015

Source: MacArthur, (1956).

The troubles in Madras had begun as far back as 1875 when due to the successive failure of the southwest monsoon for two years, famine conditions of great magnitude prevailed in an area containing a population of 19.4 million. As is too often the case, the natural calamity was exacerbated by hoarding by merchants, dealers and others. The prices asked for rice were beyond the means of the people to pay, and famine followed. Of the many diseases which occurred in the relief camps diarrhea and dysentery were the most prevalent (Figure 2).

Within the sheds which were set up for the famine victims where Porter worked, 34.4 percent of 3200 patients admitted, died. The main diseases in the camp are presented in Figures 3 and 4. In each case, except for smallpox, about a third of those afflicted died; (smallpox was remarkably

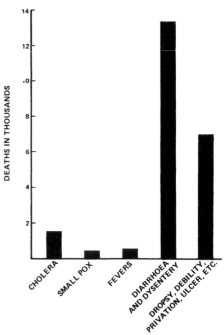

FIGURE 2.   Causes of deaths in relief camps in the Madras Famine of 1876–1878.

DEATHS IN THE FAMINE SHEDS OF THE ROYAPETTACH HOSPITAL DECEMBER 13, 1876 TO MAY 25, 1878

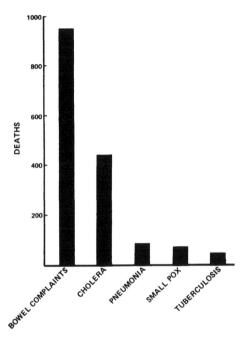

FIGURE 3. Deaths in the famine shed of the Royapettach Hospital (December 13, 1876 to May 25, 1878).

mild with only 5 deaths among 67 cases).[†] Among the 459 autopsied cases, the main cause of death was "the alvine fluxes." Alvine flux today would be translated as dysentery and diarrhea. This was responsible for 77 percent of the total, and was about equally important in adults and children. Cholera caused about five percent of the deaths. The etiology of these intestinal diseases was of course unknown at the time, and probably even the feeding therapy was incorrect in terms of present concepts, for Porter mentions that the hospital staff

---

[†] This is particularly interesting since Sprunt (1972) showed that undernourishment decreased susceptibility of rabbits to vaccinia.

had to contend against the persistent endeavors of the patients to conceal any bowel complaint, lest they should be put upon milk diet and deprived of curry and rice, the only food they considered worthy of the name.

The most common additional factor affecting the death rate was some complication of the lungs, often pneumonia (Table II) which was the direct cause of nine percent of the deaths.

Of particular interest is the description by Cunningham (1889) of microscopic aspects of the atrophy of lymphoid tissues in the gut in these cases.

In many instances not only was the epithelial coat disorganized, but the soilitary glands were either present in very small numbers, or could not be recognized at all, and Peyer's patches, in place of presenting their normal aspect, appeared as mere empty networks, composed of collections of minute depressions surrounded by slightly elevated ridges. In most cases over considerable areas of the gut, and some almost universally, the adenoid tissue appeared to be virtually absent.

Add to these descriptions the size of the mesenteric lymph nodes recorded by Porter (1889) (Table III) these scientists can be credited with an accurate accounting of great atrophy of the lymphoid system, (Table IV) long before its function was recognized.

In this first adequate study of the factor of disease in the ecology of famine, an endemic disease (dysentery) was superimposed upon the effect of famine, on starvation, wandering, exhaustion and inadequate sanitation in the relief camp.

TABLE II

Incidence of pneumonia in 459 autopsies on victims of the Madras Famine of 1876 and 1877

Complication of alvine flux	102
Complication of other diseases	8
Idiopathic	22
Total	132 (28.7%)

Source: Porter, (1889).

TABLE III

Size of mesenteric lymph glands in Indian famine victims

	Men	Women	Children
Atrophied	73 (42%)	74 (60%)	2 (3%)
Normal	57	37	51
Enlarged	36	6	11

Source: Porter, (1889) cited by Cunningham (1889).

F. B. BANG

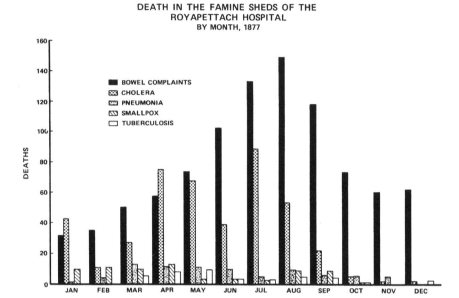

FIGURE 4. Death in the famine sheds of the Royapettach Hospital by month, 1877.

The relationship of dysentery to malnutrition has been frequently noted since then: In their famous study of dysentery in the Malay States, Fletcher, Jepps and Horn (1927) observed:

Owing to the fall in the price of tin which occurred shortly after the war many of the Chinese were thrown out of work, and as they could not obtain sufficient to eat, their powers of resistance were lowered and they fell victims to dysentery.

Several studies in wild-caught unimmunized monkeys which began as studies on Vitamin A or

folic acid (Vitamin M) deficiency ended up by showing that bacillary dysentery frequently developed in the vitamin deficient monkeys, while the normally fed controls remained healthy (Day et al., 1940).

McCarrison (1920) the first director of the Indian Nutrition Research Center at Madras, showed that monkeys kept on a poor diet similar to that eaten by a majority of the urban poor led to atrophy of the intestine and dimunition of lymphoid tissue.

TABLE IV

Ratio of spleen weight to body weight in men and women suffering from alvine flux and pneumonia and phthisis in the Madras famine of 1876

| | Alvine flux | | | | Pneumonia and phthisis |
| | Men | | Women | | |
	No.	Ratio	No.	Ratio	No.
Hypertrophied	10	1/125	9	1/127	5
Normal	22	1/258	17	1/279	18
Atrophied	135	1/540	97	1/558	13

Source: Porter, (1877).

TРАНС

Finally, dysentery is now endemic in Bangladesh, and one of the unforgettable scenes in a refugee camp was the children who lined up to demonstrate complete rectal prolapse.

The Russian Famine and Typhus

In Russia, the disruption of World War I, and the Revolution which took place towards the end of the war, were marked by massive famine and by epidemic disease.

The disease (louse borne epidemic typhus) had been present in Russia before the famine (Figure 5) but as starvation swept the country, famine and typhus combined their destructive effects. Dr. W. Horsley Gantt (1928) started work there in 1919 as part of the American Relief Administration and stayed on to work with Pavlov. Some years later he published an account of the medical, public health, and educational problems in that country during the years of devastation.

The very vastness of the scale of this catastrophe defies description.

When the smoke of battle died down in 1919, it was followed by epidemics of typhus, smallpox and cholera involving about 25,000,000 of 130,000,000 people in Russia. Although 80 percent of the Russians had probably always been undernourished to the same degree or even worse than the poor of other countries as they existed chiefly on black bread . . . there was not starvation until the drought and famine years. From 1919 through 1922 millions of refugees wandered over Russia searching for food. They covered the country, and wherever they stopped they lived and died like locusts.

Epidemic typhus is transmitted by lice. It is primarily a disease of cold and temperate climates, for body lice do especially well in clothing and in unwashed rags. With the disruption of life so vividly described by Gantt (1928), there is no wonder that it became epidemic (Figure 5). One can only speculate whether the lack of food itself caused increased susceptibility. Figure 6 shows that with the decrease in available food energy, there was an increase in infectious disease in Leningrad; but there was an equally remarkable relationship to the availability of baths (Figure 7). Most investigators of epidemic typhus in those

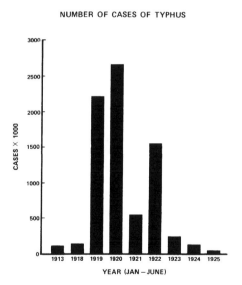

FIGURE 5. Number of cases of Typhus in Russian famine, 1913–1925.

CORRELATION OF FOOD AND INFECTION

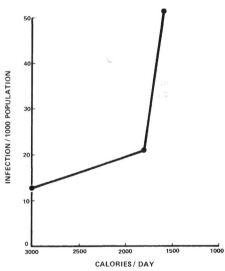

FIGURE 6. Relationship between food energy and the prevalence of infection in Leningrad during the Russian Famine of 1919–1922.

66 F. B. BANG

CORRELATION OF CLEANLINESS AND INFECTION

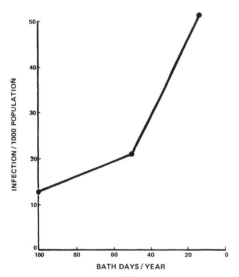

FIGURE 7. Relationship between frequency of bathing and infections in Leningrad during the Russian famine of 1919–1922.

days, ascribed the epidemic to lack of soap and hot water.

Pinkerton (1949) who studied the disease in Poland was concerned with the possibility that degrees of starvation lowered resistance to rickettsia. He investigated the effect of starvation on murine typhus in guinea pigs and rats and found much larger accumulations of rickettsiae in the copious peritoneal exudate in starved (with water *ad libitum*) than in adequately fed animals.

World War II and Tuberculosis

Tuberculosis and famine have been called the twin sisters of poverty (Gontzea, 1974). It was undoubtedly important in the Madras famine, but as Porter remarked, the deadened sensibility of the starving patient made recognition more difficult. In the framework of war and starvation, the importance of tuberculosis became apparent only after louse-borne disease had been eliminated by DDT (Keys *et al.*, 1950).

The end of World War II in Europe was accompanied by famine and starvation in many concentration camps and in civilians in a number of areas. A Danish study of returnees from concentration camps in Germany where they had been kept for an average of six months (two to eighteen) in the two closing years of the war under conditions of extreme deprivation offers unusual data (Helweg-Larsen *et al.*, 1952). The prisoners, all of whom originally came from Copenhagen, were made up of two groups: members of the resistance movement (MRM), and Copenhagen policemen. The two groups were maintained in very similar living quarters and were subjected to similar circumstances of exposure, but the policemen were allowed to receive supplemental food from Copenhagen, whereas this was denied to the MRM. Starting immediately after repatriation in May 1945, 605 MRM and 726 policemen were studied for an ensuing 5-year period, by repeated X-rays, sputum examination and general physical examination. Follow up was successful for 95 percent of the MRM and 97 percent of the police. A total of 53 cases of pulmonary tuberculosis and five extra-pulmonary cases were found. Of this total, 38 were diagnosed within the first eight months, and 13 during the next year. Thus most of the disease (51/57 cases) was found within the first 20 months after release from camp.

The differences between the two groups are shown in Table V. Thus, there was three times as much disease in the group on limited food during internment. The disease was also three times more severe in the MRM. The prisoners had been exposed to wretched sanitary conditions and had had severe calorie undernutrition with hard physical work. Thirty-six percent of the MRM and 14 percent of the police had manifest nutritional edema when they were released from camp.

There were also records on the tuberculin sen-

TABLE V
Five-year incidence of tuberculosis in 1331 Danish returning from deportation after World War II

	No. returning	No. cases	Percent
MRM	605	41	6.8
Police	726	16	2.2
Both groups	1331	57	4.3

Source: Helweg-Larsen.

sitivity of the men before deportation. A three percent incidence of disease developed among those who had been tuberculin positive and a 22 percent frequency among those who had been negative before deportation.

The degree of exposure during camp life was great. Eighty percent of the MRM who had been negative before deportation became positive, while 60 percent of the police converted. It seems likely then that the major effect of the starvation in this situation was to increase susceptibility to new disease, rather than to reactivate latent disease. There are few studies of tuberculosis and malnutrition, free of other factors such as crowding.

Current understanding of the early events in the pathogenesis of tuberculosis depends largely on the extensive detailed studies of Mackaness and his colleagues who have worked primarily with an intracellular bacterial parasite, Listeria (Collins and Mackaness, 1970). This work shows that the immunized animal responds by means of sensitized T cells (thymus derived lymphocytes). These immune T cells release lymphokines (soluble substances which activate the macrophage) so that the macrophages are better able to digest the bacteria. Furthermore, correlation between the activation of macrophages and the disappearance of tubercle bacilli from the lesion has been shown by Dannenberg et al. (1975).

There have been numerous studies on the effect of diet on susceptibility of animals to tuberculosis (Keys et al., 1950; Bhuyan and Ramalingaswami, 1973). Most of these indicate that one or another deficiency causes increased susceptibility to experimental tuberculosis. However, the mode of action of these deficiencies on the immunopathogenic mechanism is unknown. The marked atropy of lymphoid tissues, especially of the thymus, following starvation is well known. In addition, the failure of malnourished children to respond to tuberculin after immunization with BCG suggests that the defective T cell which almost surely occurs during famine may be responsible for the increased susceptibility to tuberculosis. However, there are gaps in our knowledge. First, we need to be sure that the Listeria model really applies directly to tuberculosis. In constrast to the above, activation of macrophages in some viral infections leads to increased susceptibility. Secondly, both macrophages and lymphocytes are affected in experimental malnutrition. The mechanisms involved in the effect of nutrition (itself a complex reaction) on a series of complex immunologic interactions in tuberculosis are not yet adequately understood.

Famine and Endemic Disease

Diseases which become epidemic during times of famine are chiefly diseases endemic in an area before the famine. There is a clear destructive positive feedback in the system, thus, the more famine and social disruption, the more disease yielding more famine. In the ecologic context, the potential for spread of a given endemic disease in a given area must be evaluated. Louse-borne diseases will be rare or absent in a warm delta area where people constantly bathe, but are likely to be epidemic in areas where the cold requires the wearing of layers of clothing, discourages bathing, and inhibits washing in the open. Fortunately, the endemic typhus and relapsing fever present in Ireland and Russia well before the famines of 1845–51 and 1918–21 no longer threaten to become epidemic because of effective insecticides against lice.

In the Bengal Delta, where famine has visited frequently, disease consists of a wide spectrum of bacterial and virus infections. A large sector of the human population is constantly exposed to a multiplicity of waterborne agents through the use of common sources of contaminated water for washing the body including the mucous membranes of the mouth, nose and anus. The daily ritual bath of purification assures that from the age of one year onward, there is a constant inoculation, frequently intranasal, of all infectious organisms that are able to survive in water (Bang, Bang and Bang, 1975). Whatever the mechanism of transmission, respiratory disease dominates in some areas (Ichag) and diarrheal disease in others.

One might expect that under these circumstances the population would be rapidly immunized against all of the endemic agents. There is, of course, a balance between the availability of new susceptible soil (respiratory or intestinal mucosa) for the potential pathogen, and actual immunization. Diptheria is a significant and serious disease of the respiratory tract of children during the monsoon season in some areas of the Delta and in other areas is rarely seen. Wherever it has been studied in delta areas the population is immunized through frequent infection by way of skin lesions from scabies or impetigo (Chakraborty, Bang and Hillis, 1972). Competition for susceptible soil is so great that some childhood diseases such as chicken pox or hepatitis are post-poned to adulthood (Sinha, 1976), presumably through epidemiological interference (Bang, 1975).

During famine, epidemic disease develops when individual resistance and community resistance to infectious disease are lost, the wandering starved are crowded into camps, sanitation is nonexistent, and each person is exposed to increasingly large doses of infectious agents. By the same token, the infectious agents that have been hyperendemic in an area but have not caused significant disease because of constant active-passive immunization do not break out because the great majority of the people are already immune. This is probably true of poliomyelitis, other enteroviruses and some adenoviruses.

At the other extreme, endemic diseases which are poor natural immunizers such as malaria and bacillary dysentery do become major participants in the disaster. The Bengal Famine of 1943 killed millions of people and it was accompanied by so much malaria that many of the starving people of Calcutta were found to have malaria parasites in their blood (data from the Indian Council for Medical Research).

Dysentery, primarily bacillary dysentery, is characteristic of famine. It is readily recognized as the bloody flux, which was clearly described in 1881 by Porter, and so severe and constant is the tenesmus that during the 1974 famine in Banglad-esh the virulent form (Shiga bacillus) was rec-ognized by the frequent prolapse of the rectum. Natural immunization of the intestinal tract to the several antigenic types is inadequate to protect the patient, and so one attack is followed by another. The atrophy of the Peyer's patches in starvation (Andreason, 1943) is a sign of the loss of lymphoid tissue through the intestine, and thus an absence of immune cells which might be present in the well nourished individual.

Measles is an acute viral disease of children. When transmission is intense it may be limited to children under two years of age. It has been con-sidered as a scourge of underdeveloped countries where malnutrition is common, and this severity has been apparent particularly in tropical Africa where it may kill 10–20 percent of the children who are infected. However, the severity of measles may vary dependent upon the type of prevalent malnutrition (Sinha, 1976).

It does not have a reputation for a comparable severity in the Bengal Delta, and yet malnutrition is also common and often severe. In a detailed study of clinical measles and other diseases in a small village of West Bengal, Sinha followed the courses of four epidemics of measles in the village involving 2242 people; 20 percent of the children were severely undernourished. Of these, 98.5 per-cent were marasmic and 1.5 percent had kwashiorkor or marasmic-kwashiorkor. During the epidemics 179 children contracted measles. Only two of them died, and both of them had kwashiorkor (see Table VI). Measles had such a bad reputation in relation to famine, that it was closely monitored in the refugee camps during the 1974–75 Bangladesh famine. Early in the course of the famine, it appeared in the largest camp, but died out before it could be studied.

It was possible to compare two other refugee camps in Dacca which were operated by the same administration and which received the same input of food energy. The larger one was more auspici-ously located and had better sanitary facilities. Measles developed as a small epidemic in this camp, but did not appear in the other. The con-sulting pediatrician to both camps, Dr. Rainer Arnhold, was concerned because the children in the "better" camp were failing to gain weight on a supplemental feeding of 450 Kcal given twice a day, whereas children in the poorer camp were responding to the same feeding. Measles appeared in the camp where the feeding procedures were failing (see Table VII).

The difficulty of obtaining accurate data under conditions where a small staff is responsible for 20,000 people living in tents (Figure 8) and where illness and death cannot be completely recorded is emphasized. Thus, no final conclusions can be drawn from the data, but three points can be made: mortality rates were below those for Africa, mor-tality rates were higher in hospitalized children from the camp where more children failed to gain weight, and measles appeared only in the latter camp (McGregor, 1964; Morley, Woodland, and Martin, 1963).

EFFECT OF FAMINE ON DISEASE

How does famine affect susceptibility to particular diseases? There are three aspects to this question. The first is how does famine affect the immune system, the second is how does it work epidemiologically, and the third is what are the available data on experimental infections.

TABLE VI

Mortality from measles in malnourished children in Ichag, West Bengal

	No. children with measles	Mortality	Percent
Kwashiorkor	2	2	100
Marasmic undernourished or healthy	177	0	0

Source: Sinha, (1976).

TABLE VII

Weight gain, malnutrition, death rates, measles, prevalence and sanitation status in two refugee camps in Bangladesh

Camp	M	D
Number of families	2360	4100
Malnourished children in day care	130–150	270
Children failing to gain weight over 6 weeks	19–26%	34–44%
In hospital death rate (all cases)	3/40 = 8%	27/120 = 23%
Measles	no cases	200 + cases
Sanitation	poor drainage soil clayey	excellent drainage on banks of river sandy soil

FIGURE 8. Refugee camp in the Bangladesh famine of 1975–1976.

The Immune System

The interaction of infection and malnutrition is similar in complexity to that of separating the effects of heredity and environment (Chandler, 1957). Famine is often abruptly epidemic, continues for some months and has disruptive effects for months afterwards. This is more similar to the situation which is created by the periodic elimination or severe restriction of total food in experimental animals than to the restriction or deprivation of particular types of food energy, protein, vitamins or minerals.

Following the remarkable preview of Cunningham, (1889) that acute starvation leads to depletion of the lymphoid system, the French anatomist Jolly (1915) independently showed in 1913 that there was striking atrophy of the thymus and bursa in pigeons after 6–9 days' starvation and a similar atrophy of thymus, spleen and lymph nodes in starved rabbits. Marasmus like conditions of chickens are accompanied by atrophy of lymphoid tissue throughout the animal (Bang and Bang, 1972). These same changes were found in humans who starved during wartime conditions and were then killed by shell fragments. The germinal centers which are responsible for the amplification of antibody response to a recent antigenic stimulus are particularly affected.

Recent knowledge of the dynamics of the immune response emphasizes the role of T cells, both in a direct response to bacteria and in assisting in the B cell (antibody) response. Studies on endemic malnutrition frequently show that immunoglobulin levels are usually normal in malnourished subjects, but that the immune response to some antigens is depressed (Suskind, 1977). It is generally recognized that this T cell response is inadequate in endemic malnutrition in Africa where a low protein-high carbohydrate intake leads to kwashiorkor. The number of T and B cells in the blood of malnourished children has been studied by a number of authors. T cells are frequently lowered (Chandra, 1974a, 1974b), which would explain the poor response to tuberculin first clearly outlined by Harland (Harland, 1965). The single study in which T cells were measured differentially in marasmus and kwashiorkor reported that they were specifically lower in kwashiorkor (Bang, et al., 1975). A differentiation of the two extremes of malnutrition seemed significant in another context in Sinha's village study: children who tended toward kwashiorkor had fewer posi

tive tuberculin tests after BCG than children who were marasmic (Sinha and Bang, 1976).

The ubiquity of dysentery as a major disease of starvation raises the question of immune mechanisms in the intestine. These are just beginning to be understood. The dynamics of the plasma cells which produce secretory IgA antibody in the Peyer's patches of the small intestine have recently been demonstrated (Craig and Cebra, 1971; Pierce, and Gowans 1975) but nothing is yet known of their fate in starvation or their reconstitution after refeeding.

Among the experimental data on the effects of malnutrition on susceptibility are two remarkable reports which show that the effects of induced maternal malnutrition are passed on to two succeeding generations even though the second and third generations receive normal diets. Chow and Lee (1964) showed this with rates of growth in rats derived from malnourished mothers, and Chandra (1975) showed significant reduction in antibody responses in F_1 and F_2 generations derived from mother rats which were originally malnourished even when the succeeding dams were mated with well nourished males. Lee and Dubos (1969) have shown that there is a filterable agent, presumably a virus, which can suppress growth in mice and which mimics the effect of malnutrition. Are there agents in man which may be evoked by malnutrition and may then be transmitted vertically, like murine leukemia virus? This would allow for "inheritance" of acquired characteristics.

Disruptions of Energy Flow during Famine

Famine is preceded by a change in food habits, then a rechanneling of available energy. Disease causes a loss of energy and thus a leak in the system.

During the Irish famine of 1845–51, potatoes became scarce and cereals were shipped in. Some months later scurvy became epidemic, except in people who were fed a special vegetable soup by the Quakers. In retrospect potatoes have high amounts of Vitamin C, and cereals very little. A very similar ecological result is that which occurs in the Indian sub-continent. Many varieties of peas furnish a protein supplement to the daily rice. Not only do these vary in their nutritive value, but one of the hardiest and cheapest (Lathyrus sativum) contains a toxic component which causes a progressive disease of the nervous system, namely lathyrism (Mitchell, 1971). Unfortunately this pea, (*khesare dal*) will grow when other peas fail to grow and thus is particularly favored in times of drought (Indian Council for Agricultural Research, 1970). Consumption of small amounts apparently causes no difficulty, but if it becomes an important part of the staple diet it causes a progressive spastic paralysis (Park, 1972). Its toxicity may be eliminated by adequate cooking, but this is not generally known, so that in times of famine the stage is set for dependence on a toxic plant. A recent epidemic of several hundred cases in Bangladesh is a reminder of this sequence.

The pathogenesis of famine will not be understood until there is some rough understanding of the energy flow within a community subject to famine, and of the mechanism of breakdown. Consumption of energy by the people living and working within the Bengal Delta has been studied only in a preliminary way. It has been shown that a normal sedentary adult male Bengalee consumed 10.1 ± 2 MJ (2423 ± 506 (cals) whereas a bicycle-*rickshawwalla* carrying a passenger consumed 13.0 ± 1.0 MJ (3128 ± 250 Cals) (Fariduddin, Rahman and Ahsanullan, 1975). One unusual rickshaw peddler consumed over 25 MJ (6000 Cals) daily. At least two other major factors must be incorporated into any estimate of

calorie need: infectious disease, malabsorption, with or without diarrhea. It is very difficult to estimate either of these. However, Beisel (1975) who has made special studies of metabolic changes during infectious disease estimates that the calorie intake may need to be doubled.

Malabsorption is a common but poorly understood syndrome in South and Southeast Asia (Lindenbaum, 1973; Rosenberg and Scrimshaw, 1972; Klipstein, Lipton and Schenk, 1973). It may be measured by a number of indirect methods, such as fat absorption or xylose absorption and is often manifest mainly as a failure to gain weight. When in addition one recognizes that in some areas where highly prevalent diarrhea causes direct loss of energy through failure of the food to be digested, one cannot but wonder whether the caloric demand of the average community in Bengal may not be several times that of a theoretical community which is free of these diseases.

If we turn back to famine itself, a very abbreviated adaption of an energy flow chart (Figure 9) modified from Odum (1971) shows the sequence of energy flows. Figure 10 illustrates the effects of destruction of the storage of energy by a flood or drought; this leads to epidemic disease, reduces energy output, and causes complete disruption of a very carefully balanced energy flow. With the symbol marked as storage there should be

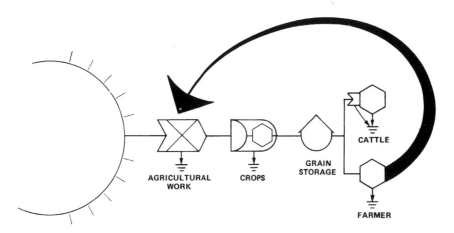

FIGURE 9. Diagrammatic presentation of the energy flow in an agricultural system (adapted from Odum 1971).

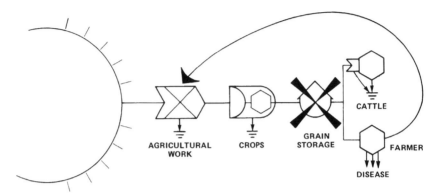

FIGURE 10.   Diagrammatic presentation showing disruption of the energy flow when personal and food energy (see text) is depleted by flood or drought (adapted from Odum 1971).

included the stored energy present in the individual (as fat), or present as resources for the future. However that may be, all stored resources are minimal in areas subject to famine. Examination of the proportion of children in the usual village who are underweight at different seasons of the year showed that the weight of the child varied with the time since the last harvest (Sinha, personal communication).

What Famine Related Diseases
Can Be Prevented Today?

Disease control in times of famine must compete with the overwhelming basic needs of food, water and shelter. Thus it must be inexpensive, culturally acceptable, highly effective and easy to administer. Control of louse borne diseases has been demonstrably successful. When future famines develop in cold climates lice must be promptly controlled.

Dysentery has been a common component of famine in Asia as long as records have been available, yet the only known effective control of dysentery is sanitation and sanitation is the first casualty in a starving community or a famine camp. In context, the Oxfam mobile sanitation feces disposal unit should be further evaluated. The effectiveness of small amounts of antibiotics in controlling dysentery should be tested even though antibiotic resistant strains of bacteria are known to have emerged.

Since tuberculosis has a period of incubation and

development of some months in individuals, it builds up slowly in a community and it is usually ignored during a famine. Presently available drugs such as isoniazid are such effective weapons that mass administration of isoniazid should be immediately instituted in the next outbreak of epidemic nalnutrition. But the correct dosage for malnourished subjects will have to be determined, because their metabolism of drugs is almost surely altered (Mehta *et al.,* 1975). The cost of isoniazid should be less than one cent per person per day.

Other diseases must be considered within the context of each situation. Vaccines like poliomyelitis are meaningless in the tropics where most people have already acquired immunity by endemic infection, but would be immediately necessary if famine struck a highly sanitary environment. Measles vaccine should be used in Africa where the disease among the malnourished nonimmunes is highly fatal, but is probably less necessary in Asia. Antimalarials are important only if malaria is already moderately endemic in an area, and would probably not be of value in hyperendemic areas. Supplementation of food with Vitamin A is essential in all rice growing countries since this vitamin is absent in rice.

Thus medical preventive preparation for famine depends greatly on the geographic area in which the famine occurs (Foege, 1971). All available data indicate the urgent need for planning specific disease prevention in given areas.

New data are certainly needed on the effects of

acute starvation on the immune response in experimental animals. It is at least possible that the effects of rapid destruction of lymphoid tissues could be retarded by a chemical substance or substances.

Finally, there is need for research. The number of immediate and fundamental unanswered questions on the causes, consequences, and prevention of famine is staggering.

PERSPECTIVE

The thesis that disease has a major role in famine and that disease control is an essential part of combating famine has been discussed. At this point the recurrent neomalthusian cry is heard: If the normal forces that eliminate excess population are controlled, human population will increase, thus human suffering will increase and the day of world calamity will be hastened. I think it is necessary to state the problem in other terms.

Both energetically and morally, I believe that it should be stated in terms of healthy person years/ km$_2$. I assume that an improved world would be one in which all people who live in it are able to have satisfactory disease-free lives. Undernutrition and infectious disease do not kill suddenly and regularly. For each person who dies there are many more debilitated, miserable and energetically inefficient. No one has yet calculated the energetic requirements of the army of inadequately nourished children who are stricken and die before puberty.

I assume that by eliminating or at least modifying disease we have carried out one half of the goal of improvement of human life on this planet—and that this is *not antagonistic* (Figure 11) to the goal of also reducing the total

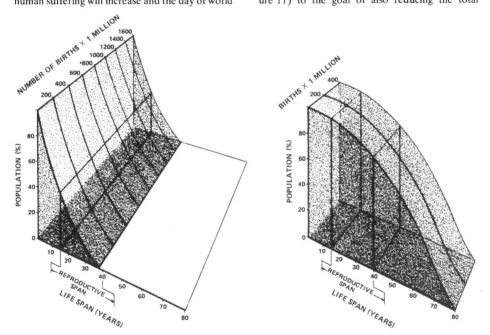

FIGURE 11. Differences in populations' use of available energy. The figure at the left represents the present situation in many underdeveloped nations. An individual in these countries uses relatively little energy, because of the short life expectancy, but because the population is so high, all of the available energy is consumed. The figure at the right represents the achievement of the combined goals of medicine (long life) and population control (low birth rate) in which the energy, roughly the same amount as available in the figure at the left, is consumed by a small population with long life expectancy.

increase of population which must be achieved in other ways.

SUMMARY

In this survey of the role of disease in the ecology of famine, we have emphasized that the same factors which lead to famine often lead to mass spread of infectious disease. In most of the famines for which adequate records are available over the last century and a half, disease has played such a significant role that it has killed as many people as starvation itself. This may be partly related to individual loss of resistance, but the population effect seems to be more important . . . the normal components of resistance within a society (immune capacity, sanitation, community spacing) break down and endemic disease flares into epidemic.

The ecological effect is a tremendous loss of energy for the community: calorie loss due to infection, malabsorption and diarrhea, and crop loss due to lack of strength for agricultural tasks. This may increase caloric need several fold so that a disruptive positive feedback loop is instituted within a community that is already on the edge of imbalance. There is a need for specific planning for disease prevention as an integral part of famine prevention. Finally, future relief procedures must be predicated on present knowledge derived from specific areas with specific disease problems and specific types of endemic malnutrition.

ACKNOWLEDGEMENT

In the preparation of this overview, I have benefited greatly by discussion with a number of people involved in administering relief in Bangladesh during and after the famine of 1974, and from visits to a number of acute relief camps especially in the Rangpur district.

Dr. M. Rahaman of the Cholera Research Laboratory, Bangladesh was especially helpful in listening to my ideas and correcting them gently. Dr. K. M. S. Aziz also of C.R.L. constantly gave me background information and assisted me in getting new material. Dr. T. W. Simpson kindly made available very scarce material from autopsy material from wartime casualties in Okinawa who had been starving when killed. Dr. R. Arnholt discussed the role of disease during the famine relief and readily furnished material for this paper. Dr. H. Gantt called on his memories of the Russian Famine and helped in location of material.

The great need that we all have for knowledge about famines and what to do about them continues. These friends have given freely of their material. I am, of course, solely responsible for errors and misinterpretations.

REFERENCES

Andreason, E. (1943). Part III. The thymolymphatic system during inanition and restitution. *Acta. Pathol. et Microb. Scand.*, **49**, 121–1515.

Bang, F. B. (1975). Epidemiological interference. *Int. J. Epidem.*, **4**, 337–342.

Bang, B. G., and F. B. Bang (1972). Malnutrition. *Amer. J. Pathol.* **68**, 407–417.

Bang, F. B., M. G. Bang and B. G. Bang (1975). Ecology of respiratory virus transmission. A comparison of three communities in West Bengal. *Amer. J. Trop. Med. Hyg.*, **24**, 326–346.

Bang, B. G., D. Mahalanabis, K. L. Mukherjee, and F. B. Bang (1975). T & B lymphocyte in undernourished children. *Proc. Soc. Exp. Biol. and Med.*, **149**, 191–202.

Beisel, W. R. (1975). Metabolic response to infection. *Ann. Rev. Med.*, **26**, 9–20. Also personal communication.

Bhuyan, Un. N., and V. Ramalingaswami (1973). Immune responses of the protein-deficient guinea pig to BCG vaccination. *Amer. J. Pathol.*, **72**(1), 489–500.

Chakraborty, S. M., F. B. Bang and W. D. Hillis (1972). Some aspects of diphtheria immunity in rural West Bengal. *Indian J. Med. Res.*, **60**, 778–788.

Chandler, A. C. (1957). Interrelations between nutrition and infectious disease in the tropics. *Amer. J. Trop. Med. Hyg.*, **6**, 195–208.

Chandra, R. K. (1974a). Rosette-forming t-lymphocytes and cell-mediated immunity in malnutrition. *Brit. Med. J.*, **3**, 608–609.

Chandra, R. K. (1974b). Immuno competence in low-birth-weight infants after intra uterine malnutrition. *Lancet* **2**, 1393–1394.

Chandra, R. K. (1975). Antibody formation in first and second generation offspring of nutritionally deprived rats. *Science*, **190**, 289–290.

Chow, B. F., and C. J. Lee (1964). Effects of dietary restriction of pregnant rats on body weight gain of the offspring. *J. Nutr.* **82**, 10.

Collins, F. M., and G. B. Mackaness (1970). The relationship of delayed hypersensitivity to acquired antituberculous immunity. II. Effect of adjuvant on the allergenicity and immunogenicity of heat-killed tubercle baccilli.

Craig, S. W., and J. J. Cebra (1971). Peyer's patches: an enriched of precursors for IgA producing immunocytes. *J. Exp. Med.*, **134**, 18.

Cunningham, D. D. (1889). In: *The Diseases of the Madras Famine of 1877–1878*, Ed. Porter, A. Government Press, India. 234 pp.

Day, P. L., W. C. Langston, W. J. Darby, J. G. Wahlin, and V. Mims (1940). Nutritional cytopenia in monkeys receiving the goldgerger diet. *J. Exp. Med.* **62**, 463–477.

Dannenberg, A. M. Jr., M. Ando, K. Shima, and T. Tsuda (1975). Macrophage turnover and activation in tuberculous granulometa. In *Mononuclear Phagocytes in Immunity, Infection and Pathology.* Ed. R. van Furth. Blackwell, Oxford. pp. 959–980

Fariduddin, K. M., M. M. Rahaman, and A. B. M. Ahsanullah (1975). Study of energy expenditure and food intake of some working class people in Bangladesh. *Bangladesh Med. Res. Council*, **1**, 24–31.

Fletcher, W., M. Jepps, and A. E. Horn (1927). *Dysentery in the Federated Malay States.* John Bale Sons and Danielsson, Ltd., London, 81 pp.

Foege, W. H. (1971). Famine, infections and epidemics. In *Famine: A Symposium Dealing with Nutrition and Relief Operations in Times of Disaster.* Ed. G. Blix, Y. Hofvander and B. Vahlquist, Almquist and Wiksell, Sweden, pp. 64–73.

Gantt, W. H. (1928). In *A Medical Review of Soviet Russia.* British Medical Association. pp. 1–112.

Gontzea, L. (1974). In *Nutrition and Anti-Infectious Defence.* S. Karger-Basel. Munchen, pp. 1–276.

Harland, P. E. S. G. (1965). Tuberculin reactions in malnourished children. *Lancet,* ii, 719–721.

Helweg-Larsen, P., H. Hoffmeyer, J. Kieler, E. H. Thaysen, J. H. Thaysen, P. Thagesen, and M. H. Wulff. Tuberculosis. In *Famine Disease in German Concentration Camps. Complications and Sequels. Acta Medica Scand.* Suppl. **274**, 330–361.

Indian Council of Agricultural Research (1970). Pulse crops of India. Ed. P. Kachroo, M. Arif. New Delhi, 334 pp.

Jolly, J. (1915). Labourse de Fabricius et les organes lymphoepitheliaux. *Arch. Anat. Microsc. Morphol. Exp.* **16**, 363–547.

Keys, A., J. Brozek, A. Hernschel, O. Michelsen, and H. L. Taylor (1950). In *The Biology of Human Starvation* Vol. II. University of Minnesota Press.

Klipstein, F. A., S. D. Lipton, and E. A. Schenk (1973). Folate deficiency of the intestinal mucosa. *Amer. J. Clin. Nutr.* **26**, 728–737.

Lee, C. J., and R. Dubos (1969). Lasting biological effects of early environmental influences. *J. Exp. Med.* **130**, 955.

Lindenbaum, J. (1973). Nutrition: role of malabsorption. In *Disaster in Bangladesh.* Ed. L. C. Chen. Oxford University Press, pp. 52–66.

MacArthur, W. P. (1956). The medical history of famine. In *The Great Famine–Studies in Irish History, 1845–52.* Eds. R. D. Edwards and T. D. Williams. Browne and Nolan, Ltd., Dublin, Ireland, Chapter V, pp. 263–315.

McCarrison, R. (1920). Effects of deficient dietaries on monkeys. *Brit. Med. J.* **1**, 249–253.

McGregor, I. A. (1964). Measles and child mortality in the Gambia. *W. Afr. Med. J.* **13**, 251–257.

Mata, L. J. (1975). Malnutrition-infection interactions in the tropics. *Amer. J. Trop. Med. and Hyg.* **24**, 564–574.

Mehta, S., H. K. Kalsi, S. Jayaraman, and V. S. Mathur (1975). Chloramphenicol metabolism in children with protein-calorie malnutrition. *Amer. J. Clin. Nutr.* **28**, 977–981.

Mitchell, R. D. (1971). *The Grass Pea: Distribution, Diet and Disease.* Association of Pacific Coast Geographers Yearbook, **33**, 29–46.

Morley, D., M. Woodland, and W. J. Martin (1963). Measles in Nigerian children—a study of the disease in West Africa and its manifestations in England and other countries during different epochs. *J. Hyg.* **61**, 115–134.

Odum, H. T. (1971). *Environment, Power, and Society.* Wiley-Interscience. New York, 331 pp.

Park. J. E. (1972). In *Textbook of Preventive and Social Medicine.* Third Edition. Banarsidas Bhanot Publishers. M. P. Jabalpur, India.

Pierce, N. F., and J. L. Gowans (1975). Cellular kinetics of the intestinal immune response to cholera toxoid in rats. *J. Exp. Med.* **142**, 1550.

Pinkerton, H. (1949). Influence of nutrition in resistance to experimental rickettsial infections. *Bact. Rev.* **13**, 112–117.

Porter, A. (1889). *The Diseases of the Madras Famine of 1877–78.* Printed by the Superintendent, Government Press, Madras. 243 pp.

Rosenberg, I. H., and N. S. Scrimshaw (1972). Malabsorption and nutrition. *Amer. J. Clin. Nutr.* **25**, October–November, 1040–1133.

Scrimshaw, N. S., C. E. Taylor, and J. E. Gordon (1968). Interactions of nutrition and infection. *WHO Monogr. Ser. No. 57,* World Health Organization, Geneva.

Sinha, D. P., and F. B. Bang (1976). Protein and calorie malnutrition cell-mediated immunity and B.C.G. vaccination in children from rural West Bengal. *Lancet* ii, 531–534.

Sinha, D. P. (1977). Measles and malnutrition in a West Bengal village. *Trop. and Geogr. Med.* **29**, March, 32–41.

Sinha, D. P. (1976). Chickenpox—a disease predominantly affecting adults in rural West Bengal, India. *Int. J. Epidem.* **5**, 367–374.

Sprunt, P. H. (1942). The effect of undernourishment on the susceptibility of the rabbit to infection with vacinia. *J. Exp. Med.* **75**, 297–304.

Suskind, R. M. (1977). *Malnutrition and the Immune Response.* Ed. R. M. Suskind. Raven Press, New York.

SECTION III

FOOD AND FAMINE

SECTION III
INTRODUCTION

John R.K. ROBSON

Famine relief is inevitably associated with the provision of food supplies, but in reality the simple concept of providing food where it is needed is very complex. In the past, considerable money and effort have been provided not only for famine relief, but also for disaster relief in general, regardless of whether it is due to earthquake, war, flood, or hurricanes. In the course of any one year, millions of tons of food are supplied to developing nations, during which time the providers divert a substantial part of their exports for the feeding of the victims of disasters. Although the benefits of these efforts have not been properly evaluated, nevertheless, some general lessons have been learned.

First there has to be a differentiation between cataclysmic disasters and long term continuing disasters. Famines tend to be of the latter type, but the customary relief offered is usually the same as that provided in times of cataclysmic disaster. Famines tend to disrupt transportation and distribution networks and may make the relief completely ineffectual. The question is also raised whether food relief is actually tackling the cause of the problem. Consideration is therefore being given to studies of the food supply system before the famine occurs. This may provide an insight, not only into the most appropriate mode of relief, but also into the causation of the famine, thereby providing opportunities for early warnings of disaster.

The stage for famine is often set long before the disaster. For example, certain areas are vulnerable to food shortages. Within these areas recognition of inappropriate agricultural practices, excessive urbanization, or overgrazing, could perhaps prevent food shortages from occuring. An examination of the food supply system itself may identify more appropriate ways of handling the problem once it has arisen. The food supply system (which is an energy supply system), has been identified as having three components: production, distribution, and consumption. Like all systems, the efficiency of the whole is dependent on the efficiencies of its component parts. The supply system is derived from two modes of food production, namely marketing and subsistence. The application of systems analysis to the famine or pre-famine situation allows a reconstruction of the main events in the food chain. This, in turn, facilitates surveillance and may provide early warnings of impending food supply problems. An analysis of the food chain may also be invaluable in demonstrating weaknesses or breakdowns in the chain, which needs to be considered when plans are formulated for relief.

REFERENCES AND ADDITIONAL READINGS

Reutlinger, M., Selowsky, S. (1976) *Malnutrition and Poverty.* World Bank Staff Occasional Papers No. 29. International Bank for Reconstruction and Development.

Idusogie, E.O. Olayide, Olatunbosum, D. (1977) *Post-harvest crop losses: The Nigerian case.* Joint FAO/WHO, OAU Regional Food and Nutrition Commission for Africa. Special Paper No. 12 Accra, Ghana.

Jolly, D.A. (1976) Food cost, farm policy and nutrition. *J. Nutr. Educ.* **8**, 56.

National Academy of Sciences, (1975) *World Food and Nutrition Study.* Interim Report, National Academy of Sciences, Washington, D.C.

Krumdiek, C.L. (1971) The Rural to Urban malnutrition gradient. *J. Amer. Med. Assoc.* **215**, 1652.

Basta, S. (1977) Nutrition and health in low income urban areas in the Third World. *Ecol. Food and Nutrition,* **6**, 113.

Haverberg, L. (1977) *An analysis of the nutritional situation in Ghana and a proposed system of nutrition planning for the Ministry of Agriculture Ghana.* UNDP/FAO Agricultural Development Planning Project — Ghana. Consultant Report No. 10, FAO. Rowe. Page 119.

Brown, L.R. (1975) The World Food Prospect. *Science* **190**, 1053.

THE CONCEPT OF FOOD SUPPLY SYSTEM WITH SPECIAL REFERENCE TO THE MANAGEMENT OF FAMINE

ROGER W. HAY†

Food and Nutrition Surveillance, UNICEF, Addis Ababa Ethiopia

INTRODUCTION

While the onset of famine may be apparently catastrophic, more often a series of identifiable events have occurred which have progressively imperilled the food supply of the area. The significance of these events, sometimes taking months or even years to gain momentum, may pass unrecognized for a time. However, in retrospect it is often possible to see that long before the seriousness of the human effects were known, the stage had been set for disaster. For, while the cause of famine may be attributed to a single unusual natural catastrophe—drought, flood or pestilence—a closer examination shows that this was superimposed on a vulnerable situation where ecological imbalance was already apparent. Overcrowding, land whose productivity has been reduced over centuries of tillage, rangelands where the animal-pasture balance had been disturbed, uncontrolled urbanization and many other factors may have combined together to destroy the equilibrium between man's needs and the resources of the environment.

Had the signs been recognized early, a whole range of preventive measures might have been applied. In other words, if it were possible to interpret predictive indicators of food shortage with a certain degree of accuracy and confidence, famines might be, if not averted, at least managed. An analysis of these indicators broadens the scope of response to serious food shortage from "famine relief" to a consideration of the inter-related causes of famine and therefore the type of intervention possible to ameliorate or prevent its effects.

This paper proposes the concept of "food supply system" as a basis for the analysis of precarious food supply situations and draws attention to its possible applications in famine prevention and management.

THE CONCEPT OF "FOOD SUPPLY SYSTEM"

A food supply system may be regarded as an energy carrying chain. It embraces the complex of factors which determine food production, distribution and consumption for a particular population group and defines the way each element relates to the rest.

Man has selected certain plants and animals for food. Most contain energy extracted from the environment, and concentrated and bound, in the first instance, by plants during the process of photosynthesis. Animals have used and re-stored some of this energy during growth and are secondary energy carriers. The production of food, therefore, may be regarded as the application of techniques to improve environmental energy concentration and storage processes. The distribution component of the food supply system is the transport of bound environmental energy to an area where human demand for it exists. After consumption the stored energy is released and used for human activity, growth and other biological functions. Thus, the energy flow in a food supply system is a particular and important example of eco-system energy transfer. As such it is amenable to measurement and analysis.

The concept of food supply system identifies population groups with homogenous *patterns* of food supply. This does not imply that within each group everyone has equal access to food. By contrast, once a population group is classified with respect to its food supply system, the way food

Based on a paper presented at the American Association for the Advancement of Science Meeting held on February 20, 1976.

† Presently Associate Research Fellow, Queen Elizabeth House, 21 St. Giles, Oxford.

resources are distributed within that group can be examined. This is rarely proportional to biological requirements but more often is skewed towards the privileged. As it cannot be assumed that within one food supply system the distribution of resources approximates to a Gaussian configuration, notions of mean per capita production and consumption have limited use in the analysis of food supply system dynamics.

The total efficiency of a food supply system is limited by the individual efficiency of its component parts. When energy extraction becomes inadequate, when distribution mechanisms become inefficient or when the food commodity available for human consumption is an inadequate energy carrier, the flow of energy along the food supply system chain declines. The extreme result of this decline is famine.

There are a number of advantages in applying this concept to the problem of impending food shortage.

1) Food supply is not the domain of a single discipline. It demands the concerted and collaborative effort of ecologists, agriculturalists, economists and nutritionists. The concept of the food supply system reflects the scope of the problem and provides a framework in which the contribution of one discipline can relate to and complement the others.

2) The multiplicity of the inter-related causes of food shortage are frequently confusing. By defining carefully the components of the food supply system chain and the way each relates to the rest, it is possible to understand the relative significance of each and therefore the causes of decline in the system as a whole.

3) The ability to define a point of inadequacy with some precision within the context of a complete system of food supply, provides a sound basis for planning corrective strategies. The concept therefore lends itself to use by the systems analyst who may make a valuable contribution in defining alternative possibilities for improving the stability and efficiency of a food supply system.

A CLASSIFICATION OF FOOD SUPPLY SYSTEMS

While many local variants may occur, less than a dozen major food supply systems exist. Man either hunts for his food, herds it, fishes for it, grows it

or buys it. Each food supply system has been developed to take advantage of the environmental resources which supply it. Each has its own characteristics and behaves in a particular manner; each has definable advantages and disadvantages and each has a limited and measurable capacity to withstand the effects of environmental changes. The stability of food supply, the velocity with which shortages develop, and the signs indicating the magnitude of food shortage are all determined by the characteristics of the system.

Market Dependent Food Supply Systems

The food supply system which operates almost universally in "developed" countries has three main components. Food is produced, a marketing system distributes it and a consumer buys and uses it. This sequence of events taken together constitutes a "market dependent food supply system." The characteristics of this food supply system are the multiplicity of its production components, the complexity of its distribution component and the total dependence of the consumer on the market. The system has been developed to produce food with maximum efficiency, without seasonal fluctuations in supply to the consumer and with enough variety to satisfy a number of food preferences.

The market dependent food supply systems of the developed world are supplied almost entirely by an international complex of high performance production elements which rely on a sophisticated agricultural technology. This implies capital investment in machinery, improved seed varieties, fertilizer and disease control. Efficiency in energy transfer is of necessity lost to some extent when food has to be processed or moved long distances to the consumer. Sophisticated storage and transport techniques to ensure minimum losses are therefore important.

Market-dependent food supply systems in developing countries are less complex. They are often supplied not only by commercial production but also by surplus producing subsistence units. The distribution component may only entail the sale of produce to the consumer at the local market. At the same time, imported food may also compete with locally produced food.

The efficiency of market dependent food supply systems depends not only on the efficiency of their production components but also on the efficiency with which food can be stored, processed and moved to areas of demand.

Their stability depends on the degree of protection which modern technology has devised, and on the extent to which their production elements can absorb the effects of localized production failure.

The chief disadvantage of market dependent food supply systems lies in the fact that most consumers have little control over the system they depend on. Minimum demand is set, not by consumer choice, but by biological requirements. Access to the market depends entirely on the consumer's purchasing power and the poor must compete with the rich in a market which is governed more by supply than by demand.

Subsistence Food Supply Systems

In contrast to the ubiquity of the market dependent food supply system in the developed world, a characteristic of a developing country is the variety of its food supply systems, which often lack a distribution component as food is produced and consumed by the same family or, in the case of co-operatives, group of families. These are subsistence food supply systems. Many are ancient and all are precursors and the building blocks of market dependent food supply systems. However, they are important as they still feed a large proportion of the world's population. While they are generally less stable and efficient than market dependent food supply systems, they enjoy advantages of their own.

Because more than one food supply system may operate in one area, the people of a locality may be identified by their food supply system. Indeed, this is necessary if food shortages are to be understood and dealt with. Subsistence food supply systems may be classified according to the nature of their production component as this determines the staple food and the character of the system as a whole. The most common subsistence food supply systems are dependent on either grain cropping, root and tuber cropping, herding or fishing. Each may be sub-classified according to local practices such as flood irrigation cropping, nomadic pastoralism and the like. Combinations also exist.

With the worldwide drive towards more efficient food production, pure subsistence food supply systems are becoming less common, but even if capital is available for investment in improved productive efficiency the word "subsistence" may still be applied if a family usually derives *most* of its food from its own holding. In an improved

subsistence economy capital is usually generated either from the sale of food crops which are surplus to the family's requirements, or from the sale of cash crops which are grown specifically for this purpose. These systems may be sub-classified according to the level of capital investment or, alternatively, according to the ratio of food bought and food grown.

Subsistence food supply systems are characterized by the relative lack of variety of their production components, their vulnerability to climatic changes and pest and disease outbreaks, the high input of labor required for production and the variable role played by the market in the food supply chain.

The stability of these systems is not great and depends to a large extent on favorable environmental conditions. Over the years, communities served by these systems have developed means of buffering shortages, but these mechanisms have their limitations and these limitations once exceeded, result in the rapid decay of food supply. It is worth noting that when shortages develop in a subsistence food supply system, the system becomes isolated from alternative sources of supply because purchasing power is already low and is exhausted rapidly. However, the essential nature of subsistence means that these systems retain a simplicity which allows the consumer a certain degree of control. Provided the essential resources are plentiful, this does a great deal to compensate for the system's inefficiency. The main food supply systems described here are classified in Table I.

APPLYING THE CONCEPT

Before the concept can be applied to a specific problem, the characteristics of the food supply systems of the area in question must be determined. A convenient method of doing this is to prepare a flow chart for each system in turn, indicating its main components and showing how each element relates to the rest.

Suppose, for example, that a hypothetical urban-rural area typical of many parts of the developing world has a population with the following occupational characteristics:

Subsistence cropping agriculturalists	50 percent
Wage, salary earners and merchants	25 percent
Commercial farmers	15 percent
Those without regular employment	10 percent

TABLE I

A Classification of food supply systems.

		PRODUCTION		DISTRIBUTION	CONSUMPTION
Market-depen-dent food supply systems	Industrialized Country	Multiple Commercial Domestic and Foreign Production Units Food processing prominent		Complex marketing system Dependent on efficient transport and storage procedures	Wide range of choice Acquisition limited by purchasing power
	Developing Country	Imported food + Domestic 'commercial' production + 'Surplus' subsistence production		as above as above local marketing for cash or barter	as above as above variable range of commodities acquisition limited by purchasing power
Subsistence food supply systems	Grain crop dependent	'UNIMPROVED' Variable surplus for sale Little or no fertil-izer, pesticides, etc., avail-able Small hold-ings, labour intensive	'IMPROVED'	Little contribution to food supply from market	quantity and choice limited to what is grown. purchasing power close to zero staple provides generally adequate energy-protein balance
			usually pro-duces surplus to food re-quirements Fertilizer, pesticides, seed may be bought farm machinery sometimes used generally labour in-tensive	variable contribution to food supply from market	variable but food generally limited to what is grown purchasing power falls to zero rapidly in bad years generally adequate energy-protein balance
	Root and tuber dependent	As above Additional protein source required to supplement staple — may be produced or bought Cash crops may be grown to provide purchasing power		Variable contribution from market	Generally limited choice Purchasing power usually low Staple rich in energy, poor in protein Protein acquisition may be limited by purchasing power (tends to produce kwashiorkor type malnutrition in times of shortage)
	Animal dependent	Common in areas too dry for rain-fed cropping often nomadic or semi-nomadic Little protection against disease May supplement with crop-ping in good years		Often exchange of animals for grain in local markets	Milk, meat, ?blood plus grain variable purchasing power dependent on herd size and animal conditions. Falls rapidly in poor years Food choice extended during good years with market purchases Staple provides excellent energy-protein balance

It is obvious that this population is served by two food supply systems—a subsistence cropping food supply system and a market dependent food supply system. The subsistence system may contribute surplus production to the market, but it is unlikely that the subsistence farmers will be able to buy much food. These general characteristics are set out in Figure 1.

By tracing the course taken by food from the point of production to the consumer, it is possible to reconstruct the main events for each food supply chain. This has been done in Figure 2 for the subsistence farmers and in Figure 3 for those dependent on the market for food.

The vulnerability of subsistence systems to drought, disease and pest is evident as capital is not

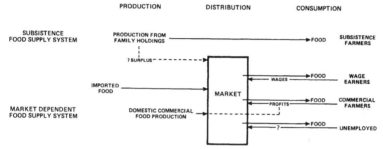

FIGURE 1   Two food supply systems serving one area common in developing countries.

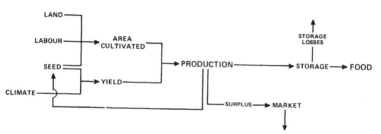

FIGURE 2   "Subsistence" cropping food supply system (main features only).

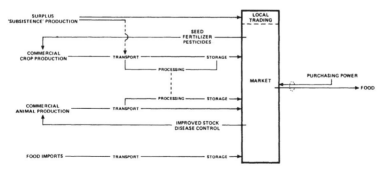

FIGURE 3   Market dependent food supply system (selected features only).

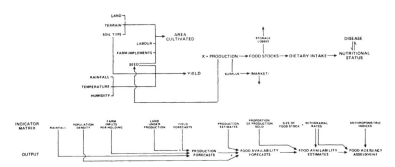

FIGURE 4   A subsistence cropping food supply system showing a possible selection of performance indicators.

available for investment in water supply systems, fertilizer and pesticides, and production is often not sufficient to store for famine years.

On the other hand the market dependent system draws on a number of production units (domestic and foreign) developed to produce with maximum efficiency and with minimum vulnerability to environmental disturbance. However, because the access of different people to the market varies enormously, true food availability is not evenly distributed. This is a striking example of the way skewness develops in a food supply system. By comparing the subsistence system shown in Figure 2, with the market dependent system shown in Figure 3, it is clear that, by "coming to town," the subsistence farmer has exchanged his vulnerability to the vagaries of climate, pest and disease, for the vulnerability of dependence on a market over which he has little control. The plight of those who have neither land nor regular employment is obvious.

The ways in which the community controls its food supply has not been shown in these diagrams, but it has already been noted that this is a complex and important feature of food supply systems. Almost all societies have developed the means to buffer fluctuations in food availability and, in particular, to ameliorate the consequences of a declining flow in food supply. These devices have the effect of creating elasticity in the relationships between elements of the food supply system chain. For a specific society, the concept of food supply system may be used to identify these devices as it provides a framework for undertaking a systematic search. It is important to take these into account when interpreting changes which are predictive of food shortage.

These diagrams are, of course, over-simplifications. To be useful, each component of the food supply system chain must be expanded to include the precise factors which determine levels of production and patterns of distribution. (See Figure 4.)

TWO SPECIFIC APPLICATIONS

The concept of food supply system may be used for a variety of purposes; as an aid in planning agricultural development strategies and food and nutrition policies, and as one input to socioeconomic development planning. However, the main purpose of this paper is to indicate ways in which the concept is useful in the management of food shortages.

Food and Nutrition Surveillance

A number of countries prone to food shortages have recognized the urgent and far-reaching problems which must be solved if food production is to be stabilized and improved. They have also recognized the value of having some warning of imminent regional shortages so that appropriate emergency actions can be taken to prevent starvation. In order to provide information for planning relief (and development activities), considerable interest is being expressed in developing national data collection systems. These will monitor the dynamics of production, distribution and consumption as an entity, with emphasis on the analysis of this data over time for predictive purposes.

Food and nutrition surveillance may be regarded as a way of monitoring the performance of food supply systems. Because the concept distinguishes homogenous patterns of production, distribution and consumption it provides a neat framework for surveillance design.

Once the food supply systems of an area have been defined it is possible to select a population sample from each and to construct a matrix of indicators representing critical points in each food supply chain. The cause and effect sequence is implicit in the concept and it can be used to identify predictive indicators and so provide a basis for estimating the likely consequences of changes observed in the determinants of food supply.

As real data is accumulated, the crude flow chart of the food supply system can be transformed into a formal model which defines more precisely the way the major parameters of each system are related. Predictions of changes in food availability can then be made with a known level of confidence. If it is possible to validate such a model, the monitoring of a small selection of predictive indicators should be sufficient to follow further trends in human food availability.

For illustration, a hypothetical array of indicators has been constructed for the system in Figure 2 and shown in Figure 4. In practice, it is probable that this indicator array would be modified considerably with experience. In some cases indicators will be found to be redundant; in others the residual variance in some postulated relationships will be so high that other indicators will be required to improve predictive probabilities.

If the promise of food and nutrition surveillance is fulfilled, the early recognition of changes liable to endanger the food supply system, and the quantitative prediction of their consequences, will provide a rational basis for introducing measures designed to improve the system's performance and thereby avert serious shortages.

Food Emergencies

Food emergencies are often the result of a complex of causes often they imply serious ecological imbalance. As such, the causes demand as much attention as their consequences. Frequently, the obvious indicators of famine—malnutrition, mass migration and disease—are treated and scant attention is paid to the factors which caused a decline in food supply.

This narrow and shortsighted view has arisen for a number of reasons. Among them is the fact that there is no single discipline which encompasses all the aspects of food supply dynamics. In fact, the field covers agrometeorology, agricultural economics, nutrition and health as well as the more general disciplines of ecology, and the social sciences; and all are interrelated. As a result there is no generally accepted framework for analyzing the causes of food shortage and no "system of thought" to which all the concerned disciplines can relate.

Further, until the dynamics of food supply have been examined thoroughly it will not be possible to plan assistance to areas where food supply is in the process of decline with any precision.

The concept of food supply system, encompassing as it does all the factors determining production, distribution and consumption, is offered as a conceptual basis for rethinking the problems of food availability. This does not imply a new discipline, but it does provide a framework for linking the contributions of a number of disciplines in a coherent manner. Much more should be known about the way food supply systems behave—their capacity to withstand environmental change, their dynamics and the way in which they signal stress. When these facts are known, it will be possible to devise ways of improving their efficiency with predictable results. The urgent need for such basic information opens up a whole field of observation and investigation.

Because so little is known, it is only possible at this stage to indicate in general terms how the application of the concept of food supply system broadens the possibilities of attack on the problem of food emergencies.

Failing Food Supply

It should be obvious by now that each food supply system demands a technique specifically related to its structure and characteristics. An analysis of a food supply system in decline should show the points in the chain where inadequacy has developed. The identification of these points will suggest the specific ways for supporting the food supply system.

If the causes appear to be short-term in nature, the correct response may be temporary measures designed to strengthen weak points in the system, or to supplement inadequate inputs. Assistance may take the form of an agricultural commodity such as seed or fertilizer, or food itself, if this is likely to be more efficient. On the other hand, if food shortages are the consequence of long standing defects in the system, more radical measures may be required. In this situation food aid is likely to be counter-productive except as a temporary expedient. The food supply system as a whole would have to be modified or even replaced.

Established Food Emergencies

Famine is not a disease in itself, but the symptom of serious food supply system pathology. Thus, the application of the concept of food supply system to the problem of famine increases the scope of response from relief feeding alone to a multi-pronged attack aimed at restoring the food supply system to functional integrity. This strategy does away with artificial distinctions between relief and rehabilitation as the problem resolves itself into a matter of rehabilitating the food supply system as a whole. While food aid may be required for a period, the main effort will be concentrated on the flaws in the food supply system which lead to its disintegration.

In particular, the dependence on food aid which frequently develops in times of chronic shortage can be placed in perspective. If the objective is to get a food supply system functioning again, aid will automatically be directed towards increasing the efficiency of food production and distribution, not reducing it with palliatives. An early, measured response has much more chance of fulfilling this objective than allowing a population to become weakened and apathetic as a result of overt malnutrition.

Finally, if enough were known about the behavior of food supply systems, the effects of corrective strategies could be measured and predicted. This would place the response to famine in a rational context. The advantages and disadvantages of a particular strategy could be weighed and assessed, possible spinoff effects could be identified, and the management of famine integrated with long term development to reduce the vulnerability of the area.

The concept of food supply system is thus, in a number of ways, a powerful planning tool in the management of famine.

CONCLUSION

The problems of famine are glaring in their fully developed form. This paper has suggested that it is more efficient to analyze the potential problem in advance and institute preventive measures. The idea of food supply system, a comprehensive expression linking the determinants of food production, distribution and consumption as a continuum, has been advanced as a conceptual framework with many specific applications. Among these, food and nutrition surveillance and the response to food emergencies have been discussed briefly as examples. The significance of a broad interdisciplinary approach to the problems of developing more stable and more efficient food supply systems is implicit in the concept.

In a world where there is enough food, but it is poorly distributed, the concept underscores the contention that food is not an economic commodity so much as an environmental resource to which all men must have adequate access.

ACKNOWLEDGEMENTS

This paper is based on a presentation to the American Association for the Advancement of Science symposium—"The Ecology of Famine" held in Boston in February 1976. It is published here by their kind permission.

I am grateful to my colleagues in Ethiopia who have contributed to the development of the concept of "Food Supply System" to Dr. L. J. Teply of UNICEF, New York, for his helpful comments, and to Dr. J. B. Mason, now of FAO, Rome, with whom the original ideas were hammered out.

ISSUES IN THE PROVISION OF FOOD AID FOLLOWING DISASTERS

FREDERICK C. CUNY

INTERTECT, Dallas, Texas

Each year, thousands of tons of food are provided to disaster-hit developing countries, primarily by means of food aid programs such as the U.S. Food for Peace (PL480) Program and the World Food Program of the United Nations. In the past, in-depth needs assessment and evaluation studies of the real impact of these programs on the societies they are intended to help have been virtually non-existent. Recent experience and a growing understanding of the problems involved in the provision of food aid indicate that the strategies used and the basic assumptions under which these programs operate should be evaluated and revised. Increased awareness of the types of disasters, of their effect on local food production and distribution systems, and of the options available to meet the needs of the affected population could substantially reduce the incidence of massive food importation and its negative impact on a developing society.

KEY WORDS: Food distribution, Food aid, Disaster, Civil War, Flood, Earthquake, Cyclone.

INTRODUCTION

Each year, millions of tons of food are supplied by food-exporting nations to the developing countries. A substantial portion of this food is made available after disasters with the intention of providing emergency and post-disaster supplies to replace food stores lost in the disaster. The United States, Canada and Australia are the world's largest suppliers of emergency food aid. Last year alone, the United States, through its PL480 program (Food for Peace), supplied 328,000 tons to disaster-hit nations† The U.S. PL480 program and the World Food Program of the United Nations are the two most important sources of supply. With the growing humanitarian concern about world hunger and the recent awareness of the role that disasters play in the cycle which retards economic and social development processes, the amount of food aid which will be available in the future is projected to increase.

In recent years, there has been a trend for post-disaster food aid programs to continue long past the initial emergency period. Droughts in the Sahel, failures of the rice crops in India and Bangladesh in past years have convinced many program administrators that a disaster will have a long-term

† Figure supplied by Food For Peace Office, U.S. Agency for International Development, based on FY78 (Oct. 1, 1977–Sept. 30, 1978).

effect on food needs in a region, and that food aid should be continued until such time as food supplies are restored and the markets are fully back in operation.

The mechanisms which exist for supplying emergency food aid following disasters have been set up to meet short-term humanitarian objectives, based upon certain basic assumptions. The first and foremost of these assumptions is that the disaster victim has lost his supply of food in the disaster. The second is that normal distribution systems are totally disrupted and will be unable to function. The third assumption is that, due to the disaster, the victims will not have the capital necessary to buy food, even if it were available.

Due to the nature of most emergency and post-disaster programs, few sophisticated evaluations of the impact of food supplied after a disaster have been conducted, and the above assumptions have gone virtually unchallenged. Only in the last several years has there been a growing concern on the part of administrators that the overall impact of post-disaster food imports may have far greater negative than positive effects. From this growing concern, six major questions have arisen:

Is food aid necessary?

What is the social and economic impact of large-scale food programs on a country's development?

Is the food provided appropriate?

If the food is necessary, how will it be provided?
Does the provision of food aid after a disaster
speed or delay recovery?
Whose needs does a food program meet?

DISASTERS AND FOOD NEEDS:
THE ISSUES

In order to understand some of the factors at play,
it is necessary to examine several different types of
disasters. The four disasters that cause the most
concern are earthquakes, large-scale floods (especially those caused by cyclonic storms), prolonged
civil disturbances, and droughts.

Case I: Earthquakes

Earthquakes are particularly violent disasters
and can affect extremely large regions. In
Guatemala in 1976, over one-third of the country's population lived in structures which were
damaged or destroyed by the earthquake.
Thousands of people were killed, and transportation and communications were disrupted throughout the entire country. On the surface, such a
disaster would seem to meet the criteria for massive importation of food; and indeed, a number of
agencies immediately began planning food programs.†

However, a closer examination is warranted.
First, most of the damage incurred in an earthquake is related to structures—houses, commercial buildings, bridges, etc., may be destroyed, but
rarely are food supplies affected. In the case of
Guatemala, most of the food was still in the fields,
as yet unharvested; thus food was still available.
What was needed was a place to store the food, and
the rapid restoration of the market network to
ensure that food supplies could be distributed. The
harvesting and marketing of the food is the primary economic endeavor of the majority of the people living in the affected area. Even after the disaster, efforts to harvest, transport and market food
took precedence over everything except immediate medical needs. In every location, functioning
markets were in operation long before massive
amounts of food could have been distributed by
outside donor agencies. Nonetheless, several
agencies continued their plans to import food,

some on the assumption that it was needed, and
others in an effort to improve the nutrition levels
of the people throughout the disaster-affected region.

Two things should be mentioned here. First, the
large-scale importation that was planned was
viewed with alarm by the small farmers and the
government.‡ They reasoned that large amounts
of food would substantially lower the price the
small farmer would receive for the food he had
produced. This concern was so great that several of
the relief agencies, after failing to persuade the
others to stop their food programs, attempted to
stabilize prices by constructing large silos and buying food at the pre-disaster price. Second, those
agencies that wanted to improve the nutritional
level, using the disaster as a vehicle for initiating
change, were working against tremendous odds.
Experience during the past few years has shown
that the primary concern of the disaster victim is to
return to normal as quickly as possible, and that
change instituted during a disaster rarely takes
hold.§

Case II: Civil War

Food importers argue that such a conflict, especially if it is long-term, disrupts transportation and
local markets; if the fighting is widespread, it may
also disrupt farming. This rationale was used by
several agencies for importing massive amounts of
food following the civil war in Lebanon in 1976–
77. In the case of Lebanon, they also argued that it
is a food-importing nation even during the best of
times; therefore, massive emergency supplies
would be necessary in the post-conflict period.

However, the Lebanese situation differed from
what was immediately evident. First, even during
the high points of the fighting, scarcity of food had
never been a problem. Each faction in the civil war
had to depend upon the loyalty of non-combatants
within their area of operation and, thus, elaborate
and rather sophisticated schemes were developed
to ensure that food supplies flowed even through
the worst of the fighting. Marketing and transpor-

---

† Among the U.S. agencies providing food aid were: CARE,
Catholic Relief Services, Church World Service, The Salvation
Army and Direct Relief Foundation.

‡ "The Appropriateness of PL480 Food Donations After the
1976 Earthquake and in Non-Disaster Times," edited inter-
view with Francisco Batzibal Pablo and Benito Sicajan Sipac,
Robert Gersony and Tony Jackson, Chimaltenango,
Guatemala, October 1977.
§ "Disaster and Coping Mechanisms in Cakchiquel
Guatemala: The Cultural Context," Dr. Margaret Kieffer,
INTERTECT, 1977.

tation of food from rural areas were indeed disrupted; but in most cases the farmers were able to cultivate and harvest basic foodstuffs and to store them safely until the transportation systems were restored. Immediate needs after the fighting ceased were met by this reserve of food which became available when the fighting stopped.

Nevertheless, major relief organizations immediately initiated large-scale importation of food for the war victims. The food was distributed through the network established by each of these organizations and not through normal markets.† Concern immediately arose on the part of the farmers about the impact of this food on prices.‡ They needed to market their own surplus in order to be able to recoup expenses lost during the periods of fighting. In order to stabilize prices and guarantee a fair price to the farmers, the government initiated a price support program. But what about the fact that Lebanon is normally a food-importing nation? While the country does import large amounts of food, it is connected to other countries in the Middle East by an intricate import/export network. Post-disaster food programs operated outside this network and, had sufficient quantities been imported in this manner, it would have had a decidedly negative impact on the recovery of this vital economic system. Had this been coupled with a widespread lethargic agricultural recovery, the net result could have produced disastrous consequences for years to come.§

Case III: Floods

Flood situations are often cited as a justification for post-disaster food programs; this type of disaster does destroy food supplies and creates an immediate need for food for the disaster victims. The primary question in this case is not whether the food is needed, but rather which sources should provide it and through which mechanisms should it be distributed.

The cyclone and tidal wave which struck Andhra Pradesh, India, in November 1977 provides an excellent recent example. The tidal wave and high winds accompanying the cyclone generated floods which destroyed between 70 percent and 90 percent of food supplies in the area where the cyclone came ashore. The tidal wave itself struck an area approximately 30 km. long and 15 km. wide. Flooding in the remainder of the cyclone-affected region did extensive damage in an area of approximately 500,000 acres (1171 square miles)—a very substantial area, especially when examined on-site.‖ To put the damage in perspective, however, the total area affected by the tidal wave represents less than two percent of the total irrigated area within the two districts where it struck. Within the entire state of Andhra Pradesh, the area affected by both wind damage and the tidal wave makes up less than ten percent of the total area under cultivation. While there was an immediate and pressing need for emergency food supplies in the cyclone-affected region, the surrounding area was largely unaffected.

There was a good crop in 1976 and again in 1977, and surplusses were available. India has a food bank for regional supplies, and the foodstuffs in it were relatively unaffected by the storm. The questions which faced program administrators were: Where should the food be obtained? How could equal distribution be assured? Should food be imported from outside the country, should it be purchased in surrounding markets, or should it be transferred from the food bank? Or should local markets in the affected areas be stimulated with cash so that normal market activities could take care of the food deficiency? Those agencies that considered importing food implied that such programs would be able to deliver food faster and more efficiently than would in-country purchase of food from existing stocks or stimulation of local markets. (In this case, massive importation would not have been more rapid. The roads were quickly restored; few vehicles were destroyed by the cyclone; and food began arriving from surrounding areas at a very rapid rate.)

The dearth of available capital for food purchases encouraged several agencies to consider food-for-work programs, while others argued that this in itself was another incentive for importing food. Again, the question of what effect food-for-work or outright gifts of food would have on the local food producers and markets was hotly debated.

---

† Information taken from reports of CRS, World Food Program and UNICEF to the Committee of Voluntary Agencies in Lebanon, December 1976.

‡ From a disaster assessment report to Save the Children Federation by Charles MacCormack, SCF Program Director, December 1976.

§ The fact that more food aid was not provided is a tribute to the coordination efforts of the American Council of Voluntary Agencies for Foreign Service, Inc., in New York.

‖ Taken from data provided in U.S.A.I.D. Sitrep No. 5, December 1977; from local reports; and from on-site inspection.

Several agencies decided that food distribution programs of any type would be a disincentive and offered instead labor-intensive projects which generated much-needed capital in the area. Their reasoning was that money injected into the area would have a far greater (and decidedly more positive) impact on recovery than would simple food distribution programs.

Case IV: Droughts

Finally, there is the special case of drought and massive crop failures. In these cases, are there adequate supplies and marketing mechanisms necessary to meet demands? The long drought in Sahelian Africa saw millions of tons of food imported over a seven-year period to supply the victims. There is no doubt that thousands of lives were saved due to this effort. But again, haunting questions remain. Did the imported food have a negative impact on the marketing of food that was available and that was produced in the region? Did the means by which the program was conducted and the way the food was distributed prove to be a disincentive to marginal farmers, adding those people to the ranks of refugees? Was the imported food similar to that to which the refugees were accustomed? Could food have been purchased in neighboring countries that were not affected by the drought?

There is no doubt that, from the relief agencies' point of view, it was simply easier to purchase food supplies in the exporting countries and ship it in.† The question remains: does a decision based on ease of administration serve the needs of the victim or the donor?

These questions and many others relating to the Sahel will take years to answer. But with the growing sophistication about how food is produced, and the necessity for working through local systems rather than outside of them, the resulting perspective is likely to be a condemnation of the wholesale importation of food.

GENERAL LESSONS

From past experience, then, what are the major lessons relating to the provision of food following

† For more complete information see: *International Disaster Response: The Sahelian Experience*, Barbara J. Brown, Janet C. Tuthill, and E. Thomas Rowe, University of Denver, June 1976.

disasters? For example, what is the effect of a disaster on food needs, and when is the provision of food really necessary?

In order to further understand these issues, it is necessary to divide disasters into two categories: cataclysmic disasters, and long-term continuing disasters. In the cataclysmic disaster, there is usually one large-scale event which occurs, doing most of the damage and destruction. Following this single event, there may be a tremendous amount of suffering and chaos, but generally things begin to get better as time passes. In a continuing disaster, the situation remains constant or may even deteriorate as time passes. Cataclysmic disasters include earthquakes, volcanic eruptions, cyclonic storms and floods. Continuing disasters include prolonged civil strife, crop failures and droughts.

The damaged area in a cataclysmic disaster is usually relatively small, while the area affected in a continuing disaster can be extremely large. In terms of food and food distribution, cataclysmic disasters are normally more disruptive and destructive. For example, they may disrupt the transport of goods and the marketing system. They can disrupt or damage irrigation systems. To a limited extent, they do destroy food supplies, but the amount of destruction depends on the season, the location of the disaster, and the total area affected. On the other hand, continuing disasters not only disrupt transportation and distribution networks, but can often bring them to a long halt and ultimately destroy the system itself. (An excellent example is the effect of the drought on the traditional barter/exchange system of the Taureg nomads in Niger. Due to the extended drought, many Tauregs were forced to become sedentary and to enter the money economy.)

When, then, is food necessary? Food must be provided whenever victims are denied long-term access to normal markets, or when the local market system is not capable of meeting the demand for food. In the vast majority of cases, these conditions exist only in the continuing disaster.

The next question for an administrator is: What is the best form of food assistance? There are no simple answers to this, and the easy access of many private voluntary agencies to PL480 and World Food Program stocks has obscured the realization that simple food distribution programs may not be the best answer and that other options exist. In most disasters, agencies find themselves responding to a problem by addressing the products of that problem rather than its causes. Most agencies are so blinded by the short-term immediate needs that they fail to examine closely the impact of the programs they develop to alleviate short-term needs, and they fail to examine the long-term impact of the program on the affected society.

If the food programs developed after disasters have had such a negative impact on the societies they were intended to help, why are they continued? First of all, the sophistication required in assessing the impact of these programs has only recently been developed. In the past, the cause-and-effect relationships at play (and especially the long-term impact of these programs on a society, both socially and economically), have not been well understood, nor have they been closely examined. Interest in this field has only recently become more widespread and as yet, few of the agencies involved in food distribution programs have acquired the capabilities to conduct such assessments.

Secondly, agencies are often caught in the "speed" syndrome. A disaster creates tremendous pressures within an organization to respond quickly, to make its choices about program options rapidly, and generally to get things moving as quickly as possible. Pressures are exerted by the disaster victims themselves, the local government, the press and, most importantly from the agencies' point of view, by the agencies' donors. Agencies fear that, if they do not take immediate action, both the opportunity and the funds will not be available at a later date. In this rush to action, needs assessment and sophisticated analysis of existing supplies, marketing systems, etc., go by the wayside.†

Public pressure exerted on an agency to import food after a disaster is based on a misunderstanding of both actual needs and of the problems involved in this type of program. The general public labors under a very unsophisticated set of assumptions about developing countries, and surplusses from the industrialized countries are often seen as a simple expedient for solving Third World problems. All the major relief and development organizations must be called to task for their failure to communicate the realities to their donors and to the public at large.

† There is much talk about improving the disaster assessment capabilities of relief agencies. While this is certainly worthwhile, a better approach would be to improve their understanding of an area long before a disaster strikes. In short, if an agency has not been involved in an area before a disaster occurs, it should not attempt to intervene in the post-disaster period.

There is a final factor which serves to perpetuate food aid programs, and it is this factor which has drawn most of the recent criticism. The food aid system has built-in incentives that reward massive distribution of surplus food. In the U.S. PL480 program, for instance, an agency that distributes PL480 food receives not only the food for distribution but also money for support of the staff involved in the distribution and a grant proportional to the tonnage delivered to defray overhead expenses. For some non-profit organizations, this arrangement can be a godsend; and a number of agencies receive a substantial portion of their operating funds for simply administering the various PL480 programs. There is nothing, of course, which would prevent an agency from purchasing post-disaster food supplies locally or from the surrounding area. But when presented with a choice of expending funds to do so with no cash return, or utilizing PL480 foodstuffs and receiving, in effect, a bonus for doing so, it can be seen that the PL480 program is a disincentive to agencies which would otherwise use their resources to stimulate recovery of local food distribution systems.

FUTURE DIRECTIONS

What then is the future of food aid programs following disasters? Most assuredly, criticism will continue to mount not only concerning the way food programs are administered, but also concerning the impact they have on the societies they are intended to help. The essential question will be raised time and again: Whose needs does the program meet—those of the disaster victims, the donor agencies, or the food producers of the industrialized nations?

Many disaster experts predict a trend away from the provision of post-disaster food assistance, toward the provision of capital-intensive projects after a disaster that will help re-start the normal food distribution processes. Other disaster specialists are calling for increased awareness of the opportunities available in adequate pre-disaster planning/mitigation measures to prevent large-scale food shortages following a disaster. For example, they point out that those areas that are subject to drought and/or crop failures are, even in the best of times, marginal areas; these areas can be identified long before a disaster strikes and agencies can work to improve the agriculture in these regions so that the effects of a disaster can be reduced, if not eliminated.

There are no simple answers to the issues raised in the provision of food aid. But it is vital that these issues be confronted and examined. Our understanding of both disasters and the impact of disaster assistance programs must continue to increase if meaningful changes are to be made in the international relief system.

ON STRATEGIES AND PROGRAMS FOR COPING WITH LARGE SCALE FOOD SHORTAGES

THOMAS J. MANETSCH

Systems Science Program, Michigan State University, East Lansing, Michigan 48824

A basic premise of the paper is that for various reasons many people in developing countries will experience food shortages in the years ahead. A main thrust of this paper is in considering strategies for managing available food resources from domestic and foreign sources during a period of scarcity in a particular population group, region or country. Historical experience, deductive argument and simulation studies are used to seek policy guidelines that can lead to reductions in mortality and morbidity resulting from food shortages. It is concluded that in a number of cases a "fair share" distribution policy can significantly reduce mortality and morbidity. The paper concludes with discussions of programs for implementing a fair share policy and the role that computer simulation models can play in the development of policies and programs for coping with food shortages.

KEY WORDS: Food shortage; food policy; famine management; computer simulation.

INTRODUCTION

It is practically a foregone conclusion that in spite of man's best efforts there will be severe food shortages in various places in the years ahead. Such shortages can arise directly by significant reductions in aggregate food supply due to, for example, adverse weather or less directly from non-uniform food distribution caused by a number of often interrelated factors such as structural unemployment, skewed distribution of land and other resources, moderate disruptions in food supply, rising relative food prices, and hoarding and speculation. Clearly no one chooses to cope with food shortages whatever the cause, we seek to avoid them by various means. However, since food shortage is a fact of life in our generation, we must continue to give serious attention to rational management of food resources when shortages do occur.

A main thrust of this paper is in considering strategies for managing available food resources (from domestic and foreign sources) during a period of scarcity in a particular population group, region or country. We will seek some general policy guidelines that can lead to reduction in mortality and morbidity. Our conclusions will be based upon historical experience, deductive argument and, to some extent, results obtained from computer simulation studies. The paper concludes with a brief discussion of programs and organizations which can contribute to implementation of effective famine relief strategies.

TWO ALTERNATIVE STRATEGIES

It is helpful to begin by considering two hypothetical food management strategies of interest which lie at opposite poles of a spectrum which includes an infinite set of intermediate alternatives. We will assume that people in a particular locale are subjected to a prolonged food shortage with a food supply fixed at some fraction of the total requirement per unit time. We will then ask ourselves what proportion of the population is likely to survive at various levels of food shortage. We will consider the following diametrically opposite strategies for allocating food to the distressed population:

a) "Enough or nothing"—if the food available is sufficient to feed x percent of the population at normal levels, x percent of the people will receive normal intake and 100 minus x percent will receive no food at all.

b) "Fair share"—food is distributed throughout the population according to need (individual differences in requirements, for instance due to size, work, age, sex, pregnancy, etc., accounted for). Then if the total food availability is x percent

95

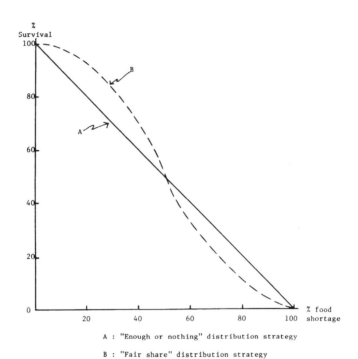

A : "Enough or nothing" distribution strategy

B : "Fair share" distribution strategy

FIGURE 1   Comparison of two strategies for food distribution and their effect on survival.

of normal, each person will receive x percent of his required intake.

These two strategies will result in significantly different patterns for survival rates in the population. These differences are compared in Figure 1. Under distribution strategy (a) we have a straight line relating the survival percentage in the population (not considering natural deaths) to the percent food shortage. Clearly the survival percentage in this case is equal to the percent the available food is of the normal food supply (100 minus percent food shortage). Since the remainder of the population receives no food at all over an extended period, none of them survive.

Under the fair share distribution strategy (b) the situation is somewhat more complex. Let us begin by asking a question. Suppose we have a given population and enough food to feed, say, 99 percent of the people at a normal rate on a continuing

basis. Is it possible to distribute the available food so that all, or nearly all, survive indefinitely? (Again we exclude natural deaths from consideration.) The answer is "yes." A population in any reasonable nutritional state can absorb significant food shortages without significant increases in mortality if food distribution is equitable. In this case, we can argue that a number of factors can intervene in enhancing survival. (For example: lowered nutritional *requirements* per capita, reduced food wastage and consumption of non-traditional foods.) At the other extreme, suppose that we have a 99 percent food shortage and that one percent of the food supply is available to feed the original population. What will be the survival rate if the available food is distributed equitably over the population? Clearly the survival rate will be zero or very nearly so.

The results of the discussion are summarized in

the backwards "s" shaped curve (B) in Figure 1. Precisely where this latter curve lies depends upon a number of factors (for example original nutritional status of the population, food in storage at the beginning of the shortage, the change in food requirements resulting from loss of body mass, the duration of the food shortage, etc.). The general shape of this curve, however, suggests that fair share, as an operating strategy, can result in higher survival rates in a number of cases. In fact, for food shortages up to some limiting percentage, there is probably no other strategy an agency, governmental or otherwise, responsible for food supply management could pursue that would result in higher survival rates. The recent experience in combating famine in Bihar, India (CIRTPR 1969; Gangrade and Dhadda, 1973; Singh, 1975) is an historical example of at least partial application of this approach. Through appropriate action a very serious food shortage was dealt with with very little loss of life. We explore the practical implementation of fair share as a guiding philosophy later in the paper. We will also briefly discuss the extremely important and complex issue of the ranges of food shortage over which fair share is a reasonable strategy to pursue.

SOME SIMULATION RESULTS

The above arguments are underscored by recent simulation studies. We will describe and compare results from two simulation models which differ significantly in scope and level of detail. It should go without saying that models can be misued and that they only offer partial guidance in arriving at policy prescriptions. (We'll have more to say later about an appropriate role for models in dealing with food shortages.) Earlier work (Manetsch, 1977) described a so-called survival model of a food deficit country that permits the model user to explore different government·and donor agency strategies for coping with food shortages.

It is not the purpose here to describe this model in detail. This has been done in the reference just cited. We will, however, present a general description that will help in understanding the simulation results to be discussed. This model disaggregates a famine-prone country according to population groups focussing particularly on the low income people most vulnerable in times of food shortage. The model includes food production, measured in cereal equivalent, as it occurs during two harvest periods. Food offered for the sale by farm families is determined as a price-dependent surplus after rural consumption and storage needs have been satisfied. Private food demand for each of the urban income classes is determined on the basis of nutritional requirements, food price and per-capita income by class. In a normal food situation the government intervenes in the food system through imports and food releases to the domestic market. Domestic food price is determined by the interaction of farm marketed surplus, government food releases and private food demand. In a normal food situation, government food releases keep the food price level down and even low income people are reasonably well fed. During a food shortage (caused, for example, by adverse weather or an inability to import sufficient food) food price soars and starvation can result in low income population groups. The model includes government programs to deal with food shortages including relief to vulnerable groups and widespread food rationing. The model also permits the user to explore the consequences of various foreign aid strategies for assisting the simulated country as it goes through a food crisis.

Figure 2 illustrates a series of simulation experiments conducted with this model in which a country of about 35 million people was subjected to food shortages of varying degrees. In all the experiments the country entered a calendar year with insufficient food to last until the upcoming (July) harvest. It was further assumed that imports and external aid were not available to make up the deficit and that the two annual harvests (July and October) were below normal. The initial nutritional status of the population was, more or less, typical of that found in the developing countries. Figure 2 displays the number of deaths that resulted in the population as determined by the severity of the crisis as measured by the private food stock at the onset of the crisis. With a stock level of about four million metric tons of grain, the food situation is normal. Therefore, in Figure 2 the severity of the food crisis increases as one moves leftward along the horizontal axis.

The two curves in the figure correspond to alternative government policies for dealing with the food shortage. In the top curve (Price Control Only) the government seeks to use its limited food stocks (on the order of 200,000 metric tons) to hold prices down. These efforts fail because of limited stocks, prices soar, the wealthy survive and many poor starve. While the intent may be other-

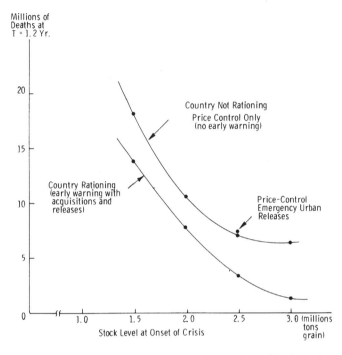

FIGURE 2   Numbers of deaths predicted for two types of intervention based on stock levels of grain at the time of onset of crisis in a typical developing country.

wise, this policy is very close to the enough or nothing strategy of Figure 1 in practice.

The bottom curve in Figure 2 represents a government attempt to implement a fair share strategy (B in Figure 1). Country wide rationing is invoked and government by various programs (food acquisition, relief programs and releases to the private market) seeks equitable distribution of available food. At all levels of crisis tested the latter policy resulted in fewer deaths related to the food shortage. Before leaving this discussion, however, it is important to point out that the rationing approach worked only when initiated early as a result of an appropriate early warning indicator based upon information such as nutritional status in various population groups, private and public food stocks, external food available from importation and aid, and time until the upcoming harvest. In fact, the survival model mentioned above pointed out a number of important areas wherein timing is

important to human survival in the event of food shortages. Timing of external food aid is another case in point.

A second set of simulation results came from a model designed to deal in more detail with human malnutrition and its impacts on energy requirements and mortality (Manetsch, 1979). Unlike the equivalent segment of the survival model above, the more detailed model considers the special nutritional requirements of young children and pregnant women and allows for supplemental feeding of young children. Also unlike the earlier model, this model permits consideration of changes in nutritional requirement due to infection and malabsorption (Bang, 1978; Rosenberg, Solomons and Levin, 1976) and varying physical work demands for energy. Both models allow for changes in basal metabolism as a function of nutritional debt. Nutritional debt in both models is computed over time as the net *accumulated* difference of food requirement minus consumption. It is measured in these models in terms of kilograms of grain equivalent. Morbidity and mortality, along with energy requirements, are influenced by nutritional debt in more or less detail in the two models.

Results from the second, more detailed, model are shown in Figures 3 and 4. In Figure 3 a number of simulation experiments were conducted with various percentages of food shortage. In each case, the shortage lasted for a period of one year whereupon the food supply returned to normal. Food was assumed in each case to be distributed among the population on a fair share basis (B of Figure 1). The curves indicate the percent survival for each level of shortage tested. This experiment was carried out for optimistic and pessimistic sets of

assumptions to be briefly described. In both cases the initial nutritional status in the population roughly approximated that typical of developing countries at the present time. The straight line on Figure 3 corresponds to the enough or nothing distribution of strategy of Figure 1 and related discussion.

The optimistic and pessimistic assumptions relate to how large mortality rates are for a given level of nutritional debt and how energy requirements per capita change as nutritional debt increases. These functional relationships will, of course, vary from population to population and must be carefully estimated on a case-by-case basis. The assumptions underlying the results in Figure 3 are very roughly optimistic and pessimistic for a developing country population. The

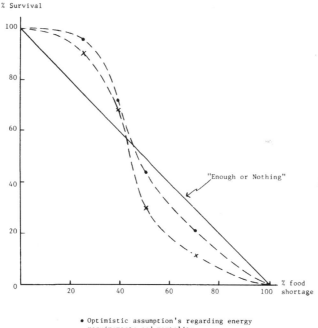

• Optimistic assumption's regarding energy
  requirements and mortality

✗ Pessimistic assumption's regarding energy
  requirements and mortality

FIGURE 3   Survival in relation to food shortage relieved by distribution of food on a fair share basis. Two curves are presented based on optimistic and pessimistic assumptions.

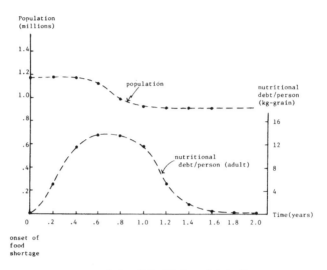

FIGURE 4   Time paths of total population size and nutritional debt for a one-year food shortage in a simulated Asian population.

specific functions included in the model were constructed from information from a variety of sources including Blix (1971), Chen (1975), Johnson (1975), Keys *et al.* (1950) and Masefield (1967). These functions require much more attention in any further modeling work of this kind.

The important point in Figure 3 is not survival rate prediction in particular cases but rather that, under a wide range of assumptions, survival rates under the fair share strategy are again substantially better than for the enough or nothing strategy for food shortages of substantial magnitudes.

Figure 4 presents an insight into the inner workings of the second model. In this simulation experiment a 39 percent food shortage of one year duration was programmed along with optimistic assumptions on death rates and energy requirements. Figure 4 displays the time paths of total population size and nutritonal debt (Kg-grain per adult) following the one year food shortage beginning at $t = 0$. In evaluating the results of Figure 3 it is helpful to know that the model assumes an Asian population with an average (over age and sex)

weight per person of about 100 lbs. (45 kg.). Figure 4 shows that the nutritional debt curve begins to level off well before the end of the food shortage (at t = one year). This, in the model, is due to somewhat reduced energy requirements as body wastage ensues and activity levels decline and to early deaths (of the more vulnerable in the population) which make more food available for survivors. Death losses prevail well beyond the peak in nutritional debt due to delayed mortality of many victims of disease, etc. This delay phenomenon (adjustable in the model) plays an important role in determining survival rates (along with mortality and energy functions) and merits further study.

MEANS OF IMPLEMENTING A FAIR SHARE STRATEGY

It is clear from the foregoing discussion that in many cases efforts to follow a fair share food distribution strategy can result in substantial reductions in human mortality and morbidity. In practical terms, this would include cases where famine strikes a limited segment of a population, for example, certain socioeconomic groups or inhabitants of a region of a country, and where an entire country experiences a food shortage of limited magnitude. In cases of restricted or small scale food shortages where relatively small quantities of food relief are involved there is an almost automatic disaster response. In other cases the decision of whether or not to adopt a fair share strategy at a governmental level will be an extremely complex one. At the outset it can be argued that there will be a political price for a government to pay where fair share means a significant reallocation of resources within the society. In addition to the humanitarian case we can argue that there is also a political price to pay for not pursuing this strategy! There are indeed complicated political issues here that will be unique to each situation. However, we will move on to other considerations that affect the decision to adopt or not adopt fair share. Clearly, human survival is only one of a number of criteria to be considered in this decision. Avoidance of possible permanent brain and nervous system impairment due to food deprivation in young children is certainly another. Other adverse consequences of morbidity due to undernutrition will have to be considered as well. We can only say at this point that the decision of whether to pursue fair share in a grey area situation can best be made with broadly based counsel (divine as well as human!) and information.

The appropriate information base here might include the nutritional status of the population (particularly that of vulnerable sub-groups), food availability in private and public storage, import and aid quantities expected, available logistic resources, food production forecasts and the likely duration of the crisis. Computer models along the lines of those mentioned above adapted to the specific situation might also provide useful information for this decision.

We continue discussion of the implementation of fair share and consider a number of programs various experiences have shown can be effective if properly implemented by government or private voluntary agency.

Food Acquisition Programs

Beyond the notion of reserve stocks at governmental levels, there are the obvious opportunities to acquire external food through normal imports, concessional loans or outright aid. Significant early warning of the impending food crisis is essential if these supplies originating in another country are to arrive in time to help those in distress. Governments can also initiate a domestic acquisition program based on purchases (perhaps enforced) from farmers, middle-men, or others in control of surplus stocks. The government of Ceylon's decisive actions in acquiring and distributing food during a World War II food emergency is a valuable precedent (Kelegema, 1957). Governments have also appealed for voluntary contributions to support food re-distribution efforts (Gangrade and Dhadda, 1973).

In the past, private voluntary agencies, both domestic and foreign, have marshalled significant food resources for meeting crisis situations; and the unfolding world situation is likely to call for a significant expansion of these efforts. For those of us in affluent countries, efficient voluntary organizations represent the most effective way of getting contributions to points of need. As with government these groups must be able to mobilize resources quickly. In some cases it is prudent to use contributed money to buy food on the domestic market of the affected country for re-distribution to those in need. The actual food distribution may take place in individual cases through government or voluntary channels. Coordination of government and voluntary efforts is clearly an extremely important matter (Gangrade and Dhadda, 1973).

Food Distribution Programs

A number of food distribution options are available and in each case there will be an appropriate blend of programs for meeting the specific and unique needs which exist. One of the more traditional distribution options in market countries is the release of government-held food into the private market. In a number of countries, governments use food acquisitions (imports and domestic purchases, etc.) and subsequent releases to the market to regulate domestic food prices. Under shortage conditions the same mechanism can provide a supply of food to those with adequate buying power. A multi-level price system involving identification cards for lower income people is sometimes used (for example, the fair price shops in India) to guarantee supplies to those with limited income. Related to this option is free distribution of a specified ration to classes of people without a means of support, for example, certain women with small children, the sick and the elderly.

At least one country, Sir Lanka (formerly Ceylon), has implemented a guaranteed food subsidy for the entire population (Edirisinghe and Poleman, 1976). Under this scheme, every person receives a free weekly rice ration at some level below minimum requirments. Such a program is not without its costs in terms of attaining more visible development goals, but lower class well-being has shown marked improvement in Sri Lanka as a result of the subsidy program. Furthermore, the people of Sri Lanka would be better prepared to face a significant food shortage than people more weakened from chronic food shortage. Clearly, design of a subsidy program such as this is a complex task, but the idea bears consideration in other situations.

The last food distribution program to be mentioned here is the so-called food for work program. This program originated, at least in modern times, in the nineteenth century as the British colonial government sought to cope with recurring famines in India (Arno, 1976). In all variations of the scheme, food is paid as a wage in return for work, usually on public work projects. The program, as then conceived, had four major impacts: the provision of emergency employment for those unemployed, distribution of needed food to those able to work and their families, the completion of worthwhile projects, and the reduction in migration and its attendant social disruption during famines. In a successful modern application of the food-for-work concept, India employed it as one means of combating the Bihar famine in 1967 (Gangrade and Dhadda, 1973). There is evidence that the program, in addition to improving food distribution, was helpful in famine mitigation and in the rural development of the country through the digging of wells, construction of roads and irrigation facilities etc.

Experience with the food-for-work concept has not been uniformly favorable, however. In certain countries, the program has been used in normal times as a means of reducing rural unemployment and poverty and improving nutritional status. A common criticism has been that it has depressed farm food prices and reduced farmer incentives to expand production. This was not necessarily the case under the original British colonial concept because the program was viewed as an "employer

of last resorts." That is, the wage in terms of food ration was set at a relatively low level. This low wage, in fact, provided an important test for the presence of a situation requiring public attention. Test programs were set up to determine whether the situation was serious enough to motivate substantial numbers to work for the low wage rate. The program was then expanded as the food situation worsened in a given area. Clearly, design of effective food-for-work programs requires careful attention to factors such as the wage rate, selection of projects that will make a positive contribution to famine mitigation and/or furthering development goals, location, number and size of projects and the magnitude of the workload imposed per day. With respect to the latter point, if a food crisis deepens the workload imposed per day should reduce accordingly in order to conserve energy/food. It is also worth noting that the famine relief project itself might well be manned with food constituting a significant part of wage payments.

Information and Organizational Considerations

Mayer (1975), Hay (1977) and others have called attention to the key role information plays in dealing with food shortages. Hay's concept of a food supply system provides a basis for defining the information set needed to monitor the food supply of a country or region. In a food crisis situation, the narrower case considered here, certain programs and variables assume central roles that dictate information priorities. Special work is needed to prescribe what this key information set is in a given crisis situation, how often the information must be acquired and how accurate it should be. Knapp's work (1979) is a useful step in this direction. He has added a more detailed information system to the original survival model (Manetsch, 1977) and studied the value of monitoring various sets of variables to effectiveness in managing food resources under the fair share strategy. For the situation studied, his work indicates that nutritional status of the various population groups, and food stock levels at key points (such as farm and government) are of key importance in effective food supply management during crisis. His work also provides a basis for the design of sample surveys to provide the required management information at appropriate times and with needed accuracy. Models that go beyond the original survival model in level of detail would be important in extensions of Knapp's approach. Of particular interest are some (now on the drawing board), that model the *distribution* of nutritional status within a population in jeopardy under various policy options.

Related to information systems for food crisis management is the need for early warning indicators that can provide substantial advanced warning of food crises with low probability of false alarms. Since there is considerable overlap with the information set required for food crisis management it's reasonable to think in terms of one information system able to address both needs. FAO and other groups provide food situation monitoring in vulnerable countries, however, there appears to be more that can be done in this area. Early warning indicators are best constructed on the basis of a number of key variables including (but not limited to) domestic food stock levels, nutritional status of vulnerable population groups, crop forecasts (perhaps utilizing remote sensing technology) and external food likely from imports and aid. Again, appropriate models appear to have a useful role to play—this time in the design of good early warning indicators.

With respect to organization for implementing programs such as described above, a couple of general considerations emerge. Firstly, an organization is required that can initiate and implement the right *mix* of food distribution programs and coordinate the many diverse resources normally available. In a bonifide crisis, military, police, volunteers, voluntary organizations, the private sector and numerous governmental organizations offer resources and organizational structure to be tapped and coordinated. In the second place, a hierarchical structure is needed that can assess overall needs and resources and allocate resources according to need. In a practical situation, these allocative decisions must be made at national, regional and local levels. The 1967 experience in India provides one important case study— Gangrade and Dhadda (1973), Singh (1975), Verghese (1967). Fortunately, there is an international cadre with experience in organizing and managing famine relief. This is exemplified in Aall and Helseng (1975) where the design and operation of a nutrition program to meet emergency food needs in the Sahel is discussed. Clearly, each famine-prone country should have well-developed contingency plans and organization for famine relief.

International Dimensions

We briefly mention the need for an international apparatus that can move quickly in allocating and transporting emergency supplies to countries in distress. At the present time, this structure, operating on both bilateral and multilateral bases, can move quickly in responding to relatively small scale food shortages. It is not at all clear that this would be the case for massive food shortages which are possible, if not likely, in the years ahead. What happens if two or more distressed countries should simultaneously clamor for limited food aid? What happens if the politics of food aid should ever become seriously intertwined with the politics of petroleum in one or more major donor nations? What happens if a faltering world shipping industry is suddenly asked to transport 10–20 million metric tons of grain on short notice? What are the implications of these issues for world level emergency stocks and their deployment around the world?

CONCLUSIONS

We have concluded that in many cases a fair share distribution strategy can substantially reduce human mortality and morbidity resulting from food shortages. In combating large scale food shortages effective domestic implementation of this strategy requires a careful blending of programs which may include food acquisition, food subsidies, releases to the private market according to various pricing options, food-for-work, and 100 percent food aid for certain selected population groups. Organization and implementation of such an effort is a challenging task. However, there are many important lessons to be learned from history. The international infrastructure for responding to large scale food shortages requires substantial further development. Further developments in simulation modeling applied to food shortage response can pay dividends, particularly in the design of early warning indicators, programs for implementing relief strategies and related information systems.

ACKNOWLEDGEMENTS

I would like to express apprecation to my colleagues L. Aronson and G. E. Rossmiller and to anonymous reviewers for their helpful suggestions.

REFERENCES

Aal, C. and E. Helseng (1975) *The Sahelian Drought II— Experiences from a Supporting Programme in Niger for Food Provision Nutrition Rehabilitation, Prevention of Malnutrition*. Report to the Norwegian Red Cross/ Norwegian Freedom from Hunger Campaign. Postbox 8139, Oslo Dep., Oslo 1, Norway.

Arno Press (1976) *Famine in India*. Reprint of report of the Indian Famine Commission (1901), first published in 1901 by Office of the Supt. of Govt. Printing, Calcutta.

Blix, G. ed. (1971). *Famine—A Symposium Dealing With Nutrition and Relief Operations in Times of Disaster*. Almquist and Wiksells, Uppsula.

Bang, F. B. (1978). Famine Symposium—The role of disease in the ecology of famine. *Ecology of Food and Nutrition* **7**, 1–15.

Central Institute of Research and Training in Public Relations (1969) *Famine Relief in Bihar: a Study*. New Delhi.

Chen, L. C. (1975). An analysis of per capita foodgrain availability consumption and requirements in Bangladesh: a systematic approach to food planning. *The Bangladesh Development Studies* **III**, 93–126.

Edirisinghe, N., and T. T. Poleman (1976). *Implications of Government Intervention in the Rice Economy of Sri Lanka*. Department of Agricultural Economics, Cornell University, Ithaca, New York.

Gangrade, K. D. and Siddharaj Dhadda (1973). *Challenge and Response—A Study of Famines in India*. Rachana Publications, Delhi.

Hay, R. W. (1977). Famine Symposium Report: The concept of food supply system with special reference to the management of famine. *Ecology of Food and Nutrition* **II**, 1–8.

Johnson, B. L. C. (1975). *Bangladesh*. Heinemann Educational Books, London.

Kelegama, J. B. (1957). Ceylon economy in the war and postwar years. *Ceylon Economist*.

Keys, A., J. Brozek, A. Henschel, O. Mickelsen and H. Taylor (1950). *The Biology of Human Starvation*. The University of Minnesota Press, Minneapolis. Vols. I and II.

Knapp, A. (1979). *An Approach to the Design of Information Systems for Famine Relief*. Unpublished Ph.D. Dissertation, Michigan State University, East Lansing.

Manetsch, T. J. (1977). On making effective use of available food resources during times of acute shortage. *Indian Journal of Agriculatural Economics* Vol. XXXII, No. 2, 12–23.

Manetsch, T. J. (1977). On the role of systems analysis in aiding countries facing acute food shortages. *IEEE Transactions on Systems, Man, and Cybernetics*. Vol. SMC-7, No. 4, 264–73.

Manetsch, T. J. (1979). *Modelling Human Under-Nutrition and Related Mortality—Model II, Working Paper*. System Science Program, Michigan State University, East Lansing.

Masefield, G. B. (1967). *Food and Nutrition Procedures in Times of Disaster*. FAO Nutritional Studies, Rome, No. 21.

Mayer, J. (1975). Management of famine relief. *Science*. Vol. 188.

Rosenberg, I. H., N. W. Solomons and D. M. Levin (1976). Interaction of infection and nutrition: some practical concerns. *Ecology of Food and Nutrition* **4**, 203–206.

Singh, K. S. (1975). *The Indian Famine 1967—A Study in Crisis and Change*. Peoples Publishing House, New Delhi.

Verghese, B. G. (1967). *Beyond the Famine*. Bihar Relief Committee, New Delhi.

SECTION IV

SELECTED CASE STUDIES
OF FAMINE

INTRODUCTION

John R.K. ROBSON

The Russian famines provide an insight into the interrelationships between political events, social and economic development and geography. Although there seemed to be little rational reason for the location and timing of the famines, it is clear that their emergence and creation were inadvertently perpetuated by man.

The studies of the famines of Bangladesh, on the other hand, reveal the vulnerability of the population. This vulnerability was due to a number of factors, many of which are difficult to control. For example, continual population growth aggravates the difficulties of the landless or those with inadequate land to support them. When crops fail, emigration from the area occurs, of necessity, the food behavior of the affected people has to change regardless of diet preferences and economic sacrifices have to be made.

Weight loss is inevitable as is protein calorie malnutrition. A relationship between malnutrition and infections has been clearly established. First, the natural body defenses such as the skin and mucous membranes are no longer able to resist invasions by microorganisms. Furthermore, the effect of protein depletion on the intestinal tract results in malabsorption. This may be aggravated by the presence of masses of parasites such as roundworms. Malabsorption, poor diet and protein deficiency lead to impaired immunity to infections which are inevitable. The tissue damage resulting, puts additional demands on the body for protein for repair and so the malnutrition is aggravated. It is not surprising, therefore, that morbidity and mortality increases.

In children, growth is stunted and may never be caught up if the food shortages are recurrent and chronic throughout the growing period. In these circumstances, whole populations may be undersized and physically incapable of producing enough to support the needs of the population. While the effects of the famine may be felt first in the rural areas, eventually the migration of the hungry begins to have its effects in the urban areas where even greater pressures are exerted on the limited food resources. It is at this time that jobs are lost and the effects are felt by everyone, regardless of whether they live in isolated farms, villages, towns, or cities.

Environment is one other important component of the famine syndrome. Bangladesh is subject to prodigious adverse environmental influences. It not only depends on a massive hydrological system, but it is subject to the vagaries of this system which are uncontrollable. For example, parts of Bangladesh are low lying and are vulnerable to flooding. The delta area is also susceptible to both riverine floods as well as the effects of oceanic monsoon storms. Bangladesh is also affected by an actively growing mountain chain formed on interlocking tectonic plates, which continually generate earthquakes. All of these influences affect the food supply to the country and add to the complexity of ensuring adequacy of food for the population.

In the following case studies, a detached scientific review, as well as personal experiences are presented. One of the more sobering aspects is the conclusion that famine control will depend on the input of knowledge from numerous disciplines and sciences. These include water resources, agronomics, transport logistics, rural demography, social anthropology, storage engineering, land use planning, international relations and public health.

Interdisciplinary co-operation even on a simple scale is always difficult to achieve and it follows that the more disciplines involved the more difficult will be the task of directing and coordinating efforts. While the task may be formidable, the first steps in achieving this objective have been achieved by the recognition of the complexity of the ecology of famine.

REFERENCES AND ADDITIONAL READINGS

Murdoch, W.W., Oaten, A. (1975) Population and Food: Metaphors and the Reality. *Bioscience,* 25, 561.

O'Keefe, P., Westgate, K., Wisner, B. (1976) Taking the naturalness out of natural disasters. *Nature,* 250, 556.

Rush, H., Marstrand, P., Gribbin, J., MacKerron, G. (1976) When enough is not enough. *Nature,* 261, 181.

Huffman, S.L., Chowdhury, A.K.M., Alauddin, Zenas M. *Lactation and fertility in Rural Bangladesh.* Paper presented at the Annual Meeting of the Population Association of America, Atlanta, Georgia, U.S.A., April, 1978. (Document 335 is available from Nutrition Planning, Ann Arbor, Michigan, U.S.A.)

Chowdhury, A.K.M. Alauddin, Huffman, S.L., Curlin, G.T. (1977) Malnutrition, Menarche and Marriage in Rural Bangladesh. *Social Biology,* 24, 316.

Gokulanathan, K.S., Verghese, K.P. (1970) Sociocultural malnutrition. *Clin. Pediat.* 9, 439.

Pimentel, D., Hura, L.E., Bellotti, A.C., Forster, M.J., Oka, I.H., Shotes, O.D., Whitman, R.J. (1973) Food production and the energy crisis. *Science,* 182, 443.

Odum, E.P. (1969) The strategy of ecosystem development. *Science,* 164, 262.

The World Food Outlook. (1974) *Ceres,* 38.

Seaman, J., Holt, J.F.J. (1975) The Ethiopian Famine of 1973-4 in Wollo Province. *Proc. Nutr. Soc.,* 34, 114A.

Holt, J.F.J., Seaman, J., Rivers, J.P.W. (1975) The Ethiopian Famine of 1973-74 in Harerge Province. *Proc. Nutr. Soc.,* 34, 115A.

Greene, M. (1974) Impact of the Sahelian Drought on Mauritania, West Africa. *Lancet,* 1, 1093.

Wisner, B. (1976) *The human ecology of drought in Eastern Kenya.* Ph.D. Thesis Clark University, Worcester, Mass.

ENVIRONMENT:
A CRITICAL ASPECT OF DEVELOPMENT
AND FOOD PRODUCTION IN BANGLADESH

LEONARD BERRY

Director, International Development, Clark University, Worcester, Massachusetts 01610, U.S.A.

Bangladesh, like Holland, is a country on a delta, though the great seasonal fluctuations in the Ganges and Brahmaputra create a season of water shortage as well as one of water plenty. Like Holland also, it has the disadvantage of not being able to control most parts of the hydrologic systems on which the country depends. The rich deltaic area, which has provided the setting for a steady growth in population and production over the past few decades, is a zone of interaction between four major earth systems and a rural population of over 50 million people. Earth Tectonic systems on a major scale, two of the world's greatest hydrologic systems, intense marine and atmospheric storms in one of the great storm hazard zones of the globe, all contribute to an intensely dynamic environment. Thus Bangladesh is close to the Himalayan mountain chain. This area is an actively growing mountain range, formed on the margins of interlocking tectonic plates. The zone south of the Himalayas, including much of Bangladesh is a zone of periodic earthquake activity. Parts of Bangladesh, especially the Sylhet basin, are depressed troughs, susceptible to deep flooding, several meters deep, each year. The Ganges and Brahmaputra, together have an average annual discharge of 707,000 cubic feet per second, only four rivers in the world have larger discharges, and peak flow in the Ganges-Brahmaptura matches all but the Amazon. The flood finds its way through a complex distributing channel system to the sea (Figure 1).

The deltaic area is just a meter or two above sea level and there has been a constant struggle to maintain such low lying land in cultivation. There is frequent river flooding but also quite common

intense storms, under certain conditions these can create storm surges flooding the low lying land with sea water.

The human interaction with these environmental systems provides the tragedy and the opportunity in Bangladesh. Careful adaptation of means of livelihood to environmental conditions has for many hundreds of years, resulted in a reasonable, if meager, living for many in the Bengal delta area. Several events contribute to changes in that pattern. First, for a variety of reasons, the number of people living in the area has increased almost exponentially; perhaps 25 million in 1850; about 30 million in 1900, 45 million in 1950, and 75 million today. Secondly, a similar rate of increase in the number of people living off the land in the Ganges and particularly in the Brahmaputra valley have resulted in changes in the upstream environment affecting Bangladesh. Third, it may be that the physical systems in the area have operated recently in ways which create greater problems for the people and the country. Fourth and not least, it may be that some of the development in the last few decades has had negative environmental effects. The effect of sea walls on the shrimp fisheries, the effect of sprays and fertilizers, meant to improve rice production, on the production of fish are two examples.

Complicated interactions are involved in all these systems at a variety of scales. This environment, at times so threatening, has stimulated agricultural settlement over a long period of time. The rivers which flood so disastrously also bring abundant nutrients to the soil. Local rice strains have become adapted to the flood situation and the low coasts, vulnerable to cyclone hazard, are ideal for a combination of rice farming and fish and shellfish culture. As in other parts of the globe, the effects of the more extreme natural events are, of course, related to the increasing density of popu-

Based on a paper presented at the American Association for the Advancement of Science Meeting held on February 20, 1976.

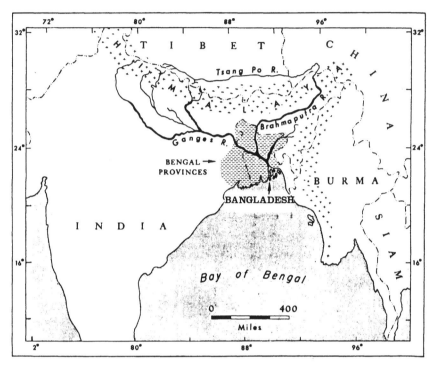

FIGURE 1   Location map of the Bengal basin.

lation in the hazard zone as well as to the intensity of flood or storm.

The pattern of settlement in the country is closely linked with the physical features of the land, every levee or other rise in the flood plain is the site of an elongated village crowding above the water line. At some times of the year, water more than land is the medium of communication. However, the seasonality of all things in the monsoonal subcontinent spreads even to the delta. In the dry season, the rivers are low and water becomes a problem for crops and for human consumption; pumping or storage are then the important needs.

THE EFFECTS OF INCREASING
POPULATION IN BANGLADESH

Population data in Bangladesh are not precise but it is nonetheless clear that rapid growth of population has taken place despite the huge toll of war and natural disasters in the past decade. Such increasing numbers have had several effects. In the year 1700 there were 1600 acres per 1000 people, a relatively high density of population for that time. People thrived mainly on rice and fish. By 1950, there were only 800 acres per 1000 people and at present there are about 400. But national statistics hide the specifics of changes in person/land relationships. First, many people have gone to live in the growing towns, especially Dacca, though they still need to be fed. For those living in the countryside, land has grown into a very scarce commodity; despite urban growth there are many more people than ever before. The increase in numbers means that some land is inevitably used for new dwellings, roads and industry. In those areas prone to flood, (nearly half the country), space for dwelling on those small parts of the land-scape above flood level is totally used. Old river levees raised further by years of house building and decay, provide precarious spots to locate villages whose inhabitants cultivate the seasonally flooded flat lands 1–3 meters below. Figure 2 shows

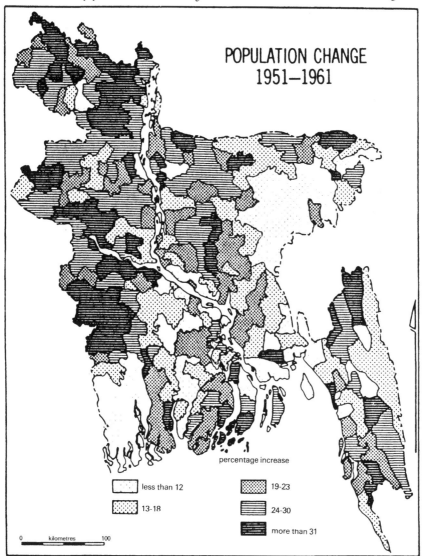

POPULATION CHANGE
1951–1961

percentage increase

less than 12   19-23

13-18   24-30

more than 31

0   kilometres   100

FIGURE 2   Percentage increase in the Bangladesh population 1951 to 1961 by thanas. Source: Johnson, B. L. C., 1975.

the change in population density over one ten year period 1951–1961. Comparing this with Figure 3, showing density of rural population per unit of cropped land, it is striking how rapid increases are most concentrated on areas with lower densities. The capacity to absorb increase in some rural areas appears to be small and the country is now in a stage of growing uniformity of rural population density. Figure 3 also reinforces our national level data on absolute density, large parts of the country have densities of over 1500 persons per square mile.

If Bangladesh is to feed itself at levels comparable to earlier eras, food production should rise four fold and must continue to rise steadily, because a population of 145 million is projected for the year 2000. This can only be achieved by moving to even more intensive patterns of production or alternatively by creating massive non-agricultural productivity to pay for imported food. The best efforts in the latter direction will still need major increases in national food production.

Up to the present, most attention has been paid to grain needs; to improving the production of rice. Increases in the quantity of production of this staple are a high priority and new hybrids and synthetics hold out some hope. But in many areas in Bangladesh, rice production has evolved in response to the peculiar environmental conditions. Because of the regular river flooding of the rice fields, but the unpredictable depth of flooding in any one year, floating rice is grown. This yields considerably lower than regular rooted varieties but is able to yield under a wide range of conditions. As it will be a very long time before close water control is achieved for some parts of Bangladesh, (at least in these flood prone areas), rice with a resilience to variable water depths will be needed. Ironically, better water control is available in the dry season where water often has to be pumped up out of the rivers. Under these high control situations, new varieties can be grown, though the social and economic problems related to the green revolution still occur.†

CHANGES IN THE GANGES — BRAHMAPUTRA CATCHMENT

The riverine systems which terminate in Bangladesh are subject to many influences. The pattern of the monsoonal rains, followed by a long dry sea-

† See for example The Green Revolution in India (Sen, 1974).

son, is reflected in the pattern of flood and low water in the rivers. Both rivers are also characterized by year to year fluctuations in flood and, to a lesser degree, low flow because of variations in the strength of the monsoon and the seasonal rainfall. These variations in flow are accompanied by fluctuations in the movement of sediment through the stream systems. Most sediment is moved in the flood period, some of that held in suspension is dropped on the flooded fields of Bangladesh, the rest is carried through to the Bay of Bengal.

The rivers may also be subject to periodic influences or trends. Much of the two basins is an area of tectonic activity, though the most intense earthquake activity has been in the Brahmaputra basin (Figure 4). Significant tectonic movement also occurs in the deltaic area particularly in north-west Bangladesh. Earthquakes in the basin trigger landslides and set up usually large flows of debris and sediment downstream. These exceptionally large sediment loads may influence changes in channel shape and position in downstream areas particularly on the delta. For example, it has been hypothesized that the Brahmaputra has been influenced since 1950 by the effects of the major earthquake of that year and that since then has been adapting its form and position to the post-earthquake conditions. This earthquake certainly caused much landsliding and many years are needed for this additional sediment to work its way through the system to the sea. There have been many changes in bed form and channel position in the last few years, but up to the present, it has, unfortunately, proved almost impossible to measure the detailed pattern of movement of bed load in a river so huge as the Brahmaputra.

Tectonic changes in the delta also may influence channel movements but the greatest overall effect has been to create the deeper inland basins and increase the flooding problems of some parts of the delta.

The other changes in the catchment are man-made. Rapid changes in land-use, particularly in the Brahmaputra basin, have created new water discharge conditions. In general, such changes result in higher flood discharges and lower dry season flows. In addition, soil erosion, from the hillslopes create new 'waves' of sediment to be gradually carried downstream. Although there is no doubt that this pattern of events is occuring, the magnitude and timing of the effects are as yet unknown.

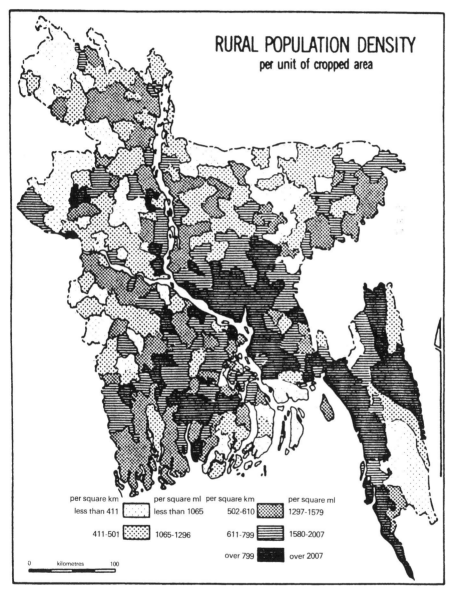

FIGURE 3 Rural population density Bangladesh per unit of cropped area, 1970 estimates. Source: Johnson, B. L. C., 1975.

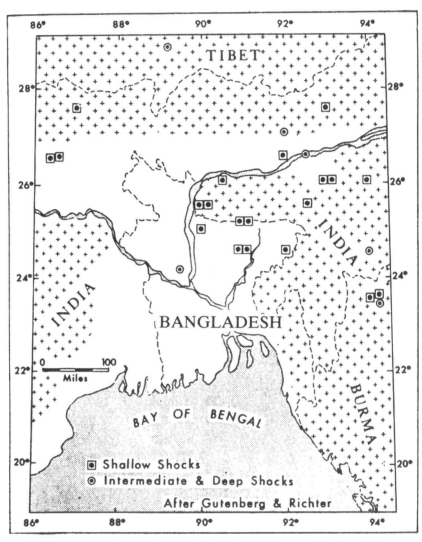

FIGURE 4 Map of Earthquake Epicenters in Bangladesh, Burma and Tibet since 1900.
Source: Morgan, J. P., and W. G. McIntire.

In the Ganges basin, other man-made changes relate to storage and removal of water in irrigation and other projects. Indian river management and future plans involve considerable diversion of water from the delta area, affecting dry season flows. The Farakka barrier currently diverts water from the Ganges, the government of Bangladesh has asserted to the United Nations that this has already had an effect on salinity penetration, reduced the fish catch and created problems for industry. In this case, it is important for Bangladesh to be able to assess not only the water supply repercussions of water control schemes on the Ganges, but also the sediment yield and nutrient flow effects.

In all of these ways, changes are occuring in the physical pattern of river flow. These changes may be critically important for Bangladesh. There is thus a need for the continuous assessment and monitoring of riverine characteristics as they influence the flow of water and sediment into the country.

PROBLEMS OF PHYSICAL SYSTEMS WITHIN BANGLADESH

In Bangladesh the physical systems of two great rivers, both influenced by intensive human activity, the effect of tectonic movements and the periodic impact of great storms combine to create a very hazardous environment (Islam, 1974).

Within Bangladesh river floods and erosion compete for attention in the newspapers (Figure 5). Except for the most severe floods the detailed pattern of the river channel changes may be the greater problem. The many distributary channels are constantly readjusting their bed, width and depth to accommodate changing amounts of water and sediment, they are also in many areas changing their location. Towns and villages situated on banksides are destroyed and the newly formed land on the other side of the channel hardly recompense for this loss because the new land is usually infertile and its use involves land ownership issues. Decisions on the location of many activities, for example, riverside docks and newly constructed road and rail bridges, as well as houses and towns, depend on good projections of future river behavior. The processes of river erosion and sedimentation in these particular situations need empirical and theoretical study. Investments on river control projects such as on embankments and water related communication projects run into many millions of dollars; research on the rivers is still comparatively slight, partly again, because of the difficulty of dealing with such large and complex systems. It may be that satellite imagery and other remote sensing devices may prove a vital tool

in acquiring and synthesizing the knowledge needed in Bangladesh.

Flooding of the rivers is often depicted as th major problem for Bangladesh, but discussions or the problem of flooding in Bangladesh is fraught with many difficulties for the uninitiated. There are obviously great problems with the unpredictability of water depths in the high water season, and there are sometimes disasters when a major flood occurs. Crops are destroyed and homes and facilities damaged. But the fact is that, quite regularly, a large part of the country is flooded by river water (Figure 6), the flood brings nutrients as well as problems, and the local rice strains are well adapted to coping with the situation. In the Northwest, where tectonic activity is actively, although slowly, creating a large trough, there are more serious regular and as yet unsolved problems. The dry season for its part also brings problems caused by pumping and water shortage, aggravated by water withdrawals upstream (Figure 7). The rivers of the Bengal basin present a major management problem at all seasons.

The flood problem is a serious one, but a combination of massive storm surges and high river floods usually creates the most critical situations. Coastal flooding results from the storm surge associated with the tropical cyclones as they regularly move up the Bay of Benegal. Such storms are more frequent here than in most other parts of the world, and they occur on average 60 times in a decade, but only exceptionally do they cause serious damage. The low lying deltaic islands of Southern Bangladesh are in places only a meter or so above sea level and sea walls and dykes have been built, to protect the land from usual storm surges. The comprehensive protective system was breached by the great 1970 storm (Figure 8) and over 300,000 people were killed. The map shows the vulnerability of these low lying but, densely peopled areas to further losses.

The greatest loss of life in Bangladesh has come through the disasters of the coastal storms, and the interaction between coastal and riverain systems needs special attention. Also the strategy for tackling the flood problem seems to need rethinking. Basic issues to be decided include: what level of flood is to be protected against; who and what is to be protected; and what costs are to be incurred for what benefits in flood protection. The emphasis should be on flood damage minimization with a variety of strategies explored for each region. Much more thought needs to be given to the costs

L. BERRY

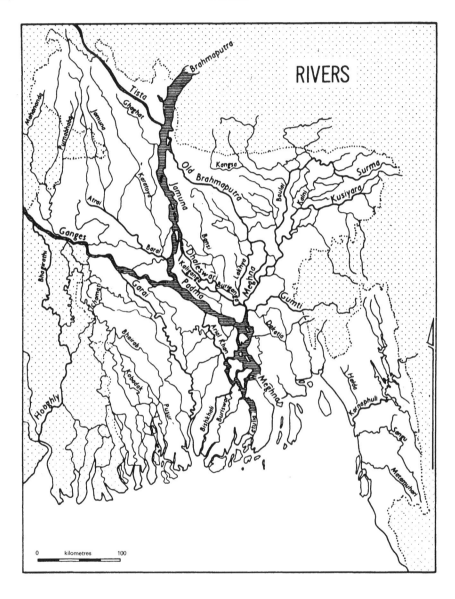

FIGURE 5 Rivers of Bangladesh.

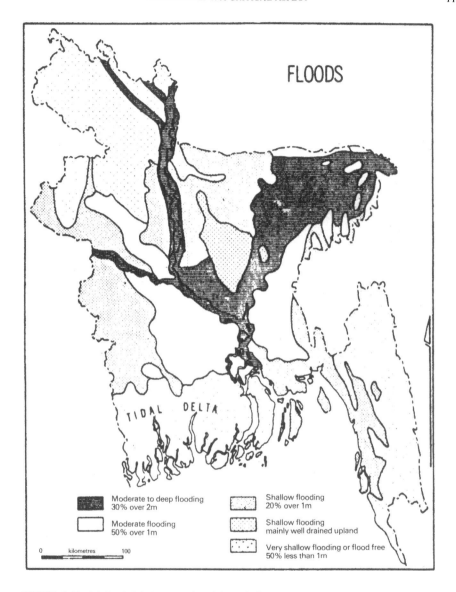

FIGURE 6   Foods in Bangladesh. An attempt is made here to indicate the relative severity of flooding by showing the proportion of the area regularly inundated to a given depth.
Courtesy of World Bank.

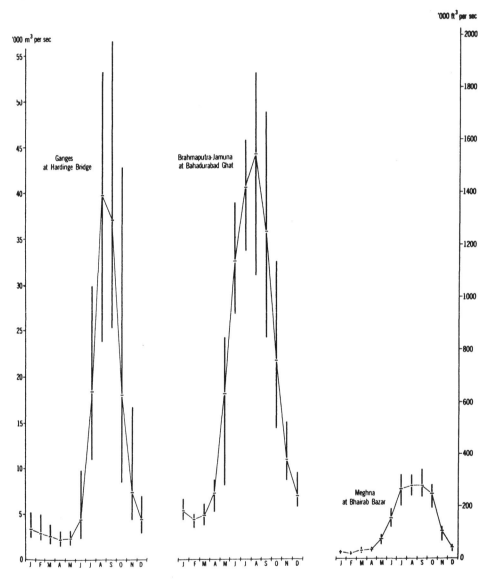

FIGURE 7   Rates of flow of three Bangladesh rivers. The vertical bars indicate the range of discharge for each month, the cross bar the mean rate. Note the very low rates of flow, particularly in the Ganges during the dry season. Source: Johnson, B. L. C., 1975.

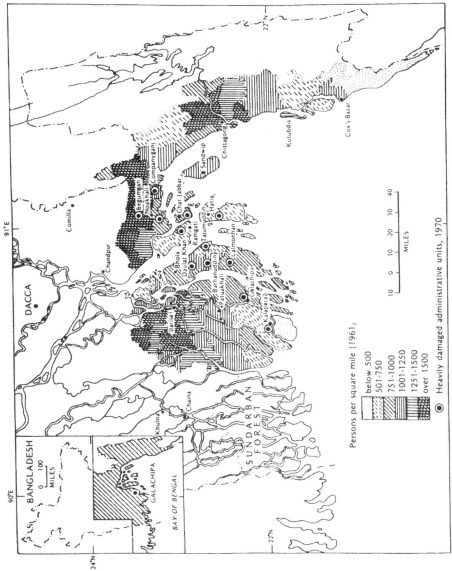

FIGURE 8 Coastal areas of Bangladesh. Population density and major cyclone-affected areas, November 1970. Source: Islam, 1974.

as well as the benefits of any particular program. The costs include not only the fiscal costs of construction, but also the losses the local agricultural system may suffer through flood protection measures; different strategies will be needed for the differing environments within the delta. A range of protective measures is possible, and since the great 1970 storm in coastal areas especially, embankments have been partly replaced and partly supplemented by raised havens within the hazard zone. It seems clear that warning systems, food stores and raised areas, together with programs for increased and continuing awareness of the hazard, are as important as embankments for this zone.

With regard to both types of flooding, there is an urgent need for continued and new study on the relations between the hydrological events and the human life systems in the area as a means of improving the effectiveness of development and protection programs.

The interaction between coastal and inland water bodies is involved also in the problem of salinity. As gradients are low, any slight change in the fresh water flow in rivers in the low flow season will allow a relatively large penetration of salt water. As water is diverted upstream, both in India and Bangladesh, this issue merits continuing attention. Salinity in water and soil is crucial to the productivity of the coastal zone and land and hydrologic slopes are so low that slight differences in level result in major differences in intrusion distances. The Harvard Study Group Salinity Model (Harvard University, unpublished data, 1972) apparently was applicable only to one rather atypical part of the coast and this problem needs new definition both in model and practical form. It is important for assessing the impact of upstream water projects on the coastal area as well as looking at the effect of water use within that area.

ENVIRONMENTAL PROBLEMS AND DEVELOPMENT CHANGE

The face of Bangladesh, in common with most of our planet, is no longer a natural environment. Man has altered the face of the earth in many ways. The cultivation pattern in the area has over the years created new ecological systems, but more recently, several types of development projects have impinged markedly on both the natural systems and the older cultivation systems, sometimes with unexpected results. No comprehensive study

has yet been made of the full measure of costs and benefits of these projects, but the side effects obviously need more detailed analysis if future projects are to avoid some of the pitfalls.

Flood protection projects in particular have brought benefit to some areas, but in these same areas have resulted in marked, partly unforeseen, changes in local life styles and production systems. Projects have often been focused too narrowly on the question of physical protection from floods and very little on broader issues of the relationship between flooding and prosperity: changes in the flooding pattern due to protection measures and what these mean for local life. For example, a number of separate trends are combining to create problems for the fish and shellfish industry. This industry is not only an important component in the family income in a number of areas, but is also vital nationally as fish is the main source of protein for the vast majority of the people in Bangladesh. The problem of flood protection which has been seen as one to be solved by engineering measures thus becomes linked with a much wider problem, that of the maintenance of the fish production levels, at the very least, while maintaining increases in rice production and protecting the population from the most harmful effects of flooding. This kind of a problem can only be tackled through a many-faceted approach to development, and probably involves national strategies. These need to be carefully worked out and combined with distinctive regional approaches tailored to the particular environment and production system of the area. The people are, of course, a vital element in both the environment and the production system.

As the efforts of the nation are mobilized to greater food (mainly rice) production, and as more sophisticated hybrid seeds are used, care is needed to ensure that the fertilizer and spraying programs do not impinge on the biological productivity of inland and coastal waters. There are signs that this may already be a problem. While attention is focussing here on the environment, the main concern is for the productivity of those ecosystems which support the people in Bangladesh. Although other factors, including the cleaning and maintenance of fish ponds, are important, the use of sprays and fertilizers appears to be greatly reducing fish production in inland waters also. The problem is one mentioned by a number of local observors, but not yet backed by sufficient detailed data. It does appear however that both local and regional attempts to improve productivity in one direction, (namely, rice production), are having adverse effects on production in fish. This need not be so and management issues are an important part of the problem, though another aspect relates to local and region organization of land use.

Even in crowded Bangladesh, there is room for a better allocation of land and water resources. The land and water resources of the nation are important assets, and while the environment imposes limitations, it seems that there are potential gains to be made through better organization and planned control of land use, including water use. Experimental approaches to developing new patterns of use of land and water might be attempted and an early start can be made by ensuring that lavish land alienation from agriculture is not made for non-essential purposes. For example, the reorganization of local land use so that fish ponds do not get polluted from fertilized rice fields is clearly possible in some areas. Considerable capacity appears to exist within the country for physical planning and if imaginative guidelines could be established, this talent might be used toward improvements in production through improvements in efficiency of land resource use. The sound basis of the study of the potential soils and land (Brammer, 1964), is an important asset to such a program.

Lastly, it appears that a regional development oriented approach may be useful even in a country such as Bangladesh which, although small, has significant differences in environment and potential for development. In each part of the country, sets of distinctive problems occur and also sets of distinctive opportunities exist. Development programs have to attempt the difficult task of solving the problems while making the most of the opportunities.

ENVIRONMENTAL DATA FOR DEVELOPMENT

One of the problems of Bangladesh is that many important aspects of environment are not yet fully understood or quantified. The dynamic aspects of the environment, the rivers and the atmosphere, for example, are the most difficult to measure. The rivers of Bangladesh present particular problems because of their great size and the fact that only a small part of the basin lies inside the country. Yet the flow and changes of course in the rivers are vital to the country. One problem needing re-examination is the question of what information about the dynamic environment is most urgently needed and how it can be obtained most effectively. There is already a good network for the collection of river flow and some sediment data. How can this be supplemented by remote sensing data? How can the network be used for other types of information, such as water quality monitoring?

More static aspects of the environment, such as the soils and land potential have already been given considerable attention, although water aspects, for example in small ponds, have been much less studied. In both cases, there is a need for the data to be examined in terms of its utility, both at the planning and the project level of development. How can it feed into the operation process?

Other kinds of information may be equally important. These include information on the effects of current development activities, the bottlenecks encountered, the side effects produced and the techniques used to deal with these problems. Such broad based monitoring needs a different approach to data gathering and may involve some selective sampling and study of particular projects or more ambitiously, the integration of this information gathering process into the project itself.

Data gathering is but the first stage in the process of learning about the problems involved. Questions arise as to techniques of storage, processing and analysis of data, but the important questions relate to how new information can be used in the development process. Encouragingly, steps are already being taken in Bangladesh to begin to build up such a network of information related to development activity.

Bangladesh is a country of many problems and a good proportion of these are not environmental. But it is in a better understanding of the relationships between productive and environmental systems that future prospects for economic and human growth reside. Although the area is densely populated and natural hazards will continue to threaten the best efforts of the people, there is still room for major increases in efficiency of use of the natural environment and consequence growth of productivity. Such growth is necessary for Bangladesh. It can only be achieved satisfactorily if development programs are set clearly in the context of the environmental systems involved.

REFERENCES

Brammer, H. (1964). An outline of the geology and geomorphology of East Pakistan in relation to soil development. *Pakistan J. Soil Science,* **1,** 1–22.

L. BERRY

Chen, L. C. (editor) (1973). *Disaster in Bangladesh*. Oxford University Press, Oxford.

Franda, M. F. (1976). *Bangladesh and India Politics Population and Resources in a Global Environment*. American University field staff problem. Hanover, New Hampshire.

International bank for reconstruction and development Asia projects DN. (1972). *Land and Water Resources Sector Study Bangladesh*. World bank documents, PS-13. (Not publically distributed).

International center for medical research, John Hopkins University. (1973). *Notes and Diagnosis on Bangladesh Famine Project. Mimeo. Johns Hopkins University, Baltimore, Maryland*.

Islam, M. A. (1974). Tropical cyclones Coastal Bangladesh in White, G. *Natural Hazards*. Oxford University Press. pp. 19–24.

Johnson, B. L. C. (1975). *Bangladesh*. Barnes and Noble, New York, p. 104.

Morgan, J. P. and W. G. McIntire. (1959). Quaternary geology of the Bengal, East Pakistan and India. *Bull. Geol. Soc. Amer.* **70**, 319–42.

Sen. Bandhudas. (1974). *The Green Revolution in India: A Perspective*. John Wiley and Sons, New York.

THE FAMINE SYNDROME: ITS DEFINITION FOR RELIEF AND REHABILITATION IN BANGLADESH

BRUCE CURREY

International Center for Medical Research and Training, Department of Pathobiology, School of Hygiene and Public Health, Johns Hopkins University, Baltimore. Maryland U.S.A. and Department of Geography, University of Hawaii, Honolulu, Hawaii, U.S.A.

The present definition of famine which emphasizes epidemic malnutrition and starvation deaths should expand to include the broader spectrum of earlier symptoms. An example from Dacca City confirms the presently accepted definition, but a second example from a famine affected area of rural Bangladesh illustrates the potential of monitoring earlier indicators. Concurrent with the change in emphasis in defining famine will come the move from belated doles of food relief towards prevention and rehabilitation through rural development.

"Famine is like insanity, hard to define, but glaring enough when recognized" (Taylor, unpublished manuscript). In Bangladesh, the culture defines three types of famine: scarcity is *akal* (when times are bad); famine is *durvickha* (when alms are scarce) and nationwide famine is *mananthor* (when the epoch changes). Different areas have different terms for scarcity and famine: on the *chars*, or newly emerged lands, of Faridpur district, the words are *ovab* and *kahath*, but within 100 yards, on the *adi*, or stable land, scarcity becomes *kahar* and famine becomes *akal*. These subtle terms contrast with the international definition accepted at the Swedish Famine symposium "Widespread food shortage leading to a significant rise in the regional death rates" (Blix, Hofvander and Vahlquist, 1971). This elegant definition lacks quantifiable thresholds for implementation and suggests that famine is only epidemic malnutrition. Famine might be more effectively defined as the community syndrome (Figure 1) which results when social, economic, and administrative structures are already under stress, and are further triggered by one, or several, discrete disruptions which accelerate the incidence of many symptoms, or crisis adjustments, of which one is epidemic malnutrition.

In Dacca City, the Swedish Symposium definition was seen to operate during the 1974–75 localized famine in Bangladesh. The widespread food shortage, although not seen in the national food grain availability figures (Figure 2), is evident

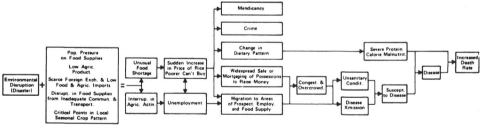

FIGURE 1   Components and Interactions of the Famine Syndrome in Bangladesh.

Based on a paper presented at the American Association for the Advancement of Science Meeting held on February 20, 1976.

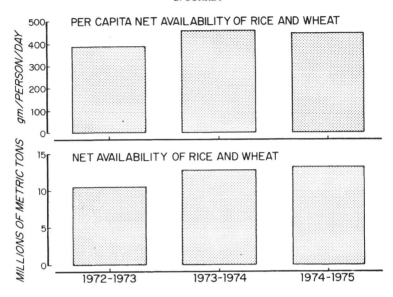

FIGURE 2   Availability of Rice and Wheat in Bangladesh, 1972–1975. (Chen and Chowdhury, 1975).

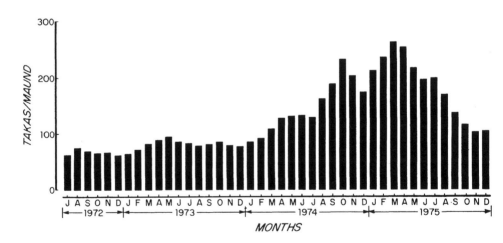

FIGURE 3   Changes in the average price of rice in Bangladesh, 1972–1975.

from the fourfold increase in the national average price of coarse-grained rice since mid-1972 (Figure 3), despite the dampening effects caused by averaging and aggregation. Simultaneously, Anjuman Mufidul Islam, the muslim burial society in Dacca, kept records of the number of unclaimed dead bodies of the poor found on the city streets. Their records show a 14-fold increase in the number of unclaimed street deaths in the last four months of 1974. Until September there were an average of only 50 street deaths recorded each month, but by December, three months later, the figure had risen to 700 per month (Figure 4). During the 15-month period between October 1974 and December 1975, 33 percent of the 6624 street deaths collected were from five urban foci: (Figure 5) near Azimpur graveyard, the railway station, at the port, the bus station, and near the burial society itself. As well as being predominantly transport points, the five foci and the areal concentration in the old city of Dacca are where the Bengali middle class disburse alms both to destitutes and to dead bodies awaiting burial. Thus at the principal focus, Azimpur Gate, people coming to visit the graveyard feel religiously obliged to give alms to the destitutes in the name of their own deceased relatives and friends.

Initially, then in Dacca City, the indigenous Bengali definition of famine as *Durvickha* (alms scarcity) appears paradoxical since alms are still being disbursed. In reality, however, the Bengali definition is intrinsically more meaningful, for it directs thoughts towards the rural context. There in the spawning grounds of famine alms-giving *is* scarce.

The rural crisis (such as that of Eastern Rangpur region of Bangladesh in late 1974) occurs when the alms giving or traditional community support through the extended family in each village is put under strain and finally breaks: relatives within the village are no longer willing to give shelter for more than one night to the destitute. The destitute must either die *in situ* or emigrate in search of food, clothes, shelter and work elsewhere. Of those community members who are vulnerable to famine, only a few leave the village; a few may go to a nearby village to other relatives, others may go to relatively prosperous areas at that time, such as Dinajpur district; and some may make a move to nearby subdivisional towns or district towns in the same division, in this case, Rajshahi division or North Bengal. Only a very few, either immediately or subsequently, cross the Jamuna river to reach Dacca, often as non-paying passengers on the roof

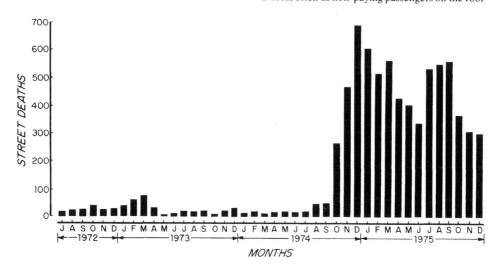

FIGURE 4   Numbers of unclaimed bodies found dead in the streets of Dacca, Bangladesh, 1972–1975.

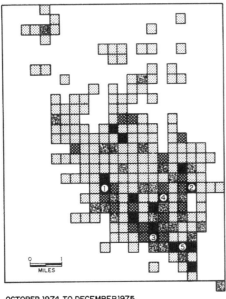

OCTOBER 1974 TO DECEMBER1975

1 667-AZIMPUR GATE   ■ 101-200
2 500-KAMLAPUR STATION   ▦ 51-100
3 486-SADAR GHAT TERMINAL   ▨ 26-50
4 316-GULISTAN BUS STATION   ░ 1-25
5 216-GANDARIA

FIGURE 5   Location and numbers of street deaths in Dacca, Bangladesh, October 1974 to December 1975.

of the train. Thus the recording of street deaths in Dacca city is only the tip of the iceberg of famine, in an area like Eastern Rangpur.

A survey of households in the ten *thanas*† (small counties) of the 1364 sq. mile riverine area of Eastern Rangpur (Currey and Malek, 1977) provides examples of the many famine syndrome

---

† A thana is the smallest administrative unit of the central government. It literally means a police station or the area that is supervised by a police station. The thana areas vary from 5 to 844 sq. miles and the thana populations vary from 10,000 to 1.3 million.

‡ The concept of "danger level" (bankful level, plus six inches) is ambiguous in Bangladesh where left and right banks vary greatly in elevation. At any recording station, however, the given danger level is taken to be relatively stable over time.

symptoms in one such root area of localized famine (Figure 6). This area was reported to be the worst affected famine area in Bangladesh in late 1974, (Ittefaq 1974). Akbar (unpublished manuscript) has already documented the slow nationwide stresses associated with the national breakdown of the political and socio-economic infrastructure after the Bangladesh War of Liberation in 1971. Single-cause catch phrases, however, like man-made famine fail to explain the acceleration mechanism by which the acute crisis occurs in particular areas at certain times.

The 1974 flooding of the Brahmaptra was more damaging than the famous flood of 1955. Although in 1974 the flood peak was 0.5 feet lower than in 1955, Figure 7 illustrates the greater destructive power of the flood in 1974 in the Eastern Rangpur area. It was above danger level‡ for 44 days compared with only 26 days in 1955: there

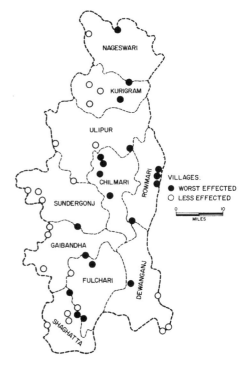

FIGURE 6   The area covered by the ten *thana* famine survey.

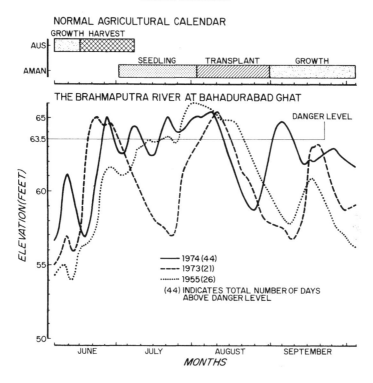

FIGURE 7   Flooding of the Brahmaputra River and its relation to the agricultural calendar in 1974.

were also six steeply rising flood peaks in 1974, not one slow rise as in 1955. Meshing the hydrographs with the local agricultural calendar above, it can be seen that the first peak in 1974 rose early and very rapidly in late June to interfere with the *aus* (summer rice) harvest and the last flood peak came as late as September when the *aman* (winter rice) is normally past both the seedling and transplant stage, and into the growth part of the cycle. Similarly the hydrograph from the Tista, the major tributary from the Himalayan foreland which joins the Brahmaputra in the area at Chilmari, indicates that the flood waters never crossed the danger level in 1955, but in 1974 they rose above the danger level for 29 days.

With these extensive high flood levels, bank line migration, averaging 1000 ft. westwards on the eroding right bank in one flood season, may be inferred from recent work on channel processes of the Brahmaputra, (Coleman, 1969). This has been substantiated by reports from local officials, and is presently being verified by satellite imagery. Such an abnormal erosion rate along the 60 miles of the Brahmaputra in the sample area alone, where riverine population densities reach 2000 per square mile, would have suddenly imposed over 24,000 people without homes or lands on the already run-down rural infrastructure between June and October 1974.

Concurrent with this extensive erosion of the right bank occurred the deposition of sterile sand on the left bank, abnormally high rainfall within the area (Figure 8), and ponding of the late flood water by water hyacinth (*Pontederia crassipes*).

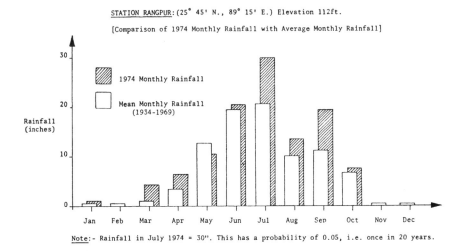

STATION RANGPUR: (25° 45' N., 89° 15' E.) Elevation 112ft.

[Comparison of 1974 Monthly Rainfall with Average Monthly Rainfall]

Note:- Rainfall in July 1974 = 30". This has a probability of 0.05, i.e. once in 20 years.

FIGURE 8   Unusually heavy rainfall at Rangpur Bangladesh 1974.

These interrupted agricultural activities and hence increased both underemployment and unemployment thus lowering the purchasing capacity of the landless labourers when the price of rice in the area was rising (Figure 9).

Households in the area were unable to afford even coarse grained rice. Between May and June, 1975, even after the acute famine crisis was over, more than 500 of the 790 households surveyed were eating less than one rice meal per day (Figure 10) which is in sharp contrast to the normal three rice meals per day in rural Bangladesh. By disregarding seasonal food fluctuations it was possible to isolate some of the alternative famine food-stuffs (Figure 11) which are not only non-seasonable, but also ubiquitous and unacceptable in normal times. In Rowmari, during the peak famine period from September 1974 to March 1975, out of 80 households interviewed, 48 were eating *kalar mocha* or plantain saplings (*Musa paradisica*) and 49 were eating *bonn kochu* or wild arum (*Araceae* spp.).

Anthropometric measurements in Rowmari in December 1974 showed that 36 percent of the children, aged between two and ten, were severely malnourished (less than 80 percent of the normal weight for height, Harvard standards). By June 1975, average nutritional status had improved either by migration and death or by harvests and feeding programmes. After the possible migration and mortality of the severely malnourished; after the harvesting of the *misti alu* or sweet potato (*Batatis edulis*) and *china kaon* or pearl millet (*Pennisetum glaucum*); and after the implementation of child feeding programmes by the Bangladesh Rural Advancement Committee, the percentage of children who were severely malnourished had fallen from 36 to 15.

In the attempt to raise money to buy food, the sale of household possessions rose abnormally high (Figure 12). During the year after the flood, the sale of household utensils *haripatil*, (cooking pots), *thala*, (brass plates), *chamuch* (brass cooking spoons), *kashar glass* (brass mugs), and *badna* (toilet jugs) was recorded by 36 percent and 37 percent respectively of the households in the thanas of Rowmari and Chilmari which were worst affected near the Tista-Brahmaputra confluence. This contrasts markedly with rates of 17 percent in the less affected northern thana of Nageswari. Land, the anchor of life in rural Bangladesh, shows a very similar areal pattern in terms of the proportion of land acreage lost per household in the nine months after the flood (Figure 13). The sen-

MARKET PRICE OF RICE BY MONTH

(AS REPORTED BY THE SUBDIVISIONAL MARKETING DEPARTMENT)

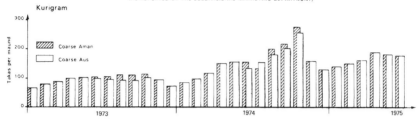

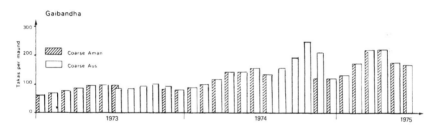

Note the absence of aman rice at the critical period in late 1974 in the price records of Gaibandha

FIGURE 9   Rice prices of summer and winter rice in the two subdivisional towns of Kurigram and Gaibandha, Bangladesh within the famine survey area.

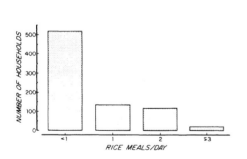

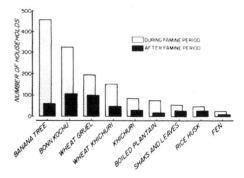

FIGURE 10   Number of households in the famine area with insufficient food for more than 1 rice meal a day.

FIGURE 11   Alternative foodstuffs during times of famine in North Bengal.

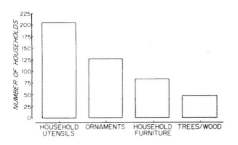

FIGURE 12   Sale of possessions during time of flood and famine in North Bengal.

sitivity of these indicators through time is illustrated in Figure 14 which contrasts the seasonal sales of land over two years in the least and worst affected thanas of Sunderganj and Rowmari. Rowmari (101 sq. miles), although smaller than Sunderganj (162 sq. miles), recorded land sales of

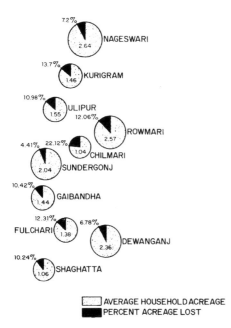

FIGURE 13   Land lost in 10 rural areas of Bangladesh during the famine.

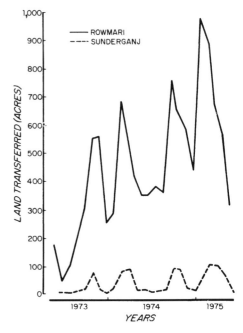

FIGURE 14   Seasonal sales of land over two years in the Bangladesh *thanas* of Sunderganj and Rowmari.

1000 acres in January 1975 while Sunderganj sales were only 100 acres. During the two-year period from May 1973 to May 1975, the revenue officer's records show the equivalent of 17 square miles of Rowmari's 101 square miles of land as having changed hands. This assumes that all sales were officially registered and does not include mortgaged land. Although in past famines, mortgaging has been less important than actual sales (Mukherji, 1944), nevertheless the real figures for land transference are probably higher.

Another symptom of famine in affected rural areas is out-migration (Figure 15). Although the total percentage of households relocating was greatest in Chilmari and Ulipur thanas a further breakdown of migration according to reason and destination may represent a more meaningful indicator of famine conditions. In some thanas, such as Shaghatta, where river erosion was reported to be as great as one mile during the 1974 monsoon, 90

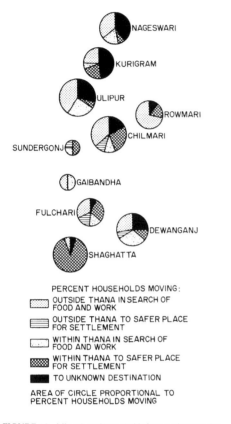

PERCENT HOUSEHOLDS MOVING:

☐ OUTSIDE THANA IN SEARCH OF FOOD AND WORK

☰ OUTSIDE THANA TO SAFER PLACE FOR SETTLEMENT

☐ WITHIN THANA IN SEARCH OF FOOD AND WORK

▨ WITHIN THANA TO SAFER PLACE FOR SETTLEMENT

■ TO UNKNOWN DESTINATION

AREA OF CIRCLE PROPORTIONAL TO PERCENT HOUSEHOLDS MOVING

FIGURE 15   Migration of households from settlements during floods in Bangladesh.

percent of the households moved within the thana to a safer place for settlement on unused flood embankments or relatives' land. In a thana like Rowmari, however, where the socio-economic structure was already overstrained before the flood, 70 percent of the households moved outside the thana in search of food and work.

Thus in a rural area it is possible to isolate and quantify several of the signs of the famine syndrome:

Dietary changes

Eating of alternative "famine foods"

Changes in nutritional status

Unusual sales of household possessions

Sudden increases in sales of land

Increased household migration in search of food and work outside the thana

These signs still need to be quantified over a period of time. Which changes significantly first, the change in foodstuffs or the drop in nutritional status? What is the lag time between an increase in the price of rice and a significant rise in the sale of household possessions? For any community is it possible, if norms are known, to forecast the ensuing levels of malnutrition and migration on the basis of trends in land sales?

Syndromes by definition not only have several signs, but also they usually have several as yet undetermined causes. As with many famines the specific causes of the 1974 famine in Eastern Rangpur are unlikely to be properly documented and weighted or even ranked in importance, but nevertheless, there are groups of associated background factors some of which seem likely to be bound up in the web of causation (Table I) and hence may suggest directions for prevention and preparedness measures. These factors operated at different scales: a few international, some national, and many at regional and village or even household scales. Some of the factors were inherent; a virtual birthright of the new nation of Bangladesh that emerged in December 1971. After the initial Joy Bangla or confidence after independence, various stress factors put increasing pressure on the administrative infrastructure. In 1974 the situation deteriorated rapidly beneath a critical threshold when the acceleration factors associated with the monsoon flooding precipitated the symptoms of famine.

As only one example of the complexity of decisions necessary for famine prevention stemming from the web of causation, land use planning may highlight some possibilities and problems:

In North America, the future policy towards the idle lands will affect the international grain market and in turn the availability of imports.

In the upper catchment area of the Brahmaputra, in Assam State, the implications of land use policy on deforestation and cover crops must be considered in relation to flood and silt levels downstream in Bangladesh.

In the country itself, national price policies could stabilise the rice-jute ratio removing many of the wild annual fluctuations in food acreages.

TABLE I

Background to the 1974–75 famine in Eastern Rangpur

	International	National	Regional	Household
Normal Conditions		High % of rural population landless High % below subsistence level Administrative unpreparedness Post-war dislocation of transport Shortage of food storage capacity Shortage of rolling stock Impared and insufficient river transport Unemployment and underemployment	Isolation and inaccessibility Vulnerable crop pattern Flooding River erosion Burial by sediment Inadequate drainage and irrigation Shortage of storage facilities	Shortage of storage facilities Position within bari kinship pattern Position in the village structure Indebtedness and lack of savings Excessive outlay on social activities High proportion of small holdings Long continued malnutrition
Strain or Normal Conditions	Depletion of foreign exchange reserves Rise in world oil prices Loss of credibility with aid givers Panic on international grain market Possible environmental changes in the Ganges-Brahmaputra basin Carryover effect of returning war refugees	Breakdown of traditional social structure Smuggling Hoarding Profiteering Irregularities in the rationing system Lack of confidence and speculation Misappropriation of aid Failure of procurement policy Terrorist activities Crop failures in 1972 and 1973 Complacency over 1973 bumber crops	Population pressure especially in vulnerable char areas through in migration Several years of recurrent flooding Increased smuggling in a border area Continued westward migration of the Brahmaputra	Underemployment and unemployment Labour exploitation: energy loss without increased purchasing power Functional weakening of joint family as an economic unit Inability to buy amidst rising prices
Disruption			1974 flooding: rapidly rising, with early multiple and late peaks 1974 accelerated bank erosion 1974 sediment dumping Outbreaks of diarrhoea and dysentery Lack of labour demand due to crop, seed, cattle and fertilizer losses	Irrational crisis desire for rice Migration in search of food Eating of abnormal foodstuffs Linkages in nuclear family change to linear linkages – e.g. weaking child – grandmother,

In each vulnerable region alternative crops whose growing seasons harmonise with the hazards or else seed banks for recovery crops after the flood must be encouraged especially if they provide employment and hence purchasing power at the vital seasons. (After Brammer, 1975).

Just as prevention must not confine itself to any single variable, like the example of land use so the quest for famine warning systems must not confine itself to any single indicator such as food price but rather investigate a wider gamut of possible predictive variables. These will fall into four broad groups:

The food producing capacity of any particular area:

– state of crop acreage
– estimated yields
– state of irrigation and drainage systems
– fertilizer stores
– labour availability

The effects of imminent or present natural and man made disasters on the area and supply lines to the area:

– rainfall
– erosion rates
– extent of sterile sand dumping
– cyclone damage

The ability of the community to utilize either local or imported food supplies:

– economic levels—savings and stocks
– employment and underemployment levels
– disease levels

Food storage levels:

– in the government godowns (warehouses)
– in private traders' stocks
– in household and village stores
– of already designated aid

In conclusion, this paper has stressed the possibilities of a more eclectic approach to the understanding and hence prevention of famine. Before the much needed research on various aspects of this syndrome is begun, it is necessary to select the types of expertise needed. Initially, I would suggest they be drawn from water resources, agricultural economics, transport logistics, rural demography, social anthropology, storage engineering, land use planning, international relations, and public health. These fields may suggest the directions of research and the type of information that can in practice be made available. Those making the decisions from the available data which will ameliorate the effects of famine must similarly not stem from one ministry alone. Famine prevention must not fall under the lone jurisdiction of a health, agriculture or food ministry. An eclectic group of policy makers need, and must not exclude, a dynamic leader. Famine and its prevention require a strong moderator when so many sectors are involved in the crisis syndrome.

ACKNOWLEDGMENT

The author gratefully acknowledges the support of the Johns Hopkins University, I.C.M.R., Dacca and UNICEF, Bangladesh whose financial support made this paper possible. In particular Md. Abdul Malek co-supervised the field survey and Kamrul Islam and M. Shahidullah co-researched the urban street death data courtesy of Dr. Abdul Wahed and the Anjuman Mufidul Islam, Dacca.

REFERENCES

Blix, G., Y. Hofvander and M. D. Vahlquist, M.D., Eds, (1971). *Famine: A Symposium Dealing with Nutrition and Relief Operations in Times of Disaster.*, Almqvist and Wiksell, Stockholm.

Brammer, H. (1975). *Disaster Preparedness Planning: Precautionary and Rehabilitation Measures for Agriculture*, Department of Soil Survey, Dacca.

Chen, L. C., and R. H. Chowdhury, (1975). Demographic change and food production in Bangladesh (1960–1974): *Population and Development*, Vol. No. 2, pp. 201–228.

Coleman, J. M. (1969). The Brahmaputra River: channel processes and sedimentation, *Sedimentary Geology*, Vol. 3, pp. 129.

Currey, B., and A. Malek, (1977): *Ten Thana Famine Survey, 1975: The Development of a Famine Survey Model for Bangladesh*. UNICEF–Johns Hopkins University, Dacca.

Ittefaq (1974). Famine in Rangpur. *The Daily Ittefaq*. Thursday, Oct. 24, Page 1, Cols. 2,3,4.

Mukherji, R. K., (1944). The effect of the food crisis of 1943 on the rural population of Noakhali, Bengal. *Science and Culture*. Vol. X. Nos. 5 and 6, pp. 185–191 and pp. 231–238.

THE CAUSES AND EFFECTS OF FAMINE IN THE RURAL POPULATION: A REPORT FROM BANGLADESH

M. MUJIBUR RAHAMAN

Cholera Research Laboratory, Dacca, Bangladesh

INTRODUCTION

To many people, Bangladesh has become synonymous with disaster, poverty and misery. Natural calamities like the cyclone of November 1970 and the man-made crisis like the army operation and war of 1971 were the two most recent examples. Basic ecological factors such as a booming population growth at three percent per annum, a stagnant economy, primitive agricultural practices have made Bangladesh extremely vulnerable to famine for a long time.

Even in the best of times, some parts of Bangladesh are affected by local scarcity which causes considerable regional distress. The famine of 1974, as it is now called, had its beginning in 1971. It has caused widespread and severe distress in many parts of Bangladesh and has been responsible for substantial mortality due to the combined action of severe malnutrition and of increased disease prevalence.

I have no special qualification as a famine watcher, if I may use that term, except for the fact that I saw the 1943 Bengal famine as a boy in my village and now I have seen famine in my home district, Rangpur, in 1974.

I would like to describe the advent of famine from a villager's point of view, thus I will try to relate the experiences of 1943 and 1973–74, particularly the reactions of rural people and their attempts to avoid starvation and death. As part of the latter topic I will describe the effects of the famine on the population. Finally, I will mention my own interest: the role of infectious disease as a source of mortality in the 1974 famine.

CAUSES OF FAMINE IN BANGLADESH

Famines, with few exceptions, are seldom precipitated by a single factor, be it natural or man-

made. Both the 1943 famine of the then British Bengal and the 1974 famine of Bangladesh were the results of consecutive crop failures due to drought and/or flood. At present, one third of the rural population of Bangladesh consists of either landless laborers or has extremely small plots of land which are grossly inadequate to support them. This has been primarily due to population increase, resulting in fragmentation of the plots which make them uneconomical for investment of labor and money. The significant proportion of the population, which constitutes the vulnerable, or at-risk, group, suffers most at times of scarcity. Throughout the year these people usually work for survival as day laborers, sharecroppers, fishermen or occasionally as artisans or petty businessmen. At times of unemployment their survival is almost always at the mercy of others, mainly their neighbors. During the best of times, the bulk of this vulnerable section of the population lives from hand to mouth. When a natural disaster, like flood and drought, hits them, they are the first group of persons to be affected by the scarcity. For example, a day laborer in rural Bangladesh works gainfully 90 percent of the working time as an agricultural laborer. When a flood washes away the planted crop, he has nothing to do and begins to starve almost immediately, unless he has some savings. Failure of a single crop may mean that he will not starve completely, but may face temporary hardships. His friends and neighbors, particularly those who are in a relatively better position, will advance him money or, more often, a sack or two of rice or paddy to tide over the immediate emergency. If for some reason, however, the next crop also fails or becomes unsatisfactory, problems of survival become much more serious. He finds it considerably more difficult to borrow or raise a loan. If his neighbors are also affected by crop failure, their ability to help him becomes severely restricted. He and his family try to stretch the

135

meager supply of food by eating one meal a day or one every two days. This is the beginning of a distressing situation which may be called a pre-famine condition. If for some reason there is an unsatisfactory yield from the crops during the third harvest, these people are literally ruined and have almost no way of surviving. Most often the failure of crops is regional so that these landless labor populations move from the worst hit places to better areas and earn a living by selling their labor. If for some reason the crop failure is widespread, affecting a large part of the country, the pre-famine situation turns into real famine. Free distribution of food, or what is called gratuitous relief, helps only a small part of the population. The larger proportion of these people and their families starves and suffers.

NATURAL FACTORS IN FAMINE

In the Rangpur famine of 1974, it was estimated that more than 70,000 people died of starvation. Rangpur is situated near the foothills of the Himalayas. The melted snow and rain coming down from the upper hills sometimes cause unseasonal floods, even in the absence of local rain. This area has always been vulnerable and subject to flood and erosion of the river banks causing shifts of river beds.

EFFECT OF WAR ON RICE PRODUCTION

Table I shows the domestic production of rice, the staple diet in Bangladesh. Following the crackdown by Pakistan during early 1971, it was evident that there was a partial failure of the crops which became more serious in 1971 and 1972, causing a nearly 20 percent decrease in the rice harvest over the 1969–70 production. This was due to a sense of general insecurity and the mass migration of the population from the then East Pakistan to India. More than 10 million people moved away, mainly from the border belt of some 30 miles width. The war ended in December 1971 and this huge population moved back to Bangladesh. On their arrival they found that most of the land had not been cultivated. There was a complete failure of crops in many areas. The following year was a busy one for rebuilding the roads and houses. In 1972–73, there was a partial failure of the monsoon in some reg-

TABLE I

Estimated production of rice in Bangladesh during 1967–74

Year	Total domestic production
1967–1968	110.53
1968–1969	112.57
1969–1970	119.19
1970–1971	110.79
1971–1972	98.87
1972–1973	100.20
1973–74[a]	118.01

[a]Estimated.

ions and flood in others. This deteriorating situation continued from 1971 through 1973. The domestic rice production reflected this. Immediately following the war, deaths and starvation were temporarily averted by massive international aid, mainly in the form of wheat, that was sent to feed the Bangladesh population. However, in 1973, and again in 1974, there were serious floods. Immediately after the flood of 1974 it suddenly became clear that Bangladesh was in the midst of a big famine. If one looks carefully at the pictures in the newspapers of the affected population of Kurigram in Rangpur taken during the flood of 1974, it is clear that the people were already famished. It was the flood that brought their plight to the attention of the newsmen and the rest of the world.

EFFECT OF FAMINE ON RURAL POPULATION

Immediately after the advent of the famine, economic pressure on the population mounted. There was a reduction in their income and a shrinking of their purchasing power. The laboring class could not find work and the men were forced to move away to the nearby towns in search of jobs, leaving their families behind. Quite often they never returned. In this way the families became separated. Small and sick children were often deserted on the roadside. Table II shows the relationships between the price of rice and the number of deserted children in Kurigram. These children were left to die or fend for themselves. They were picked up and put in an orphanage. Before and for eight months after the war, the price of rice was

TABLE II

Price of rice and the arrival of deserted children in an orphanage in Kurigram, Rangpur, 1974–75

Month	Rice price in taka	No. of children	% of all children admitted during the year
January 1974	110		
February	110		
March	135		
April	160	20	5
May	155		
June	162		
July	170		
August	170		
September	240	50	13
October	280	100	27
November	130	51	14
December	130	109	29
January 1975	135	62	17

around 50 *taka*† per maund of 40 kg. By January 1974 this had increased to 110 taka. With the very sharp rise in the price of rice in July/August of 1974, which followed the flood, the number of deserted children also increased sharply.

At times of scarcity the following events usually occur in rural areas:

Unusual drop in labor price. Normally, a day laborer gets one seer (kilogram) of rice, or two meals and an amount of money equivalent to the price of one seer of rice. When jobs become scarce, it is not uncommon to work for food alone, in which case the laborer's family members go without food.

Unusual crowding at the Land Registration Office. A large number of people try to sell or mortgage their properties.

Unusual items appear for sale in the village markets. Used items such as the *dheki,* or paddy husker, ploughs, hoes, as well as ornaments, corrugated iron sheets, brass pots, seed-paddy (but not in the sowing season), are often seen in the markets. Old clothing is often sold, even in winter. These items are usually never sold unless one is forced to do so. Their presence in the rural markets is a sure sign of distress and famine.

† One taka is equivalent to six U.S. cents.

Unusual and paradoxical prices of food materials. A large number of cattle and goats appear in the market. Many of these are bullocks used for ploughing the land and are sold as a last resort. Prices of beef or mutton in some areas become unusually low compared to the price of rice, wheat and legumes, as too many people try to sell off their belongings at the same time. At normal times, the price of a kilogram of rice is half, or one third, of that of meat. However, at times of scarcity, as in 1974 meat may become equal to, or even cheaper than, rice.

The villagers look unusually thin and the children even more so. Most forms of village entertainments, like *jatra* or folk theatres and village singing parties, come to a complete halt. All animals, including dogs, cats, cattle as well as poultry, look thin and emaciated. The whole area affected by the famine becomes unusually quiet.

Numbers of beggars increase tremendously. They are particularly visible on a bazaar day or in the front of a mosque on Fridays in areas hit by scarcity.

People resort to eating unusual items of food. These are wild *arums* (wild Calla or *Calla palustris* or *Kachu* in the local language), and similar items which grow plentifully on the roadside or in the field. They are never eaten at normal times, but during scarcity they may be difficult to find. The green leaves are eaten first and if scarcity is severe, its roots containing an irritant (responsible for itching in the mouth and throat after eating) may be boiled with rice or cooked as curry and eaten. Lack of green leaves on the wild arum plants in a village is a sure sign of scarcity and famine. Bangladesh jungles have several varieties of root vegetables not unlike yams or potatoes which are dug out and eaten mainly to substitute for the scarce rice.

An unusual increase in petty crimes. Stealing of chickens, goats or other easily saleable items also signifies scarcity. Most of these crimes, however, are not reported to the police.

Changes in moral values. Famines are associated with drastic changes in moral values. Prostitution, selling and buying of children for money or food become quite common.

High incidence of suicides. Parents unable to feed their families often commit suicide to escape slow and lingering death. Sometimes they poison their children first.

THE ROLE OF INFECTIOUS DISEASES IN CAUSING MORTALITY IN 1974 FAMINE

With the beginning of the mass movement of the population and the return of the refugees from Indian camps to Bangladesh in 1971 and 1972, a number of diseases made their appearance in epidemic proportion. Smallpox, cholera, hemorrhagic kerato-conjunctivitis and viral hepatitis are examples. However, the most significant of all was the advent of shigellosis, which had been an unimportant disease in Bangladesh before the war.

Shigella dysenteriae, or Shiga's bacillus, which was resistant to almost all the locally available antibiotics, such as tetracycline, streptomycin and chloramphenicol, began to cause widespread cycles of epidemics in many areas of Bangladesh. A similar organism, interestingly enough, was responsible for a major pandemic in Central America in 1969–70. This severe epidemic of dysentery newly occurring in Bangladesh continued through the famine of 1974. As will be apparent from Table III, dysentery was one of the two most important causes of death among the unclaimed bodies picked up from the roadside. The large majority of deaths occurred without any record of the cause of death. However, where it was recorded, the history of dysentery became a significant cause of death. This is not surprising in view of the presentation on disease and famine.

TABLE III

Cause of death by sex and disease in Dacca between October 1974 and January 1975 (percentages are of all diseases)

Cause	Male	Female	Total	Percent
Dysentery	335	393	728	36
Diarrhea	4	7	11	0.5
Malnutrition	172	142	314	15
Measles	—	2	2	0.1
Exposure	14	8	22	1.1
Fever	369	466	835	41
Smallpox	—	1	1	0.1
Other inf.	16	19	35	1.7
Others	51	31	82	4.3
Total	961	1069	2030	100

Emaciated and starving populations seem to fall easy prey to shigellosis, as has been documented in many famines in India and elsewhere. The population in the northern part of Rangpur also suffers from malaria; therefore, malaria was probably another important cause of death during the famine wherever fever was recorded as its cause.

The year following the famine yielded a good crop of rice. It is hoped that the massive international food aid under the United Nations' Food for Work Program will help in augmenting the food production further by digging canals, sift rivers, and improving irrigation. It will also help in building a buffer reserve of food. If scarcity comes in another year, as it well might, suffering hopefully will decrease considerably in magnitude.

MAN-MADE FAMINES: SOME GEOGRAPHICAL INSIGHTS FROM AN EXPLORATORY STUDY OF A MILLENNIUM OF RUSSIAN FAMINES

W. A. DANDO

Department of Geography, University of North Dakota, Grand Forks, North Dakota, U.S.A.

Famines were a regular but unexpected calamity in Russia and in the Soviet Union from A.D. 971 to 1970. An analysis of seventy-seven famines revealed that famines were not confined to specific natural regions, certain cultural areas, or select racial groups. Famines appeared throughout this millennium in the nation's best agricultural regions. Five famine zones were delimited and mapped for there was order in the diverse locations of famines. Famines tended to cluster temporally as well as geographically, but were not restricted to any zone during a specific time period in this millennium. Certain zones were subjected to many famines during specific time periods, but famines occurred in all zones at the same time period. Four basic famine types were identified, namely Transportation, Political, Cultural and Overpopulation. Droughts were not the primary factor in the creation of situations which eventually led to famines. Though natural factors contributed to famine situations, Russian and Soviet famines were largely man-made.

"He who does not work, neither shall he eat."

> *Constitution of the Union of Soviet Socialist Republics, Chapter I, Article 12.*

INTRODUCTION

Hunger, starvation and famine are visible manifestations of problems in spatial organization, human conflicts, or exploitative systems. Famines have existed throughout human history and have generally been short term events, confined to restricted geographical areas and to relatively small local populations. Contemporary reporters and most generalists when writing on famine occurrence have consistently labeled natural disasters, particularly drought, as the cause of famines; albeit, chroniclers who recorded famine occurrence and those who lived through a famine cite numerous factors which led to a famine situation, least of all a drought. In the past decade or so, a number of respected population specialists and researchers in human ecology have postulated that the famines of tomorrow will be long term events, covering broad geographic areas, and involving tens to hundred of millions of people (Paddock, 1967; Ehrlich, 1970; Williamson, 1973; Ehrlich, Ehrlich, and

Holdren, 1973; Greenwood and Edwards, 1973). They predict the population-food collision is inevitable, imminent famines in Latin America, Africa and Asia, and some are actively striving for a worldwide contingency plan to alleviate these impending famines or to shorten their length.

Yet a geographic analysis of the famine literature reveals that: rarely did one factor directly cause a famine (particularly a drought); famine duration has varied greatly in the past; famine regions differ significantly in time, size and intensity; famine deaths or deaths related to famine ranged from the thousands to the millions; famines were not restricted to certain cultural areas; and famines did not occur more frequently in selected racial groups (Walford, 1970; Nicol, 1971; de Castro, 1952; Prentice, 1939; Desrosier, 1961; Golod, 1893; Graves, 1917). Using a millennium of Russian† famines as a case study,

---

† Russia in this study is that portion of the Eurasian continent which once constituted the Russian Empire and which after the first World War was included in Soviet Russia and eventually the Union of Soviet Socialist Republics. Neither map (Plates 3 and 5) includes the Caucasus, Central Asia and Siberia. The reason for this is that the Caucasus and Central Asia were incorporated into Russia late in the famine study period (for example the Khanate of Bukhara did not become a Russian vassal until 1868 and the Khanate of Khiva until 1873; they were not merged into the Russian system until the 1920's). Siberia was incorporated into Russia by 1860, nevertheless few settlers migrated into this

139

the purpose of this paper is to determine if Russian famines were confined to specific natural regions, to certain cultural areas, to select racial groups, and to ascertain if droughts were the primary cause of famine formation. Evidence from this exploratory study may be utilized to further our knowledge and understanding of past famines and to prevent or reduce loss of life in future famines.

in one section of Russia may have been, and in most cases was, remembered as a good agricultural year by the inhabitants of another (Plate 1). A Russian famine, historically, was a protracted shortage of total food over a restricted geographical area causing widespread disease and death from starvation. Gradual disappearance of food and food substitutes first produced emaciated, listless, weak

PLATE 1   Thousands of famine stricken villagers, who fled their homes, slowly trudging towards St. Petersburg in hope of relief; famine year, 1892. (Wood-engraving which illustrated an article by a "special correspondent", printed in the *Illustrated London News*, and secured from the Prints and Photograph Section of the Library of Congress, LC-USZ62-42825.)

RUSSIAN FAMINES: A.D. 971–1970

Famines have been recorded in Russia since the first chronicles were written. They were a regular but unexpected calamity dispersed over an area larger than all of western Europe and they varied in severity, location, and frequency. A famine year

vast geographical area until the construction of the Trans-Siberian Railway in the 1890's. Even today, not more than 10 percent of the total population of the USSR lives in Siberia and few alimentary problems have been recorded. Thus time-scale and data limitations resulted in both Maps emphasizing European Russia.

individuals; then inactive, skeletonized, animal-like creatures. Regardless of racial group or socio-economic level, the young, the small, the nervous or highly active perished first; less nervous or less active, larger and older individuals perished last. Concomitant with starvation was the weakened body's lack of resistance and its susceptibility to disease which led to horrifying epidemics (Plate 2); (Golodanie, 1952; Golodanie, 1958; Ivanovsky, 1923).

But survival in a period of scarcity, or complete unavailability of food for any period of time, was dependent upon an individual's general

PLATE 2   Children who died from starvation being carted away from a Collection Station in Samara Province; famine year, 1921. (Photograph by Dr. Hill of the American Red Cross, secured from the Prints and Photograph Section of the Library of Congress, RC-10073.)

health, which in itself was a resultant of many factors including food consumption in non-hunger, non-famine periods. It appears that the food habits developed on the basis of experience and survival through successive generations provided an adequate, balanced diet. However, changes in lifestyles related to economic conditions (in particular serfdom, commercial agriculture, and collectivization) led to less freedom of choice in foods and reduced dietary variety. Peasants were forced to consume less and less relatively high-cost complete protein foods and to rely upon low-cost grain. Occasional acute quantitative diet limitations which produced hunger and famine in the first eight hundred or so years of this millennium evolved into extended periods of persistent quantitative diet limitations compounded by serious qualitative diet limitations.

SURVEY OF FAMINE AND HUNGER YEARS

A survey of famine and hunger years in Russia from 971 to 1970 revealed that one hundred and twenty-one famine years and one hundred hunger years were recorded in this millennium, one famine or hunger year out of every five. The number of famine years increased gradually, reaching a high in the nineteenth century, after which they declined. A famine year in the period between 971 and 1599 was recorded every seventeen years. Famine years increased to approximately one out of every five in the 1600 to 1799 period, and one out of every three in the 1800 to 1899 period. Famine frequency decreased in the period 1900 to 1970 to one famine year in five.

In the nineteenth and early twentieth centuries when the greatest number of recorded famine and hunger years occurred, the peasant, even when harvests were below average or even if there was a crop failure, would still sell grain for he was dependent on the cash earned from the sale of grain to pay his redemption payments and taxes, and to buy salt, cloth, some tools, etc. Famine catastrophies were greater in this crude form of commercial agriculture than in the previous subsistent agricultural system. After the revolution, Military Communism and the socialization of agriculture disrupted all aspects of rural life. The state took by force or by decree all agricultural surpluses to feed the urban proletariat and for export to pay for industrial equipment. Granted, these changes in basic rural economics, growth of markets, commercialization, and socialization of agriculture would not have been a serious problem if production had been such as to provide adequate grain for the rapidly growing population and for market. However, an examination of crop yields throughout Russian history and, particularly when Russia was a major exporter of agricultural products reveals that yields were unbelievingly low (Kushner, 1958; Liaschenko, 1949; Robinson, 1932; Timoshenko, 1932, Truog and Pronin, 1953). Thus, an archaic agricultural system, perpetual undernourishment, and a complex combination of recurring events and situations not all related to natural factors made deaths in this period from malnutrition and starvation common-place.

A multifactored physical system (with climate playing a leading role) limited the sown area, types of crops grown and yields. In northern Russia, yields of traditional Russian crops are primarily determined by heat since this is an area of moisture surplus in relation to heat. While in southern Russia, yields or crop productivity are determined greatly by the moisture available to the plant in its life cycle. Only in limited parts of Russia are the agroclimatic resources adequate to produce surpluses in sufficient amounts that would warrant great investments of time, capital, or labor. Yet climatic aberrations in the best agricultural areas of a particular stage in the evolution of the Russian state were common. In the past as in the case today, droughts and low winter temperatures resulting in plant "winter-kill" sporadically affect large sections of the country (Borisov, 1959; Davidova, et al., 1966; Kirienko, 1948). Nevertheless, the whole history of Russian agriculture has been one of continuous field experimentation with the ill-defined variables of a limited agroclimatic resource base. Through time, bad agricultural practices were discarded and acceptable agrotechniques prevailed; errors in judgement, mistakes and most innovations were eliminated by the brute force of hunger and famine.

LOCATION OF FAMINES

An attempt to locate the general area affected by famines, famine frequency and their primary causes led to the construction of Table I. This table is by no means complete but the general location of 90 percent of the cited famines has been noted and also the location of all the famines in which a crop failure was directly attributed to drought. From this, three significant observations can be made at this time. First, specific and general locations of famines moved as the Russian state expanded to its present size and famines have appeared throughout a millennium in Russia's best agricultural regions. Second, droughts were not the primary factor in the creation of situations which eventually led to famine. Buchinskii (1957), while studying climatic changes, gathered statistics on droughts recorded by chroniclers for over a thousand years. He lists sixty droughts from 994 to 1954 and less than 25 percent of these droughts could possibly be considered a significant factor in famine formation. When Buchinskii's statistics are collated with Alpat'ev and Ivanova (1958), then compared with Table I a myth is shattered: when drought occurred in Russian history a famine did not necessarily follow, that is to say, drought and famine were not synonymous. Droughts were a primary factor in not more than 15 to 16 percent of the total Russian famine years since 971. Third, there seems to be an order in the diverse locations of the famines. This becomes apparent when they are mapped according to time zones (linear combinations of regions focused upon economic-administrative centers). Five famine zones are delimited on Plate 3. Within these zones famines tended to cluster temporally as well as geographically. It should be noted that not only were certain zones subjected to famine during specific time periods but famines did occur in all zones at the same time period.

Zone I

Novgorod is located in a landscape dominated by the effects of glaciation and where insufficient summer heat and excessive soil moisture perennially inhibit agriculture. It emerged as the largest city in Russia and a major cultural and commercial center between the 12th and 15th centuries. A pattern of trade developed in which most of the cash income was derived from exporting or transshipping raw materials or finished products to the Orient, Constantinople, and Hansa towns. As a spatially interdependent enclave in a food deficit area strongly influenced by Western ideas, Novgorod was able to remain apart from the contemporary Russian trend towards a spatially restricted

TABLE I

FAMINE YEARS IN RUSSIA
971 - 1970

YEAR	LOCATION	CAUSE	YEAR	LOCATION	CAUSE
971[e]	Belobereg	War	1630[a,f]	No recorded indication of location	?
997[o]	Belgorod	War	1636[a,f]	No recorded indication of location	?
1024[a,e,f,g]	Suzdal	Fear and panic	1650[a,f]	Pskov	?
1070-71[a,c,f,m]	Rostov-Volyn	(Women?)	1660-61[a,h]	Tobolsk, Solikamsk, and other locations	Food speculation
1092-93[a,c,f]	Kiev	War and drought			
1127[d,m]	Novgorod	Frost and floods	1671[k]	Vologda	?
1128[a,m,f,x]	Polotsk, Novgorod, Pskov, Suzdal, and Smolensk	Excessive rain and floods	1673-74[a]	Voronezh	?
			1682-90[a]	In many parts of Russia; Tobolsk in 1696-97	?
1137[d,m]	Novgorod	Frost and rebellion			
1161[d,m,x]	Novgorod	Frost. and drought	1716[a]	No recorded indication of location	(Poor crops?)
1188[d,m,x]	Novgorod	Frost			
1193[e,m]	Southern Russia	?	1722[a,r]	Exact location undetermined, believed to be Solikamsk	(Poor crops?)
1215[a,d,f,h,m,x]	Novgorod and Suzdal	Frost and transportation			
1230-31[a,d,f,g,m, x,AA]	Most of Russia except Kiev	Frost	1733[z]	Smolensk	?
			1734-35[a,f,w,z]	Nizhny Novgorod	Food shortage aggravated by speculators
1279[a,f]	Many regions of Russia	?			
1308[d]	Novgorod	Epidemics, mice, grain speculation	1748[a]	Little Russia	?
			1749-50[w]	Moscow, Belograd, Smolensk and Riga	?
1309[a,f]	Most of Russia	?			
1332[a,b,f,x]	Southern Russia	Drought	1757[a]	Lithuania and Estonin	?
1364-65[b]	Central East-European Plain	Drought	1770[h]	Solikamsk	?
1366[b]	Land of Novgorod	Drought	1773[b,DD]	Ukraine	Drought
1371[b]	Moscow and most of the Central East-European Plain	Drought	1774[b,DD]	Voronezh and Kharkov	Drought
			1777[h,DD]	No recorded indication of location	?
1421-22[a,d,f]	Land of Novgorod	Snow, rain, and floods			
1442-43[a,b,f]	Tver	Drought	1785-86[a,h,DD]	No recorded indication of location	(Poor crops?)
1445[d,L]	Novgorod	Internal disruptions and bandits	1787[z]	No recorded indication of location	?
1468[b]	Lands north and south centered on Pskov	North: heavy rain, floods South: drought (Poor crops?)	1788[a]	Moscow, Kaluga, Tula, Ryazan, Belograd, and Tambov	?
1512[a,f]	No recorded indication of location	Poor crops	1820-22[a,f]	Vilna, Kherson, Belorussia, St.Petersburg, Novgorod, Tver, Pskov, Smolensk, Orlov, Kursk, Ekaterinoslav and Chernigov	?
1525[b,v]	Most of Moscovy	Drought and transportation			
1553[a,f]	No recorded indication of location	?			
1557[a,f]	Trans-Volga	?	1827[a]	Tavricheskaia	?
1570[a,f,o,s,t]	Moscovy, especially Novgorod	Political and massacre	1830[f,h]	Volyn and Pskov	?
1601-03[a,f,g,i,k,o, u,z,AA,DD]	Most of Moscovy	Mist, rain, frost, and anarchy	1833-34[a,f,i,AA]	Novorussiia, Bessarabia, Vitebsk, Poland, Smolensk, Pskov, Orlov, Tambov, Ryazan and Chernigov	Drought
1608[a,f]	Central East-European Plain	Anarchy			

TABLE I (continued)

YEAR	LOCATION	CAUSE	YEAR	LOCATION	CAUSE
1839-41 [a,f,i,AA]	Tula, Ryazan, Kursk, Chernigov, Kostroma, Saratov, Vitebsk, Perm, Arkhangelsk, and Liflan	?	1891-93 [a,b,c,f,h,i,z,DD]	Kazan, Vyatka, Perm, Tobolsk, Simbirsk, Samara, Saratov, Orenburg, Nizhny, Novgorod, Moscow, Tver, Penza, Ryazan, and other locations in Russia	Drought and political
1843-45 [a,f,h,i,DD]	Pskov, St. Petersburg, and Novgorod	?	1897-98 [b,c,h,BB,CC,DD]	Western East-European Plain	Drought
1846 [h,DD]	Bessarabia, Kharkov, Voronezh, Saratov, and Orenburg	?	1901 [b,c,g]	Ukraine and areas along the Volga	Drought
1848-50 [a]	Novorussiia and in many other sections of Russia	?	1905-06 [b,c,g,h,i,k,DD]	Ten provinces along the Volga and in Ukraine	Drought
1851 [h,DD]	Moscow, Kaluga, Chernigov, Tver, Yaroslav, Tula, Kazan, Riga, Kharkov, Voronezh, Saratov, and Vyatka	?	1911-12 [b,c,g,h,i,DD]	Along the Volga and Eastern Slopes of the Urals	Drought
1855 [h,DD]	No recorded indication of location	?	1921-22 [b,c,g,h,o,w,BB,DD]	Ten provinces along the Volga and in Ukraine	Drought, war, and transportation
1863 [a]	No recorded indication of location	?	1933-34 [b,c,h,n,q,w]	Ukraine, North Caucasus, along the Volga, and in Kazakhstan	Political and "anti-social obstinacy"
1867-68 [a,h,DD]	Finland	?			
1873-74 [a,f]	Samara and Orenburg	(Crop failure?)	1941-43 [p,BB]	Leningrad and in many parts of the USSR	War
1877 [DD]	No recorded indication of location	?			
1879-80 [a,f,g]	Saratov	?	1946-47 [b,c,g,n,EE]	Ukraine and Central Industrial Region	Political and drought
1883-84 [a,f,h,AA,DD]	Kursk, Kazan, Kharkov, and Vyatka	Drought			

SOURCES

(a) F. K. Stefanovskii, Materialy dlia Izucheniia Svoistv Golodnago Khleba (Kazan, 1893); (b) I. E. Buchinskii, "O Zasukhakh na Russkoi Ravnine za Poslednee Tysyacheletie," from B. L. Dzerdzeevskii, ed., Sukhovei ikh Proiskhozhdenie i Bar'ba s Nimi (Moskva, 1957), pp. 23-28; (c) A. I. Rudenko, ed., Zasukhi v SSSR (Leningrad, 1958), pp. 162-165; (d) M. N. Tikhomirova, Novgorod: k 1100 Letiiu Goroda (Moskva, 1964), pp. 299-309; (e) S. H. Cross and O. P. Sherbowitz-Wetzor, The Russian Primary Chronicle: Laurentian Text (Cambridge, 1953), pp. 90, 123, 134-135, 146, 150, 173, and 178-179; (f) _____, "Golod'," Entsiklopedicheskii Slovar' (Tom IX) (Moskva, 1893), pp. 102-104; (g) _____, "Golod'," Bol'shaia Sovetskaia Entsiklopediia (Tom II) (Moskva, 1952), pp. 623-626; (h) A. Keys, J. Brozek, A. Henschel, O. Mickelsen, and H. L. Taylor, The Biology of Human Starvation (Vol. I and II) (Minneapolis, 1950), pp. 1249-1251; (i) Baron von Haxthausen, The Russian Empire (London, 1968), pp. 68 and 439; (j) G. T. Robinson, Rural Russia Under the Old Regime (New York, 1932), pp. 18, 116, 152, and 245; (k) V. O. Kluchevsky, A History of Russia (New York, 1960), pp. 55, 345, and 265; (l) A. Rambaud, The History of Russia; From the Earliest Times to 1877 (Vol. 1) (New York, 1890), pp. 85 and 158-159; (m) G. Vernadsky, Kievan Russia (New York, 1948), pp. 315-316; (n) V. Kubijovyc, ed., Ukraine: A Concise Encyclopaedia (Toronto, 1963), pp. 200-201, 820-822, and 898; (o) E. Seeger, The Pageant of Russian History (New York, 1950), pp. 148-149, 162, and 340; (p) L. Goure, The Siege of Leningrad (Stanford, 1962); (q) S. and B. Webb, Soviet Communism: A New Civilization (Vol. II) (New York, 1936), pp. 258-272; (r) S. Graham, Peter the Great (New York, 1929), p. 322; (s) J. Koslow, Ivan the Terrible (New York, 1961), p. 192; (t) H. von Staden, The Land and Government of Muscovy (Stanford, 1967), p. 29; (u) S. Graham, Boris Godunof (New Haven, 1933), pp. 145-146; (v) H. Lamb, The March of Muscovy (New York, 1948), p. 107; (w) P. N. Miliukov, C. Seignobos, and L. Eisenmann, History of Russia (New York, 1968), Vol. Two, p. 55, and Vol. Three, pp. 362, 381-387, and 410; (x) M. Tikhomirov, Towns of Ancient Rus (Moscow, 1959), pp. 69, 101, 102, and 146; (z) M. T. Florinsky, Russia: A History and An Interpretation (New York, 1953), Vol. I, pp. 225, 485, and 601 and Vol. 2, pp. 474-481, and 1159; (AA) P. I. Liaschenko, History of the National Economy of Russia, to the 1917 Revolution (New York, 1949), pp. 101, 197-198, 364, and 468; (BB) J. de Castro, The Geography of Hunger (Boston, 1952), pp. 50 and 277; (CC) E. P. Prentice, Hunger and History (New York, 1939), pp. 112-113; (DD) H. H. Fisher, The Famine in Soviet Russia, 1919-1923 (Stanford, 1927), pp. 475-480; (EE) N. S. Khrushchev, "Report to the Central Committee of the Communist Party of the Soviet Union," Pravda, Dec. 10, 1963, p. 5.

(A more detailed listing of sources can be secured from the author by request.)

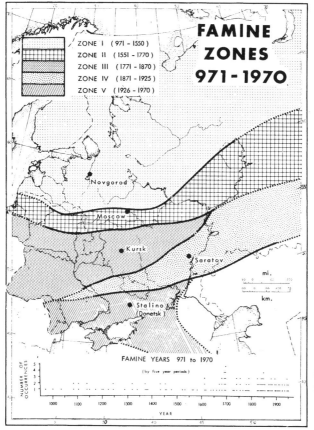

PLATE 3   Famine Zones 971–1970.

neofeudal agricultural society. An examination of twenty-one famines located in the racially diverse area dominated by Novgorod from 971 to 1550 shows that frost and floods were considered the primary contributing factors to a crop failure, followed by drought, rebellion and internal disruption, and grain speculation. Vernadsky (1948) noted

In 1127 untimely severe frosts ruined the harvest in the land of Novgorod. Scarcity of grain and prohibitive prices of bread resulted in famine and starvation: people ate linden leaves, birch bark, straw, and moss—mortality was high and corpses were strewn in the streets and the market place in the city of Novgorod.

Since Novgorod's hinterland did not produce sufficient food in good years to supply its population, a crop failure was extremely serious and famine could only be averted by importing food. When the main routes of transportation were open, a bad agricultural year would simply result in a shortage of food and a concomitant increase in food prices. When the main routes of transportation were closed for any reason, a one or possibly two year famine of serious proportions taking the lives of thousands occurred in Novgorod (Tikhomirov, 1959; Tikhomirov, 1964). Rambaud (1878) reported that in 1216,

Their communications with the Volga were intercepted; he prevented the arrival of corn, and reduced the town to starvation. The Novgorodians were obliged to eat the bark of pines, moss, and lime-leaves. The streets were filled with the bodies of the wretched inhabitants, which the dogs devoured.

The prince, *boyar*,† merchant, or group that controlled the important transportation and communication town of Torzok on the Volga, controlled the destiny of most Novgorodians in times of food scarcity. Decisions not to permit food shipments to Novgorod led to many famines such as the winter of 1230–31 when, as Lawrence (1957) cited

. . . some of the common people killed the living and ate them; others cutting up dead flesh and corpses ate them; others ate horseflesh, dogs and cats; but to those they found in such acts they did—thus some they burned with fire, others they cut to pieces and others they hanged.

Zone II

Moscow is situated in a region where agricultural production is limited by a short, cool growing season, low annual rainfall, and generally infertile soils. It became the new focal point of Russian power and culture as the result of Novgorod's seizure by Ivan III in 1478 and Novgorod's destruction by Ivan IV in 1570. As a central place, Moscow functioned as the hub of Russian secular and religious activities, as the major focus for the exchange of goods and finally as the heart of nascent processing and industrial activity. Here, a galaxy of Muscovite leaders shrewdly exploited the complete spectrum of Slavic and Mongol-Tartar social stratification to pursue a policy of national unification and growth. Muscovite Russia's agricultural base, although far from ideal, was adequate for the feeding of its people. Between 1551 and 1770 six severe famines were recorded in a zone dominated by the Moscow node. Not one famine in this time period was directly attributed to drought but there was a political character to famine in this zone. Koslow (1961) in his study of Ivan the Terrible stated that in the famine of 1570

The Oprichniki had cut down the amount of acreage under cultivation by driving large numbers of landowners and their

† In the eleventh, twelfth, and thirteenth centuries, each prince found it necessary to maintain a group of professional men-at-arms. The upper ranks of these developed into a separate class, known as *boyars*. Boyars were assigned land in return for furnishing military contingents in times of troubles, and for performing other military or administrative duties. As a result, boyars developed into a landholding aristocracy.

peasants into exile and burning the fields of *boyars* suspected or implicated in treasonable activities. Still others, both nobles and commoners, had fled to faraway places to escape the terror, leaving large fertile areas unplanted, or in some cases, already planted to crops that rotted in the fields.

During the same famine, von Staden (1967) noted

In the Podkletnye sela of the court, the Grand Prince had many thousand ricks of unthreshed grain in straw, which belonged to the household, but he would not sell them to his subjects, thus many thousand people died in the country and were eaten by dogs.

Famines did not simply occur in this zone, they were inadvertently created and in many instances prolonged up to nine years by political decisions or indecisions, non-recognition of hunger and famine, and refusal to aid tens of thousands of famine victims (Kochan, 1962; Kluchevsky, 1960; Stefanovskii, 1893).

Zone III

Centered approximately on Kursk in the hilly forest steppe underlain by leached but fertile *chernozem* soils, this zone recorded eleven famines between 1771–1870. As Imperial Russia expanded its borders south and westward at the expense of the Poles and Turks, Russian agriculturalists and invited foreign settlers poured into the newly acquired lands. At first the number of settlers was small, agricultural land was plentiful and yields of crops by Russian standards were considered good. But by 1820, the growth and density of the rural population had become a problem and was compounded by intensive migratory shifts, chiefly from districts with poorer soils. Twenty-nine famine years were recorded in this hundred year period, eight prior to 1820 and twenty-one after. The average duration of a famine was two to three years, hundreds of thousands of people perished and only three famines were considered in part to be an outgrowth of a drought. Famines in this time period were not a creation of natural factors. Serfdom, rural overpopulation, then pseudo-emancipation and reductions in land allotments, led to severe quantitative and qualitative diet limitations. Von Haxthausen (1856) observed

The principal food of the Russian people consists of bread; potatoes are unknown in most districts; cabbage is the only vegetable which is much used. Animal food, milk, and butter are little eaten. In the army each soldier receives two pounds and a half of bread daily, besides groats, etc. A healthy Russian peasant cannot subsist without three pounds . . . There is always a deficit. . .

The transition between a spatially restricted extensive subsistence agricultural society to a spatially interdependent extensive semi-commercial agricultural society came too quickly and without marked changes in the social system and advances in agrotechniques or crops that would make it possible to support a larger rural population (Morokhovets, 1931; Clarkson, 1969). In an anonymous approved Soviet interpretation of Russian history (Anonymous, 1960), it was concluded that

... serfdom hampered the development of the production forces of the country, perpetuated backward farming methods with their low productivity. It hindered the growth of the home market, including the labour market, restricted the accumulation of capital and hampered the development of more progressive, capitalist methods of production.

Zone IV

Saratov, a major food processing, transportation and commercial center located in the steppes of southeastern European Russia, was the focal point of a famine zone where between 1871 and 1925 nineteen famine years were recorded. At first, the settlers who moved from the forest and humid forest-steppe into the subhumid, flat, immense, grassy steppe were not overly cognizant of a decrease in total precipitation coupled with increased variability of annual receipts. However, it soon became cruelly apparent that severe droughts can and do occur here once every four or five years. Drought was a primary contributing factor in two out of three famine years between 1871 and 1925. This zone, delimited by the extent of six major famines, was an agricultural frontier into which land-hungry Russian peoples moved in response to some improvements in agrotechnology and overpopulation in certain rural areas. Grain from this zone played a major role in setting the price of wheat on the world market, yet one of every three years was recorded as a famine year.†

Russian famines at the end of the nineteenth century and the beginning of the twentieth were not specifically caused by drought, although a crop failure in an afflicted area without food reserves or food relief could lead to a famine (Queen, 1955;

† According to the agricultural census of 1917, Samara Guberniya had 97.1 percent of its cultivated area in grain crops; Orenburg Guberniya 97.3 percent; Ufa Guberniya 94.2 percent and Saratov Guberniya 93 percent (Balzak, Vasyutin and Feigin, 1949).

Miller, 1926; Way, 1889; Philippot, 1953; Pavlovich, 1892). Famines in this zone prior to 1917 were created primarily by economic controls rather than the intimate relations of an agriculturalist to the land he tilled. Eventual overpopulation on marginal agricultural land, high taxes, and an emphasis upon exports of grain all imposed upon a backward agricultural system in a habitually hostile environment, contributed to abject rural poverty, hunger and famine. Smith (1892) reported that the peasant

... saves little or nothing, but one harvest carries him to the next. The crop means not only food but, clothing, fuel, fodder, taxes, farm necessities, and all the requirements of his simple life. When it fails, everything fails with it.

Extended rural-urban interaction which mushroomed in this spatially interdependent extensive commercial agricultural society created an extreme form of regional specialization and abandonment of certain critical facets of regional self-sufficiency. Rubinow (1906) concluded that

Every shortage of crops means actual starvation in some part of Russia, and practically all the time in Russia there is starvation in some part of the country because of failure of crops.

To most of the peasants of Russia, and particularly those who survived the numerous famines which took place in Zone Four, commercial agriculture became commensal agriculture, namely, an association beneficial to one partner (Plate 4).

The Russian revolution was proclaimed as the great modern experiment in the eradication of man's exploitation by his fellow man and the elimination of want. Yet rural disruption related to the revolution and civil war led to one of the most terrible famines recorded in Russian history. Soviet Russia in 1920 was severely weakened by the burden of World War I and internal strife, disrupted by the shock of social revolution, and isolated from the world by a wall of fear and suspicion. Industrial production had declined to less than 25 percent of preWorld War I; internal trade was restricted by Soviet law; cities were being abandoned by peasant workers who returned to the countryside and claimed their share of confiscated noble estates; agriculture had reached a point where it scarcely produced sufficient surplus to maintain a minimal diet in the nation; and transport facilities had deteriorated to such a degree that internal distribution of agricultural products was very difficult. When the grim forerunners of drought

PLATE 4   Men and women begging for bread at the house of the mayor in a village near Simbrisk; famine year, 1892. (Wood-engraving from a sketch by a Russian officer, printed in the *Illustrated London News* and secured from the Prints and Photograph Section of the Library of Congress, LC-USZ6-42826.)

were recognized, the government instituted a number of policies which increased panic (Arnautov, 1922; Fisher, 1927; Tulaikov, 1930).

Maxim Gorky appealed to the world for bread and medicine in June 1921. A number of organizations from many nations, including the United States, responded. Hoover (1961) recorded we were

confronted with famine in about 750,000 square miles of the Volga Valley and 85,000 square miles in the Ukraine. About 25,000,000 people in these regions were in the midst of absolute famine, with death for the whole population of these areas only a few months away.

The peasants became panic stricken and some fled their villages in hope of finding food, while others remained to wait for death. The famine of 1921–22 took the lives of five to nine million Soviet citizens, and its long-range social and economic consequence are inestimable.

Zone V

Centered on Stalino (Donetsk), this zone encompasses steppe, dry-and-salt steppe, semi-desert, and merges with deserts on the east. Spatially interdependent extensive private or socialist planned agriculture was possible without artifical irrigation, but was subject to periodic droughts and excessive variability of harvests. Droughts occur here on the average of one every three or four years (Matskevich, 1971; Verbin, 1948). In the period between 1926 and 1970, seven famine years were recorded, four in the dry, droughty zone and three elsewhere.[†] Not one famine which took place in this zone in forty-four years can be attributed solely to drought. However, in each of the famines a drought occurred and there was a decrease in total grain production but not so drastic a reduction as to produce famines which claimed millions of lives. The famines recorded in this period were not caused by natural factors but by man.

A decision was made by the Communist party in the late 1920's to industrialize as rapidly as humanly possible. The party considered it imperative to have at the state's disposal large internal supplies of low cost grain. Grain was needed for export to secure credits and to pay for imported industrial equipment. Grain was needed also to feed the expanding urban-industrial population. The

solution to the state's grain need was to collectivize agriculture and to eliminate, at the same time, the more prosperous and more productive peasants. Small peasant farms were to be brought under the control of large collective farms where the state could closely scrutinize the production of grain; *kulaks* were to be liquidated.[‡] Initially the collective campaign was voluntary but it soon gravitated to the use of "extraordinary measures" when the peasants balked. A pall of terror enveloped the villages in 1929 and 1930. When groups of peasants chose to resist collectivization, they did so with pitchforks against machine guns and clubs against grenades (Kravchenko, 1950). Volin (1951) stated

... local authorities thus had a 'green light' to proceed with collectivization as rapidly as possible and to deal severely with recalcitrant elements. More than 5 million of the peasant population were uprooted, their property confiscated, and many of them deported to remote regions.

The ramification of collectivization and dekulakization was famine. Laird (1958), in his study of collective farming, quoted from Fedor Belov and he wrote

In spite of a 'good harvest' in 1932 in the area in which his *kolkhoz* was located, the 'red broom' that passed through the land, assertedly looking for surpluses, actually swept everything before it including the grain needed to sustain peasant life. As a result, the man-made famine of 1932–33 'was the most terrible and destructive that the Ukrainian people had ever experienced.§

The famine of 1933–34 was centered on the Ukraine, the most productive wheat producing region in the Soviet Union at the time. Estimated deaths ranged from five to eleven million. This famine is attributed largely to the loss of individual initiative and unexampled pauperization of the peasants by collectivization (Webb and Webb, 1936; Fainsod, 1963; Belov, 1955; Dalrymple, 1964; Dalrymple, 1965; Lewin, 1965).

‡ *Kulak* is an old Russian term meaning fist, and was applied to wealthy peasants because they were known as tight-fisted money lenders. During collectivization in the 1930's, a kulak was any peasant who opposed the socialization of agriculture.

§ A *kolkhoz* or collective farm has been officially described as a voluntary cooperative agriculture organization. In fact it may be described as a state implanted institution created to subject agriculture labor, production, marketing and income to a network of comprehensive state controls. The farm's production is primarily determined by a centralized plan imposed from above, and the kolkhoz's chief responsibility is to meet its obligations to the state.

† For more information regarding droughts and the effects of droughts on agricultural productivity, see Nuttonson, 1949; Lydolph, 1964; Dando 1969; Ventskevich, 1961.

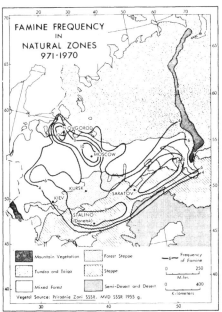

PLATE 5   Famine frequency in natural zones.

The radical transformation from spatially inter-dependent extensive commercial agriculture to centrally planned spatially interdependent extensive socialist agriculture unquestionably disrupted food production in the Soviet Union for decades. Agriculture under socialist central planning did not reap the presupposed benefits of increased efficiency, additional capital, new technology and the dissemination of information. Instead, planning errors and administrative misjudgements were cannonized and rigidly applied throughout the country with dreadful repercussions. Following World War II, the Soviet Union experienced another agricultural crisis prompted by a political decision. A decision to rigorously restore the provisions of the collective farm charter which was relaxed during World War II, coupled with the use of scarce grain in other segments of the world to promote party goals, produced the last famine recorded in Russian history (Mills, 1947; Jasny, 1948; Hutchinson, 1946; Khrushchev, 1963). The famine of 1946–47 came after a devastating war which left over twenty million people dead and another twenty-five

million homeless, and after a drought which was described as the worst since 1891. A bad harvest in 1946 was the official explanation for the grain shortage, yet the 1946 yield of farm commodities was 98 percent of the year's planned quota (Bergson, 1947). Deaths attributed to this famine have been estimated between two and five million.

FAMINE FREQUENCY

The sequence of events which produced famine in each time period was complex and multifactored. It would be extremely difficult if not impossible to specifically identify the one cause of most famines. Also, it is very difficult to identify the one place where famines occurred most frequently in the past one thousand years. Yet four major famine nodes are identifiable (see Plate 5), Novgorod, Moscow, Saratov, Stalino (Donetsk) and a transitional area centered on Kursk. Novgorod, Moscow and Saratov famine nodes recorded more than ten famine years, the Stalino (Donetsk) node

PLATE 6   A starving seven-year-old child, using the door-frame of her home for support, in the village of Osekovo, Samara Province; famine year, 1921. (Photograph by Dr. Hill of the American Red Cross, secured from the Prints and Photograph Section of the Library of Congress, RC-10075).

TABLE II

Factors contributing to the development of Russian famines 971–1970

Natural Factors	Human Factors
1. Climate	1. War
A. Excessive rainfall	A. Blockages and sieges
B. Paucity of rainfall	B. Foraging
C. Drought	C. Displacement of farmers
D. Dust storms	D. Disruption of planting schedules
E. Late frost	E. Desolation of fields
F. Early frost	F. Redistribution of land
G. Abnormal heat	G. Destruction of farm equipment
H. Cold	H. Slaughter of farm animals
I. Fog or mist	I. Fear
J. Excessive wind	
K. Hail	
L. Sukhovei	
2. Disease	2. Political Decisions
A. Blight	A. Non-recognition of hunger and famine
B. Rusts	B. Refusal to aid famine victims
C. Nematodes	C. Lack of concern for rural problems
D. Fungus	D. Contrived agricultural product-manufactured goods price imbalance
E. Virus	E. Agricultural products export policies
	F. Agriculture by decree
	G. Food requisitions
	H. Collectivization
	I. Distorted priorities
3. Rodents	3. Transportation
4. Insects	4. Serfdom
5. Floods	5. Communication
	6. Incompetence
	7. Perennial Rural Poverty
	8. Disease and/or Pestilence
	9. Panic
	10. Food Speculation

Source: Refer to Table I.

eight and Kursk at least six. Famines were recorded in the Novgorod node from 1127 to 1893; Moscow node from 1128 to 1947; Kursk transitional area from 1673 to 1947; Saratov node from 1839 to 1922; and the Stalino (Donetsk) node from 1193 to 1934. Novgorod is located in the Tundra and Taiga Natural Zone, Moscow in the Mixed Forest, Kursk in the Forest Steppe, and Saratov and Stalino (Donetsk) are located in the Steppe. Plate 5 graphically emphasizes that famines occurred in all natural zones.

The primary natural factors in the creation of situations conducive for famines to develop, as outlined in Table II, were climate, disease, rodents, insects and floods. The primary human factors recorded were war, political decisions, transportation, serfdom, communications, incompetence, perennial rural poverty, disease and/or pestilence, panic and food speculation. But food shortages resulting from any one or a number of natural factors should not have led to hunger, starvation or

famine. In every instance, there appears to have been adequate foodstuff for everyone in need and more than enough to carry the stricken area or areas through their time of troubles. The suffering which resulted from acute food shortages and famine in Russia (Plate 6) was in large measure man-made, that is to say, the failure of man to accord relief. In essence then, all of the famines which have occurred in Russia from 971–1970 can be predominantly attributed to human factors.

SUMMARY

Specific and general locations of famines moved as the Russian state expanded to its present size and famines have appeared throughout a millennium in Russia's best agricultural regions, in all natural zones, and have not been restricted to one cultural area or one racial group. Four basic famine types were identified:

Transportation or Novgorodian-famines in commercial or industrial food deficient regions dependent upon distant food sources and supplied normally by a well developed transportation system.

Political or Muscovite/Stalino-famines in regions that are nominally self-sufficient in basic foodstuffs but where regional politics or regional political systems determine food production, food distribution and food availability.

Cultural or Kursk-famines in food surplus regions induced by archaic social systems, cultural practices and overpopulation.

Overpopulation or Saratov famines in drought prone, overpopulated, marginal agricultural regions with primitive agricultural systems, and whose inhabitants' perennial food intake was only slightly above starvation.

CONCLUSIONS

Future famines involving large numbers of people, covering broad geographical areas and lasting for extended periods of time are not inevitable. But future famines could occur anywhere on the face of the earth, they will undoubtedly be man-made and they will be of Transportation, Political, Cultural or Over population famine type. With the increased use of chemicals in agriculture and use of improved agrotechniques, with reduction of food losses and improved transportation-communication networks, and with a functioning United Nations, short term natural events which in the past contributed to famine formation should only lead to food rationing in restricted areas. But, the problem in the future may be long term shortages of total food triggered by global war, seemingly permanent revolutions, or prolonged social and economic upheavals in overpopulated marginal agricultural regions.

Historically, acute limitations to a traditional diet were multifactored in cause and lay deep in the physical-social geography and economic-history of an area at a particular time. There was little reason for Russian famines to have emerged in the past and no reason why a famine should occur anywhere in the world in the future. If famines occur, they will be overtly created or inadvertently perpetuated by man.

ACKNOWLEDGEMENTS

Research for this exploratory study was conducted in the Hoover Library (Stanford), Library of Congress (Washington, D.C.), Leningrad Publichnaia Biblioteka (Leningrad), and the Gosudarstvennaia Biblioteka SSSR imeni V. I. Lenina (Moscow), and was financed in part by funds received through a University of Maryland Faculty Research Grant.

REFERENCES

Alpat'ev, A. and V. Ivanova (1958). Kharaktika i geograficheskoe rasprostranenie zasukh. In A. Rudenko (Ed), *Zasukhi v SSSR*, Leningrad, pp. 31–45 and appended material on pp. 162–165.

Anonymous (1960). *Outline History of the U.S.S.R.* Moscow, p. 119.

Arnautov, V. (1922). *Golod i leti na Ukraine.* Kharkov.

Balzak, S., V. Vasyutin, and Y. A. Feigin (1949). *Economic Geography of the USSR.* Macmillan, New York, p. 345.

Belov, F. (1955). *The History of a Soviet Collective Farm.* Praeger, New York, p. 12.

Bergson, A. (1947). The Fourth Five Year Plan: Heavy versus Consumer's Goods Industries. *Pol. Sci. Q.* **62**, 216.

Borisov, A. (1959). *Klimati SSSR.* Moskva, pp. 193–202.

Buchinskii, I. (1957). O zasukhakh na russkoi revnine za poslednee tysyacheletie. In B. Dzerdzeevskii (Ed), *Sukhovei ikh proishkozhdenie i bor'ba nimi.* Moskva, pp. 23–28.

Clarkson, J. (1969). *A History of Russia.* Random House, New York, p. 256.

Cross, S. and P. Sherbowitz-Wetzor (Eds), (1953). *The Russian Primary Chronicle.* The Mediaeval Academy of America, Cambridge.

Dalrymple, D. (1964). The Soviet Famine of 1932–34. *Soviet Studies* **XV**, 250–284.

Dalrymple, D. (1965). The Soviet Famine of 1932–1934; Some Further References. *Soviet Studies* **XVI**, 471–474.

Dando, W. (1970). *Grain or Dust: A Study of the Soviet New Lands Program 1954–1963.* University Microfilms Ltd., Ann Arbor.

Davidova, A., A. Kamenskii, N. Nekliukova and G. Tyshinskii (1966). *Fizicheskaia Geografia SSSR.* Moskva, pp. 57–82.

de Castro, J. (1952). *The Geography of Hunger.* Little, Brown and Company, Boston, pp. 50 & 277.

Desrosier, N. (1961). *Attack on Starvation.* Avi Publishing Company, Inc. Westport, pp. 3 & 284.

Ehrlich, P. (1970). Looking Backward from 2000 A.D. In E. Odum, *et al.*, *The Crisis of Survival,* Scott, Foresman and Company, Madison, pp. 238–245.

Ehrlich, P., A. Ehrlich and J. Holdren (1973). *Human Ecology: Problems and Solutions.* W. H. Freeman and Company, San Francisco, pp. 69–112.

Fainsod, M. (1963). *Smolensk Under Soviet Rule.* Vintage Books, New York, pp. 240–241.

Fisher, H. (1927). *The Famine in Soviet Russia 1919–1923.* Stanford University Press, Stanford, pp. 496–497.

Florinsky, M. (1953). *Russia: A History and An Interpretation.* Macmillan, New York, *Vol. 1,* pp. 225, 485 & 601; *Vol. 2,* pp. 474–481 & 1159.

Golod. (1893). *Entsiklopedicheskii Slovar'*, *Tom IX*. Moskva, pp. 102–104.

Golodanie. (1952). *Bol'shaia Sovetskaia Entsiklopediia*, *Tom 11*. Moskva, pp. 626–627.

Golodanie. (1958). *Bol'shaia Meditsinskaia Entsiklopediia*, *Tom 7*, Moskva, pp. 950–966.

Goure, L. (1962). *The Siege of Leningrad*. Stanford University Press, Stanford.

Graham, S. (1929 & 1971). *Peter the Great*. The Macmillan Company, New York, p. 322; reprinted by Greenwood Press, Westport.

Graves, R. (1917). Fearful Famines of the Past. *The National Geographic Magazine* **XXXII**, 69–90.

Hoover, H. (1961). *An American Epic. Famine in Forty-Five Nations. The Battle on the Front Line 1914–1923. Vol. III*. Henry Regnery Company, Chicago, p. 436.

Hutchison, K. (1946). Russia's Food Crisis. *Nation* **163**, 381.

Ivanovsky, A. (1923). Physical Modifications of the Population of Russia Under Famine. *Amer. J. of Phys. Anthro*. **6**, 331–353.

Jasny, N. (1948). The Plight of the Collective Farms. *J. of Farm Econ*. **XXX**, 304–321.

Keys, A., J. Brozek, A. Henschel, O. Mickelsen and H. Taylor (1950). *The Biology of Human Starvation*. University of Minnesota Press, Minneapolis, pp. 1249–1251.

Khrushchev, N. (1963). Khrushchev's Report to Central Committee Session. *The Current Digest of the Soviet Press* **XV**, 5.

Kirienko, I. (1948). *Zasukha i bor'ba s nei*. Nal'chik.

Klepikov, S. (1920). *Pitaniye russkago krest'ianina*. Moskva.

Kluchevsky, V. (1960). *History of Russia, Volume 3*. Russell and Russell, New York, p. 345.

Kochan, L. (1962). *The Makings of Modern Russia*. Jonathan Cope, London, p. 63.

Koslow, J. (1961). *Ivan the Terrible*. Hill and Wang, New York, p. 192.

Kravchenko, V. (1950). *I Chose Justice*. Charles Scribner's Sons, New York, p. 96.

Kubijovyc, V. (Ed), (1963). *Ukraine: A Concise Encyclopaedia*. University of Toronto Press, Toronto, pp. 200–201, 820–822 & 898.

Kunitz, J. (1933). Food in Russia. I, Food and Politics. *New Republic* **74**, 359–362.

Kushner, P. (Ed), (1958). *Selo viriatino v proshlom i nastoiaschem*. Moskva.

Laird, R. (1958). *Collective Farming in Russia*. University of Kansas Press, Lawrence, p. 64.

Lamb, H. (1948). *The March of Muscovy*. Doubleday, New York, p. 107.

Lawrence, J. (1957). *Russia in the Making*. George Allen and Unwin, Ltd., London, p. 75.

Lewin, M. (1965). The Immediate Background of Soviet Collectivization. *Soviet Studies* **XVIII**, 162–197.

Liaschenko, P. (1949). *History of the National Economy of Russia to the 1917 Revolution*. Macmillan, New York, pp. 179–181.

Lydolph, P. (1964). The Russian Sukhovey. *Annals of the A.A.G.* **54**, 291–309.

Matskevich, V. (1971). *Sel'skoe khoziaistvo*. Moskva, pp. 11–21.

Miliukov, P., C. Seignobos, and L. Eisenmann (1968). *History of Russia*. Funk & Wagnalls, New York, *Vol. Two*, p. 55; *Vol. Three*, pp. 362, 381–382 & 410.

Mills, T. (1947). Soviet Collective Farm Decree. *Foreign Ag*. **II**, 64–69.

Miller, M. (1926). *The Economic Development of Russia, 1905–1914*. P. S. King & Son, Ltd., London, p. 49.

Morokhovets, A. (1931). *Krest'ianskoe dvizhenie 1827–1869*. Moskva.

Nicol, B. (1971). Causes of Famine in the Past and in the Future. In *Famine, A Symposium Dealing With Nutrition and Relief Operations in Times of Disaster*, Almqvist & Wiksells, Uppsala, pp. 10–16.

Nuttonson, M. (1949). USSR: Some Physical and Agricultural Characteristics of the Drought Area and Its Climatic Analogues in the United States. *Land Econ*. **XXV**, 347–351.

Paddock, W. and P. (1967). *Famine 1975! America's Decision: Who Will Survive*. Little, Brown and Company, Boston, pp. 8–9.

Pavlovich, V. (1892). *Materialy dlia geografii i statistiki Rossii, sobrannyye ofitserami general'nago sktaba, Yekaterinoslavskaya Guberniia*. St Petersburgh.

Philippot, R. (1953). L'aggravation des Famines et la Legislation des Subsistence en Russia, 1891–1914. *Revue Historique* **209**, 58–64.

Prentice, E. (1939). *Hunger and History*. Harper & Brothers Publishers, New York, pp. 4–12.

Queen, G. (1955). American Relief in the Russian Famine of 1891–1892. *Russian Review* **14**, 140–150.

Rambaud, A. (1878 & 1890). *The History of Russia*. John B. Alden, New York, p. 89.

Robinson, G. (1932). *Rural Russia Under the Old Regime*. Longmans, Green & Co., New York, pp. 97, 244 & 245.

Rubinow, I. (1906). *Russia's Wheat Surplus: Conditions Under Which it is Produced*. U.S. Dept. of Agriculture, Washington, D.C., p. 51.

Rudenko, A. (Ed), (1958). *Zasukhi v SSSR*. Leningrad, pp. 162–165.

Seeger, E. (1950). *The Pagent of Russian History*. Longmans, Green & Co., New York, pp. 148–149, 162 & 340.

Smith, C. (1892). The Famine in Russia. *North Am. Rev*. **154**, 541–551.

Stefanovskii, F. (1893). *Materialy dlia izucheniia svoistv golodnago kleba*. Kazan.

Tikhomirov, M. (1959). *The Towns of Ancient Rus*. Moscow, pp. 101–102.

Tikhomirov, M. (1964). *Novgorod: k 1100 letiiu goroda* Moskva, pp. 299–309.

Timoshenko, V. (1932). *Agricultural Russia and the Wheat Problem*. Stanford University Press, Stanford, pp. 273–293.

Truog, E. and D. Pronin (1953). A Great Myth: The Russian Granary. *Land Econ*. **XXIX**, 200–207.

Tulaikov, N. (1930). Agriculture in the Dry Region of the U.S.S.R. *Econ. Geog*. **6**, 54–80.

Ventskevich, G. (1961). *Agrometerology*. Israel Program for Scientific Translations, Jerusalem, pp. 153–155.

Verbin, A. (1948). *Zasukha i bor'ba s nei v stepi Ukrainy*. Odessa.

Vernadsky, G. (1948). *A History of Russia: Kievan Russia*. Yale University Press, New Haven.

Volin, L. (1951). *A Survey of Soviet Agriculture*. U.S. Dept. of Agriculture, Washington, D.C., p. 16.

von Haxthausen, B. (1856). *The Russian Empire*. Chapman and Hall, London, p. 163.

von Staden, H. (1967). *The Land and Government of Muscovy.* Stanford University Press, Stanford, p. 29.

Walford, C. (1970). *The Famine of the World: Past and Present.* Bert Franklin, New York.

Way, C. (1889). *Consular Report 106.* Washington, D.C., p. 278.

Webb, S. and B. Webb (1936). *Soviet Communism: A New Civilization, Vol.II.* Charles Scribner's Sons, New York, pp. 258–272.

Williamson, F. (1973). Population Pollution. In M. Micklin, *Population, Environment, and Social Organization: Current Issues in Human Ecology,* Dryden Press, Hinsdale, pp. 446–447.

ADJUSTMENT OF FOOD BEHAVIOUR DURING FAMINE

ADEL P. DEN HARTOG

Department of Human Nutrition, Agricultural University of Wageningen, The Netherlands.

Communities frequently confronted with food shortages have gained experience in the course of time on how to overcome such a difficult situation. Different kinds of measures and specific actions which a rural community may take in order to cope with famine are discussed. This comprises among others: trials to adjust agriculture, hoarding of food and sale of property, money lending, various ways of reducing food intake, consumption of non conventional foods, roaming for food, migration, as well as prayer and magic. Particular reference is made to situations in Tropical Africa, India and the Netherlands during the "hunger winter" of 1944-1945. It is not always fully realized by food donors, that a famine threatened community is not apathetic and just waiting for food aid. In actual fact all possible has often been done in the hope that the situation would be alleviated.

KEY WORDS: Famine foods, Food Behaviour and Famine, Food Behaviour and Relief.

INTRODUCTION

The aim of this paper is to discuss how a community may adjust itself when it is confronted with the grave problem of a famine, and how it reacts to food relief supplied by National and International Agencies. In this paper particular reference is made to tropical Africa, India and the Netherlands. Tropical Africa and India are chosen because these regions are often confronted with problems of famine. The case of the Netherlands during the hunger winter 1944-45 has been selected as an example of a highly technically developed society which had no previous experience of famine.*

It is not within the scope of this paper to give proposals for food relief programmes. Those interested in this matter may consult the report of Aall and Helsing (1974). A very useful annotated bibliography on medical, sociological, and organizational aspects of disaster technology has

---

* Until the middle of the 19th century famine occurred from time to time in the Netherlands. Some notorious famines were the famine and farmers revolt of 1491-1492 in North-Holland, the widespread hungry year of 1566 caused by economic and political misery, the siege of Leyden in 1574 when many people perished of hunger and disease, and the disastrous potato famine of the years 1845-1847. Although no widespread famine occurred during the First World War when the country was neutral, the food supply situation was very critical indeed in 1917 and food riots occurred.

been prepared by Manning (1976) of the London Technical Group, a group of scientists and technologists concerned with surveys of disaster affected areas for relief organizations.

Before discussing this subject it is necessary to make a distinction between two terms, famine and undernutrition. Famine should not be confused with the ordinary chronic situation of undernutrition and malnutrition. Famine is in the first place related to an acute situation of extreme scarcity of food and overall shortage of dietary energy.

SOME GENERAL NOTES ON FAMINE AND SOCIETY

Famines are caused by several interrelated factors such as drought, inundation, or earthquake, but also by weak agricultural systems, political upheaval or war (Aykroyd, 1974; Cepede and Gounelle, 1967; Roch, *et al.* 1975). Dando (1976) has given an interesting account of the occurence of famines in Russia covering the period from A.D. 971-1970. One of his major conclusions is that though natural factors contributed to famine situations, most of these famines were largely man-made.

Death from starvation occurs if about one third of the body weight in health has been lost. Weight loss of lesser degree can result in disturbances of water balance leading to famine oedema, diarrhoea, caused by atrophy and ulceration of the intestines as well as psychological changes. (Aykroyd, 1971; McCance, 1975).

It is well known that people in famine affected areas are depressed and apathetic. In those regions of tropical Africa faced with the yearly recurring phenomenon of the hungry season (*periode de soudure*), social activities are considerably reduced. In Onicha, Nigeria for example, there are no public rituals involving feasting and extensive hospitality in this period. New marriages are rarely contracted and men who have been recently married fear that their wives may desert them to return to their parents (Ogubu, 1973; Hunter, 1967, Richards, 1939). Fortunately, the hungry season is generally followed by the harvest season and food will become available so that social life can return to normal.

As famine progresses, however, normal social behavior is increasingly affected. Initially, there will be mutual help between family or families but at a later stage everybody tends to care only for themselves (Jelliffe and Jelliffe, 1971). Josué de Castro (1964) has given a very impressive account of the implications of the frequent occurrence of drought on society in North East Brazil. He describes the breakdown of normal social relationships, the search for unusual foods and migration in order to escape starvation. Turnbull (1974) described how famine effected the Ik, a nomadic hunting people living on the border regions of Uganda, the Sudan, and Kenya. Being driven away from their hunting grounds to barren mountains during the colonial period and with insufficient knowledge of farming, the results were disastrous. Plagued with regularly returning food shortages, family life becomes disintegrated, children steal food from old people and parents lose much interest in the care for their children. Outbreak of diseases such as typhus, often connected with famine, are more due to the social disruption of the famine which may have been caused by civil war or earthquake, than to lowered physical resistance. Reports of famine show that children and the elderly people are usually the first victims.

Recent research shows that the human brain is more vulnerable to the effects of hunger and malnutrition than was originally thought. This is particularly true of children up to two years after birth. Such a situation can lead to intellectual and social defects (Kallen, 1973; Lewin, 1974; Stein *et al.*, 1975). These studies indicate that intelligence,

language, motor skills, and social interaction are impaired.

HOW COMMUNITIES TRY TO OVERCOME PROBLEMS OF FAMINE

Communities frequently confronted with food shortages have gained experience in the course of the time on how to overcome such a difficult situation and have often developed some kind of a survival mechanism which consists of a number of measures at family and community level in order to cope with the situation. Or as Mbithi and Wisner (1972) stated for rural communities in Kenya, "The peasant farmer is not apathetic, childlike, waiting for a famine relief or government officers to tell him how to feed his family".

Seaman, Holt, and Rivers (1974) mention how the Somali pastoralists of the drought stricken Haranghe Province of Ethiopia have established ways of attempting to deal with the problem so long as there is any possibility of survival. The authors say:

The major factors are the skill with which they find a sufficient combination of pasture and water in harsh conditions; the way in which they divide their herds and thus the resources of labour in their families; the degree to which there is redistribution between kin, by outright gifts of animals, cash or grain, by loaning of cash or animals, by the increased sale of animals, by the temporary redistribution of children amongst relatives, and lastly by the use of force against groups competing for the same scarce resources.

In Eastern and Central Tanzania a number of farmers have been interviewed concerning their perception of drought and drought-reducing adjustment (Berry *et al.*, 1971). Although the individual farmer seldom suggested more than a single alternative adjustment on the question, "If the rains fail, what can a man do?", the collective list of answers presented in Table I is of interest. It indicates that only around 20 per cent of the respondents will probably do nothing and wait for the coming drought. Communities confronted with food shortages and famine may take a number of measures which will be briefly discussed below.

Before discussing this, one should realize that famine threatened communities often have attempted to adjust their agriculture and animal husbandry by planting reserve famine crops, resowing of cereals, and other food plants which

TABLE I

Perception of feasible drought adjustment among a group of farmers in Eastern and Central Tanzania.

Kind of adjustment		% of respondents*	Kind of adjustment		% of respondents*
a)	Do nothing, wait	23	g)	Change plot location	5
b)	Rain making, prayer	22	h)	Change timing of planting	1
c)	Move to seek land, work elsewhere for food	18	i)	Change cultivation method	0
d)	Use stored food, saved money, sell cattle	8	j)	Others	6
			k)	Not ascertained	13
e)	Change crops	11			
f)	Irrigation	8			

Source: Berry *et al.*, Bureau of Resource Assessment and Landuse Planning, University of Dar-es-Salaam, 1971.
   * Percentages are of total respondents, not total replies as mutliple answers are recorded.

may be repeated many times before these actions are abandoned. Alternatively, a search may be made for more suitable agricultural lands and pastures.

Faced with the threat of a food shortage, households hoard foods in order to help overcome the expected difficulties. This alone will lead to an increase in the food prices. A widespread phenomenon with very dangerous consequences is the hoarding of food stuffs by traders and shopkeepers in hope of a later rise in food prices.

Families confronted with famine are not only forced to reduce the amount of food to be consumed but also the number of meals a day. For example, an established three meals a day pattern may change to a two or only one meal a day pattern (Ogubu, 1973). In some circumstances people may eat one meal every other day. It is clear this will not relieve the situation very much.

Another step may be to dilute meals such as paps or stews with more water, (provided sufficient water is available) in order to obtain some feeling of satiation. Foods are also mixed with unusual substances such as bark. In the Scandinavian countries and some other parts of Europe, it was not uncommon to mix cereal grain meals with tree bark. In some Asian countries, cereals may be mixed with seeds of grasses. Clay is also consumed, but it should not be confused with the habit of eating edible earth during normal periods which may be of some importance as an additional source of minerals (Hunter, 1973).

Many communities are forced to subsist on nonconventional foods during the period of food shortage. Gupta and Kanodia (1968), Bhandari (1974) describe plants used during scarcity and famine periods in the dry region of India. According to the authors, many of these plants contain much woody tissue and substances which are neither digestible nor nutritive and may therefore produce adverse effects on health. On the other hand they may temporarily appease hunger. It is of interest to note that in the Netherlands during the Second World War when food supply was diminishing, many people were ignorant of the fact that a number of still widespread wild plants and fruits could be consumed as human food. The Bureau of Nutrition Education (1942) therefore issued a brochure describing how to collect and prepare a number of these wild foods.

In the Savannah zones of West Africa a grasslike millet with tiny seeds called "hungry rice" (*Digitaria exilis*) is often consumed during food shortage. A description of supplementary and emergency food plants for West Africa has been made by Irvine (1952). In the western part of the Netherlands, during the hunger winter of 1944/45 the food situation became desperate and unusual foods such as sugar beets and tulip bulbs were consumed (Dols and van Arcken, 1946; Burger, Drumond and Sandsteed, 1948). In order to overcome problems of food shortage authorities in countries such as Indonesia and East Africa have encouraged the cultivation of cassava as a famine reserve crop.

A very dangerous situation occurs when seeds and tubers kept aside for the next planting season are consumed as food and in this way famine will be prolonged.

It is known that a very extreme situation of famine may lead to the killing of man for food (anthropophagy or cannibalism) or the consumption of dead bodies (necrophagy or burial cannabalism). (Rosenstein, 1973; Tannahil, 1975.)

People tend to rely on food from better-off relatives and other households of the community.

A.P. DEN HARTOG

Some times children may temporarily be sent into the care of more fortunate relatives. In most cases this will not even serve as a temporary solution and the affected family may be forced to sell property or borrow money in order to buy food. Food prices rise tremendously and often the poorest households lose all their possessions such as land, cattle, etc. in order to survive. Cattle will be slaughtered for family consumption or for sale. Usually livestock is as vulnerable as human beings due to shortages of fodder.

In order to survive, people roam the neighbouring areas for food. Cuypers (1970), mentioned that the Shi, a people of Zaire, in periods of famine demanded or begged the neighbouring regions for food. It is obvious that the search for food can create great social unrest in the non-affected areas.

The last stage of a severe famine is that people migrate from their homelands to other areas. A classical example is the mass migration of the Irish to North America caused by the potato famine of 1845-1851 (see Woodham-Smith, 1962). The death toll is very high among the groups of people on the move, particularly among children and the elderly. For instance, during the 1975 famine in Ethiopia, there had been increased migration from the worst areas to towns (Hussein, 1975). The poorest people came first, but small landowners followed having pawned, sold or simply deserted their holdings to seek work (Miller and Holt, 1975). In the urbanized Western part of the Netherlands during the hunger winter of 1944-45, a stream of hungry city dwellers went looking for food in the less affected areas and many died from exhaustion by the roadside. The declining strength of the people makes the search for food extremely difficult.

Apart from the above-described measures, it should be borne in mind that a community threatened with famine may tend to rely on a completely different kind of solution such as prayer.

In several drought-stricken regions it is well known that people will resort to the magic of rain-making or witchcraft in order to secure a new harvest. One may question the practical effects of these modes of accommodation to the threat of famine. Berry et al., (1971) notes, however, that, "The efficaciousness of rainmaking might be questioned, but not its importance. It is widely spread in East Africa and plays an important role in helping men to cope with the great uncertainties of semi-arid agriculture".

The different kind of measures and specific action which a rural community confronts with famine may take in order to alleviate the situation is presented in Table II.

SOME GENERAL NOTES ON FOOD RELIEF

When famine is ravaging an area, the population will turn to the local authorities and the central government for aid. Governments have the duty to protect the population against famine and they often request food relief from outside the country when the situation is beyond their capability. Food relief is, despite its humanitarian character, a very delicate matter. Local authorities will not always admit the severity of the situation to the central government in order to avoid the risk of being blamed for the causes. The central government may for prestige reasons hide the situation from the outside world. On the other hand ambassadors of potential food aid countries are usually anxious to maintain untroubled relations with their host country and are generally reluctant to declare disaster without the approval of the government of the country regardless of the severity of the situation (Sheets and Morris, 1974). Another very important aspect is that powerful food suppliers may exploit the situation by trying to impose political influence through food aid.

The administration of food relief is a very complicated and complex matter. It includes: location of the area affected by the famine; estimates of the number of people in need; supply, and distribution of food to those who are most in need (see Masefield, 1967). It is often difficult to estimate the nature and extent of a famine; even on the widely publicized drought of the Sahel in West Africa little accurate information is available (Seaman et al., 1973).

A symposium dealing with nutrition and relief operations in times of disaster had recommended speedy actions in circumstances of famine and calling for able, decisive leadership with high managerial skills (Blix, Hofvander and Vahlquist, 1971).

The Bengal famine in 1943 is an example of disaster with a very high death toll due to the failure of the government to take appropriate measures early enough. It is revealing to read Berg's paper (1972) on how the 1966-67 drought famine in Bihar, India, could have been contained and a catastrophe prevented. When faced with disaster, however, the government reacted

TABLE II
Measures and specific actions taken by rural communities in order to cope with famine

Measures	Specific Action
Trials to adjust agriculture and animal husbandry	Planting of famine reserve crops Re-sowing (this may be done many times) Search for other agricultural lands Search for other pastures
Building up of food stocks	Hoarding of foods Sale of property for food Money lending for food

Adjustment of dietary habits	Reduction of food intakes:
	    Restriction of consumption in order to save food for other persons such as children
	    Reducing number of meals a day
	    Adding extra water to the meals
	
	Consumption of non-conventional foods:
	    Wild plants, fruits and animals
	        (hungry foods)
	    Cattle fodder
	    Mixing the food with non-edible substances
	    Seed for sowing, slaughter of domestic animals
	    Anthropophagy
	    Necrophagy

Roaming for food	Begging for food from better-off households Collecting wild foods Food procurement from less affected areas Pillaging for food
Migration	Temporary distribution of children to better-off households Temporary or permanent migration to towns or less affected rural areas
Spiritual measures	Prayer Magic, for instance — rainmaking, witchcraft

effectively. The food distribution system followed the traditional Indian plan for meeting scarcity conditions. The basic outlet was the fair price shop of which 20,000 were established in Bihar. The logistics of food were found to be much simpler than of water supply. To provide each person with a minimum of two gallons of water daily, the government developed a two-pronged programme of well-drilling and water transport. The core of the programme was the hand-digging of small mudwells and the conversion of mudwells to good wells by lining them with brick.

One lesson learned from the Bihar experience was the need for a permanent national body to anticipate disasters, to monitor them as they unfold, and then to conduct the necessary relief operations. At the international level, the FAO early warning system and the World Food Council may play an important role in preventing famine. As a result of recommendations made by the World Food Conference held in November, 1974,

in Rome, FAO in close collaboration with WHO and UNICEF is now engaged in developing a system of nutrition surveillance. The general objective is to provide on-going information about the nutritional conditions of a population and the different factors which influence these. This information will provide a basis for decisions and actions to be made by the responsible authorities in order to promptly avoid food and nutritional problems (Mason, 1975). At present, FAO is assisting the government of Upper Volta in establishing nutritional surveillance for its rural population and a number of other countries are expected to be assisted soon.

REACTION OF A COMMUNITY FOOD RELIEF

What is the reaction of a famine stricken community towards the food distributed by food relief organizations? A realistic but often very unpleasant aspect of the present situation is that food stuffs made available by donor countries are not precisely the foods the recipient communities are used to. People who desperately need food are more prepared than those suffering from short-term scarcity to accept less known foods. Though a high incidence of disease such as famine diarrhoea may reduce the willingness of the community to eat unfamiliar foods (Masefield, 1967).

On several occasions foods were refused because they did not fit into the existing dietary patterns. Such experiences occurred mainly during a long term food relief when the first energy needs had already been satisfied. In order to assist food donor countries in selecting the right foods during a food emergency, FAO has prepared a provisional list of major foods using a number of selected countries (FAO, 1976).

People may have great difficulty even in severe famine conditions to accept unfamiliar food whose processing and incorporation into a meal may be unknown. The writer has personally observed the difficulties of a rural community in Northern Ghana in using a powdered chocolate flavoured instant breakfast as part of a food aid programme. It may also happen that in societies where the men or adults have the first choice of food, the relief foods are distributed at the expense of women or children (den Hartog, 1973). Another aspect is that people on the move in search of food do not have the necessary kitchen utensils to prepare the foods.

The specific social structure of the country and the special conditions of a famine stricken area may result in foods not reaching groups most in need. A weak administrative structure and the upheaval of the society as a result of famine will invite corruption so that foods will disappear into the blackmarket. On the other hand, in countries with diverse cultural groups, famine may tend to discriminate in the food distribution, for example, sedentary farmers may receive more food than nomads. It should also be realized that a sedentary population is easier to reach by food relief than the mobile nomads.

Despite its humanitarian character, food distribution to the community may cause serious social and economic side effects. In one West African country emergency food was distributed in such a way that it did not involve the traditional local leaders. It threatened to destroy local traditional leadership. Later aid was distributed with the collaboration of the local leaders (Muller, 1974). When the famine situation is alleviated a prolonged food relief programme may cause a collapse of normal food prices so that farmers will not have an incentive to increase local food production. Another aspect is that too much free food over a long period is not an incentive for a return to hard work and efficient agricultural production (Butcher, 1971). An interesting and very balanced point of view on this matter is given by Isenman and Singer (1975) taking India as an example. According to the authors, food aid has created some short term disincentive in food production, but in the long run food aid should be considered positive and compared favourably as an incentive for development with non-food aid projects. Aall and Helsing (1974) warn us for the danger of creating a so-called relief dependency and of establishing new demands for imported foods which cannot be followed-up.

CONCLUSIONS

It is not fully realized by food donors that a famine threatened community is not just waiting for food relief to come from external sources. Particularly in regions with famine experience, the community is certainly very concerned by the situation but still hopes that measures such as agricultural adjustment, reduction of meals, consumption of unusual foods (hungry crops) or substances, sale of livestock or of other property and money-lending for food may carry them through this difficult period.

It therefore often occurs that such communities will turn at a very late state to the appropriate authorities for food relief. When the situation becomes desperate the community may indeed show signs of disintegration.

Under such circumstances people may on a short-term basis accept practically any food offered to them until the hunger is somewhat appeased, provided their health situation or lack of knowledge and means of how to prepare these foods does not prevent this.

It is here that unusual foods such as army rations or, if available, specially prepared relief foods may be used. In long term relief operations, however, it is absolutely necessary to take local food habits into account in order to avoid food acceptability problems and the creation of a taste and demand for foreign foods which may later on not be fulfilled when the emergency operations cease to exist.

REFERENCES

Aall, C. and Helsing, E. (1974). The Sahelian drought, proposals for a supporting programme in Niger for food provision, nutrition rehabilitation and malnutrition prevention. *Environmental Child Health*, Vol. 20, pp. 304-329.

Aykroyd, W.R. (1974). *The Conquest of Famine*, London, Chatto and Windus.

Aykroyd, W.R. (1971). Definition of different degrees of starvation. In: Blix, G., Hofvander, Y. and B. Vahlquist, *Nutrition and Relief Operations in Times of Disaster.* Uppsala, Almquist and Wiksells, pp. 17-24.

Berg, A. (1972). Famine contained: notes and lessons from the Bihar experience. *Tropical Science*, No. 2, pp. 115-129.

Berry, L., Hankins, T., Kates, R.W., Makil, L., and Porter, P. (1971). Human adjustment to agricultural drought in Tanzania. *Dar-es-Salaam, Bureau of Resource Assessment and Land Use Planning*, University of Dar-es-Salaam. Research paper no. 13.

Bhandari, M.M. (1974). Famine foods in the Rojasthan Desert, *Economic Botany*, 28, No. 1, pp. 73-81.

Blix, G., Hofvander, Y. and B., Valquist. (1971). *Famine, a* symposium dealing with nutrition and relief operations in times of disaster. Uppsala, Almquist and Wiksells.

Bureau of Nutrition Education. (1942). Voorlichtingsbureau v.d. Voedingsraad. Onze wilde groenten en vruchten. (Our wild vegetables and fruits). The Hague.

Burger, G.C.E., Drumond, J.C., Sandstead, H.R. (1948). *Malnutrition and Starvation in Western Netherlands.* Sept. 1944-July 1945. The Hague, General State Printing Office. Vol. 1 and 2.

Butcher, D.A.P. (1971). *An operational Manual for Resettlement.* Rome, FAO. (FI:SF/GHA).

Cépède, M. and Gounelle, H. (1967). *La Faim*, Paris, Presses Universitaires de France.

Cuypers, J.B. (1970). *L'Alimentation chez les Shi.* Tervuren. Musée Royal de L'Afrique Centrale.

Dando, W.A. (1976). Man-made famines: some geographical insights from an exploratory study of a millennium of Russian famines. *Ecology of Food and Nutrition*, 4, no. 4, pp. 219-234.

de Castro, J. (1967). *Géographie de la Faim.* Paris, Editions du Seuil.

den Hartog, A.P. (1973). Unequal distribution of food within the household, a somewhat neglected aspect of food behaviour. *FAO Nutrition Newsletter*, 10, no. 4, pp. 8-17.

FAO, List of major foods consumed in selected countries. (1976). Provisional version. Rome, FAO, Food Policy and Nutrition Division.

Dols, M.J.L. and van Arcken, D.J.A.M. (1946). De voedsel voorziening in Nederland tijdens en onmiddellijk na den tweeden Wereldoorlog 1940-1945. Voeding, *Netherlands Journal of Nutrition*, 6, No. 7, pp. 193-207.

Gupta, R.K. and K.C. Kanodia. (1968). Plants used during scarcity and famine periods in the dry regions of India. *Journal d'Agric. Tropical et de Botanie Appliquée*, 15, No. 7-8, pp. 265-285.

Hunter, J.M. (1967). Seasonal hunger in a part of the West African Savanna: a survey of body weights in Nangodi, N.E. Ghana. *Institute of British Geogr. Trans*, 41, pp. 167-185.

Hunter, J.M. (1973). Geophagy in Africa and the United States, a culture-nutrition hypothesis. *Geographical Review*, 63, No. 3, pp. 170-195.

Hussein, A.M. (1975). Drought and famine in Ethiopia. *African Environment*, Special, Report 2, London, p. 121.

Irvine, F.R. (1952). Supplementary and emergency food plants of West Africa. *Economic Botany*, 6, no. 1, pp. 23-40.

Isenman, P.J. and Singer, H.W. (1975). Food aid, disincentive effects and their policy implications. Institute of Development Studies at the University of Sussex, AID Discussion Paper no. 31.

Jelliffe, D.B. and E.F.P. Jelliffe. (1971). The effects of starvation on the function of the family and society. In: Blix, G., Hofvander, Y. and B. Vahlquist, *Nutrition and Relief Operations in Times of Disaster.* Uppsala, Almquist and Wiksells, pp. 54-63.

Kallen, D.J. (1973). Nutrition, Development and social behaviour. *Proceedings of the conference of the assessment of tests of behavior from studies of nutrition in the Western Hemisphere.* Washington, U.S. Government printing Office.

Lewin, R. (1974). *The poverty of undernourished brains.* New Scientist, Vol. 64, 24 October, pp. 268-271.

Manning, D.H. (1976). *Disaster Technology, an Annotated Bibliography*, Oxford, Pergamon Press.

Masefield, G.B. (1967). *Food and Nutrition Procedures in Times of Disaster.* Rome, F.A.O.

Mason, J.B. (1975). Nutritional Surveillance. *Food and Nutrition*, FAO quarterly review. Vol. 1, no. 4, pp. 24-27.

Mbithi, P.M. and Wisner, B. (1972). *Drought and famine in Kenya, magnitude and attempted solutions.* Discussion paper no. 144, Nairobi, Institute for Development Studies, University of Nairobi.

McCance, R.A. (1975). *Famines of history and to-day. Proceedings of the Nutrition Society*, 34, No. 3, pp. 161-166.

Miller, D.S. and Holt, J.F.J. (1975). *The Ethiopian Famine. Proceedings of the Nutrition Society*, 34, No. 3, pp. 167-172.

Muller, M. (1974). Aid, corruption and waste, *New Scientist*, 7 Nov., 64, pp. 398-400.

Ogubu, J.O. (1973). Seasonal hunger in tropical Africa as a cultural phenomenon: the Onicha Ibo of Nigeria and Chakaka Poka of Malawi examples. *Africa*, 43, No. 4, pp. 317-322.

Richards, A.I. (1939). *Land, Labour and Diet in Northern Rhodesia: an Economic Study of the Bemba Tribe.* London, Oxford University Press.

Roch, J., Hubert, B., Ngyrie, E. and Richard, P. (1975). Selective bibliography of the famines and the drought in the Sahel, *African Environment*, 1, No. 2, pp. 94-116.

Rosenstein, L. (1973). La psychopathologie de l'extrême famine, *Cahiers Nutrition Diététique*, 8, no. 4, pp. 291-297.

Seaman, J., Holt, J., Rivers, J. and Murlis, J. (1973). An inquiry into the drought situation in Upper-Volta, *The Lancet*, Oct. 6, pp. 774-778.

Seaman, J., Holt, J.F.J. and Rivers, J.P.W. (1974). Hararghe under drought, a survey of the effects of drought upon human nutrition in Harerghe Province. Addis Ababa,

ERRATUM

THE REFERENCES TO DEN HARTOG'S
ARTICLE CONTINUE ON PAGE 170.

INDEX

163

Ethiopian Government Relief and Rehabilitation Commission.

Sheets, H. and R. Morris. (1974). *Disaster in the Desert: Failures of International Relief in West African Drought.* Washington, Carnegie Endowment for International Peace.

Stein, Z., Susser, M., Seanger, G. and Marolla, F. (1975). *Famine and Human Development, the Dutch Hunger Winter of 1944-1945.* London, Oxford University Press.

Tannahill, R. (1975). *Flesh and blood: A history of the Cannibal Complex,* London, Hamish Hamilton.

Turnbull, C.M. (1974). *The Mountain People,* London, Pan Books.

Woodham-Smith, C. (1962). *The Great Hunger,* New York, Harper.

Printed in Great Britain
by Amazon

54718791R00101